A Genuine
Faith

A GENUINE FAITH

How to Follow Jesus Today

RODNEY REEVES

BakerBooks
Grand Rapids, Michigan

Published by Baker Books
a division of Baker Publishing Group
P.O. Box 6287, Grand Rapids, MI 49516-6287

Printed in the United States of America

Library of Congress Cataloging-in-Publication Data
Reeves, Rodney, 1957–
    A genuine faith : how to follow Jesus today / Rodney Reeves.
       p.   cm.
    Includes bibliographical references.
    ISBN 0-8010-6567-4 (pbk.)
    1. Christian life. 2. Jesus Christ—Example. I. Title.
BV4501.3.R435 2005
248.4—dc22   2005008934

For Andrew, Emma, and Grace:
Three disciples of Jesus

Contents

Preface

Writing is a community effort. And, I'm grateful for the community of believers who have supported me from the beginning. I am especially thankful for the members of the Central Baptist Church, Jonesboro, Arkansas, who reconfirmed my faith in the loving grace that is found in the body of Christ. Two academic communities—Williams Baptist College and Southwest Baptist University—have given me opportunities to give what I have received. Christian higher education is a noble work that yields little worldly gain. I thank God for my colleagues and their sacrificial investment in the kingdom of God. And, finally, I am especially grateful to our heavenly Father for the family he has given me. Every day I offer praise to our Lord and Savior for my wife, Sheri, our children, Andrew, Emma, and Grace, our parents, Clarence and Carole Reeves, Bill and Judy Richardson, and our extended family. Their love makes me rejoice. God has been good to me. It will take an eternity to thank him.

Family, friends, and former colleagues and students have read parts of the manuscript: Sheri, Andrew, Carole, and Denny Reeves, Jeph Holloway, Ken Startup, Duane Bolin, Jo Davis, Steve Corder, Buck Rusher, Jim Jones, J. R. Madill, Stacy and Joey Pyle, Jon Clemence, Josh Jacobson, Ben Schatz, Nathan Pierce, David Capes, and Robbie and Stacey Johnson. Their insightful comments and words of encouragement came when I needed them the most. My project editor Paul Brinkerhoff improved the quality of this manuscript beyond measure with his keen eye, graceful spirit, and helpful suggestions. Thanks to Bob Hosack, senior acquisitions editor, for taking a chance on a new author. Thanks, also, to Jim Wells for the laptop computer. Your copy is in the mail.

Above all else, I pray that the Gospels of Matthew, Mark, Luke, and John will help us all learn how to follow Jesus. He is worthy.

Introduction

Strapping on Sandals

There are entrepreneurs among us who see the wide-spread hunger for spirituality as a marketplace and are out there selling junk food.

Eugene H. Peterson, *Living the Message*

I want to follow Jesus. I believe he's my best hope of finding God. It is not simply because he claimed to be the way to God. Many make claims. He lived the life. When I read stories about him, I see God. The beauty of God's handiwork is there. The mystery of the meaning of God is there. All that Jesus did, and all that he said, reminds me of what I have known all along. There is an appealing reality about him that seems too familiar to be customary. His life rings true. This is why I want to follow Jesus. I want my life to look like his. I want to treat people like he did. I want to have a passion for life like he did. I want to have his godly confidence in knowing origin and destiny. He came from God; he returned to God. He showed us the way. I want to follow him. I want to find God.

But I have a problem. He was a Galilean Jew; I'm an American Gentile. He was celibate; I'm married. He was homeless; I'm a resident. It was his practice to give away everything; I have a bank account. These are not small things. When I compare his life to mine, it's apparent that we've made different decisions—his ways are not my ways. So, what am I supposed to do? How am I to follow Jesus? Can I be a disciple of his, *literally*? What is that life supposed to look like?

These questions have been haunting me for quite some time. The fact that Jesus lived his life so radically different from the way I live my life has always been a bit unsettling for one who claims to follow him. The hardest part has been reconciling my penchant for storing things with Jesus's habit of giving things away; or, my tendencies to fight for my rights when he relinquished his without a word; or, envying his itinerant ministry when I faced the prospect of preaching to the same crowd every Sunday (somehow, in my darkest moments, I would find comfort in reminding myself, "Jesus never had to deal with a pulpit!"). At dif-

When I compare his life to mine,

it's apparent that we've made different

decisions—his ways are not my ways.

ferent times and under different circumstances these troubling doubts would invade my mind, forcing me to question the authenticity of my acculturated Christianity. Then, for only a moment, I would toy with the idea of what I would need to do to be like him. "If I weren't married," I would reason, "and had no children, then I would sell all my goods, give up my job, and head for some remote part of the world and live in anonymity, helping everyone I met. *Then* I would be a real disciple of Jesus." But, of course, I knew that fiction wasn't possible for me. My wife and children have always been the surest signs of God's blessing on my life. Besides, the monastic life is no guarantee of assuaging doubts over genuine commitment (see Merton's diaries!).[1]

The obvious difference in my life and his life, however, didn't come home to me until a few years ago when my ten-year-old son made this poignant observation. We were driving home from Sunday services—it was "Father's Day"—and I had offered some remarks about the fatherhood of God based on Jesus's parable of the prodigal son. Andrew rarely made any comments about my sermons and I never asked. We were headed to our usual restaurant for Sunday lunch, meeting Sheri and the girls (it always took two vehicles to get to church), when Andrew said, "You know what, Dad? I feel sorry for Jesus." Of course, his empathy surprised me—not so much coming from him (Andrew has always been a sensitive, thoughtful person). I couldn't figure out how my sermon had provoked such a comment. Then, after a moment, I asked what he meant. "Jesus wasn't married," he said bluntly. "And, therefore he never knew what it was like to be a father or have a son or daughter." Then, after another pensive pause, he said, "That's too bad; isn't it, Dad?"

Jesus cannot teach me how to be a good father because he was never married, and that is too bad—not just for him but also for me. If he had been married, if he had fathered many children, then his example would provide another model of Christian behavior. Instead, sons learn to be fathers by watching their own dads—good or bad. Jesus cannot teach me how to be an American Christian because he was a Galilean Jew. There were many issues that troubled Jesus in his time, for example, calling someone a fool, swearing an oath, praying in public. Yet these "Jewish" things don't bother me at all; they appear as trivial matters to this Gentile who belongs to a complicated, postmodern world. My "issues" seem very different from his. Jesus cannot teach me how to be a devoted minister, teaching at a Christian university, since he was an itinerant prophet who taught twelve Jewish men about the kingdom of God. I'm not prepared to invite my students to live with me, much less to have them learn *only* from me, to follow me. Jesus, on the other hand, expected it.

Wherever he went, the disciples followed. That must have been a much simpler life. To follow Jesus required no guesswork, no interpretation. If he went to Capernaum, to Capernaum the disciples would go. If Jesus sent them on a special task, then special instructions followed: "Do this; don't go there; when you greet someone say this; take this with you; don't bring this; if you're snubbed, do this." When it was time to move on, they moved on. There were no discussions about direction, about mission strategy, about damage control, about long-term goals, about effectiveness. The twelve did what he did, said what he said, went where he went, lived as he lived.

Jesus came not only to tell us what God thinks, he lived to show us what God requires. That's why he challenged disciples to follow *him*. To follow Jesus is to do what God wants. Twelve apostles, several women, seventy messengers, and thousands of Galileans followed him wherever he went. If he crossed the Sea of Galilee they met him on the other side. If he left the country, they left jobs, families, hometowns, and followed him. The clarion call of Jesus was simple. He did not say, "If anyone wants to be my disciple, read this book," or "sign this document," or "pass this test," or even "champion my cause." He simply said: "Follow me." And he meant it—he expected his disciples to follow him *literally* to Jerusalem, to Golgotha, to the Father.

Many followed him to Jerusalem. Few followed him to the cross. It remains to be seen how many of those Galilean pilgrims followed him to heaven. But the invitation did not end with them. Since then, many

> *Jesus came not only to tell us what God thinks,*
>
> *he lived to show us what God requires.*

people have responded to his call, as if Jesus were still inviting anyone who had ears to hear to follow him. But how do we do that? For the Galileans, the call of discipleship was unmistakable: go where Jesus goes. But how does one follow him now, for our time, in our world?

Quest for the Historical Christian

There's a scene from Monty Python's *Life of Brian* that has always bothered me. In fact, to most Christians the whole film is offensive—a sacrilegious story parodying the Jesus movement. The setting is first-century Galilee. Brian is mistaken by the masses as the Messiah. Soon, the crowds follow Brian wherever he goes. Despite his attempts at dissuading his disciples, trying to convince them of his commonness, they ever more persuade others to follow "the Messiah." Fed up with the crowds, at one point Brian tries to slip away without notice. Instead, the huge throng gets wind of where he is hiding and chases after him. Realizing that he's been discovered, Brian tries to run away. But the crowd is too fast for him. Exasperated, he turns to the crowd, and with the voice of a desperate man, he asks, "What are you doing?" Puzzled, they reply, "We're following you!" The next morning, as the crowd gathers outside his door, Brian makes his plea. "Look. You've got it all wrong. You don't need to follow me. You don't need to follow anybody. You've got to think for yourselves. You're all individuals. . . . You've all got to work it out for yourselves. Don't let anyone tell you what to do." This is the gospel of our generation; this is the way of the world. Believe in yourself; create your own destiny; find your own identity; be unique; follow no one.

I'm tempted at this point to make riposte in response to this popular caricature of Christianity. Instead, I'll wait until the story of the Samaritan woman in John's Gospel to respond to the cynicism of our age. I recalled this vignette for another reason. It didn't offend me at first. I laughed it off because it was so untrue. I thought to myself, "What a ridiculous picture of the disciples of Jesus. Everyone knows that Christians don't mindlessly follow Jesus. There isn't a Christian I know that has left everything behind to do exactly what Jesus did." At that point, I saw the implicit criticism of the parody. The reason the caricature is so funny is that it is so unreal. Disciples of Christ don't behave that way—that's the point. We claim to follow him, but we don't. We look pretty foolish making all of these outlandish claims about being "Christian" and we're not even close to living up to the moniker.

As a matter of fact, I don't care for the title. It sets the bar too high. The first followers of Jesus *earned* the nickname from their contemporaries. Unbelievers of the first century called those who belonged to "the Way," "Christians" ("Christlike" or "little Christs") because they tried to walk in Jesus' steps. The first "Christians" thought following Jesus meant that they should live like Jesus. They sold all of their possessions, helped the needy, overcame bigotry, treated Jews and Gentiles the same, spent many days in prayer, showed kindness to strangers, traveled to preach the gospel to all people, performed miracles, visited prisons to help the needy, and died martyrs' deaths. They lived like Jesus; they died like Jesus. They were aliens to a world dominated by greed, hatred, violence, and selfishness. The world didn't know what to make of them. So they labeled them, "little Christs," a pejorative term meant to ridicule such a foolish life.

At this point, some readers might object to this idealized picture of the early church, and with good reason. After all, the first Christians weren't perfect. The New Testament is filled with stories of disputes, arguments, jealousies, factions, immoralities, and other undesirable attitudes and behavior hardly becoming of a "little Christ." For example, it is obvious that the "experiment" of "sharing all things in common" didn't work. After realizing all of their capital, laying their wealth "at the apostles' feet" (Acts 4:37),[2] the "poor ones" in Jerusalem (later called "Ebionites") became a burden on Christians who were still trying to "work with [their] hands" (1 Thess. 4:11). Support for the impoverished Christians in Jerusalem was expected of everyone (Gal. 2:10). As a matter of fact, Paul devoted his third mission trip to collecting a relief offering for the impoverished members of the mother church. Yet no one else was encouraged to follow their example. In fact, those who refused to work were considered "unruly." Paul advised his congregations to withdraw fellowship from those who refused to work for their own bread (2 Thess. 3:6–15). To follow Jesus did not mean to quit work.

There were other issues that divided the early church. Should all disciples follow Jesus in circumcision? Keep the dietary code? Observe Sabbath? Support the temple? As more Gentiles came into the church, more differences emerged. What about eating meat offered to idols, or observing the Jewish calendar, or drinking wine? Should a disciple of Jesus support the same Roman Empire that crucified his Lord? Were women equal to men in the eyes of Jesus? Do women have to wear prayer shawls? Can Gentiles teach from the Hebrew Scriptures? Does a man have to eat his steak well done? Are angels worthy of worship? Can a disciple of Jesus seek reparations in a court of law? Different opinions led to conflicting advice. From the very beginning, Christians were struggling with the same questions that face us today. What is a disciple of Jesus supposed to do? What does it mean to follow Jesus when so many Christians disagree? Who is right? Who could be counted on to show the way? Who is really following Jesus? In the midst of this sea of opinion regarding genuine discipleship, Paul came forward with a bold claim: "Imitate me." In essence he was saying, "Follow me and you'll follow Jesus" (see 1 Cor. 11:1).

Today the church is plagued with the same problems. There is a massive difference in the way many Christians live their lives. Different denominations of the church have enshrined their brand of Christianity as a safe haven for those who share similar beliefs. Do you take your Christianity with or without politics? Would you like a few social causes thrown in for good measure? Do you take your doctrine straight, or do you prefer Christianity lite? How do you want your worship: high octane or slow burn? So many choices, so many possibilities. Not to worry, we have some self-appointed apostles who think they're Paul incarnate; they can show us the way. Sadly, these pretenders create disciples in their own image, styling "good news" to promote their own kingdoms—their latest *Christian* book, their latest *Christian* CD, their latest *Christian* "last days" scenario, their latest *Christian* video, their latest *Christian* conspiracy theory, their latest *Christian* self-help study Bible. Of all the sins of the American church, it's the marketing of Christianity that bothers me the most. Does the body of Christ truly need another study Bible? (The last count I made was well over sixty.)

Since we can't think for ourselves, we now have Christian gurus for everything: weight loss, parenting, career counseling, education, karate, marriage counseling, finances, political activism, cooking, computing. But what if I don't *buy* it, literally? What if I choose not to "grow kids God's way," or refuse to join a "Christian coalition," or watch CNN rather than CBN, will I be "left behind"? That's the implication. The pressure to measure up to these myriads of expectations can be unbearable. Self-doubt is the force that drives us to buy Christian fads. Most believers want what's best; we want to feel right about our faith. So, we tend to gravitate to the sounds that please us. Personal preferences end up governing spiritual decisions. We like it, we believe it, we buy it. All we like sheep have gone to market.

What I'm looking for is a little perspective. I don't trust my proclivity to act like a consumer. I'm very good at it. I've been trained to think like one ever since I was a child. Now I'm afraid that my American-born, American-made faith has led me down a path that is broad, that many others have found, and that it leads to self-deception. I want to be spent for Christ because he was spent for me. But most of what I spend is for me, not for him. Good things come to them that wait. Jesus talked much about saving for heaven. Yet, I'm more inclined to demand the rewards

Personal preferences end up governing spiritual decisions. We like it, we believe it, we buy it. All we like sheep have gone to market.

of right living right now. Jesus commanded us to make disciples; I'm too busy trying to make a living. Jesus challenged his listeners to lose their lives to find them. I can't sleep if I've lost my billfold. What's wrong with this picture? "Oh wretched man that I am, who will save me from this body of death?"

Models to Picture

The Gospels were written for two reasons: to evoke faith and to inspire faithfulness. Of course, Jesus is the main subject of the Gospel story. The evangelists wrote their tributes to him in order to get readers to believe in him. Theological purposes notwithstanding, John's Gospel was written "so that you may believe that Jesus is the Christ, the Son of God; and that believing you may have life in His name" (John 20:31). At the same time, the story of Jesus is also about those who heard him, saw him, talked with him, disagreed with him, followed him. In other words, the evangelists can't tell the story of Jesus without relating how different persons, under different circumstances, responded to him. Therefore, the Gospels served another purpose: to encourage believers to live as faithful disciples. The Gospels were meant to be read by believers as well as unbelievers. Their literary purpose was not only to convince readers to follow Jesus—believe in him—but to show believers how to be disciples of Jesus.

We cannot follow Jesus by ourselves. It takes twelve persons to follow him. That's what the Gospels teach us. Yet, the individualism of our culture inspires us to think for ourselves, to prize the power to choose as the only creative force of our own destiny, to seek the identity of the self-made person, to find our own way. Such thinking is alien to Jesus and his ways. He created a community in order to make his disciples follow him *together*. We, on the other hand, try to live out our personal convictions with the approval of like-minded individuals. Most of us join congregations of believers who think like us, dress like us, talk like us, have the same goals, belong to the same social groups, live according to the same standards, share the same identity—a collective individualism. Ironically, this "one-size-fits-all" approach to "designer" Christianity has a cloning effect—seeking our uniqueness we observe the customary, preserve traditions, replicate what is common. (Where will we find a genuine model of discipleship in this sea of sameness?)

Provincialism reigns in denominational life. How many of us think of our own brand of discipleship as the purest form of Christianity and all other expressions mere aberrations of the same? (The worship wars prove the point.) At the same time, individualism in the body of Christ produces a "Lone Ranger" mentality among disciples. Our arrogance leads to a solitary life of spirituality without context—historical, racial, political, or social. Without dialogue, without conversation, without

We cannot follow Jesus by ourselves.
It takes twelve persons to follow him.
That's what the Gospels teach us.

communion—left to myself—I tend to think that my Christian convictions are absolutely right for all persons for all time. And yet, even as I try to deal with my own ambitions, my own selfish ways, my own pretentiousness, I am left to wonder (quoting the apostle Paul): "Who is adequate for these things?" Who will be my model disciple?

This is where the Gospels come in. In the pages of Matthew, Mark, Luke, and John we learn how to follow Jesus. Yet, each Gospel writer does discipleship differently. Matthew shows how disciples are made when Jesus is absent. Throughout the Gospel story, Jesus looks past the present to instruct his followers for the future. For Matthew, Jesus is present when disciples make disciples in his absence. The story ends with the "great commission"—Jesus sends his disciples away to make disciples without him. And, in his absence he promises: "I am with you always, even to the end of the age." Matthew's Gospel, then, is a manual for making disciples—it shows the reader how to follow Jesus by making followers of Jesus. Mark, on the other hand, makes the reader wonder: "Who are the real disciples of Jesus?" The twelve do not get very good press in Mark's story of discipleship. He doesn't give the most flattering picture of those upon whom the success of Jesus's ministry rests. In fact, the disciples become a huge question mark in the kingdom initiative of Jesus. Jesus assumes they understand his parables, but they don't. He expects them to perform miracles, but they can't. They are hard-headed and hard-hearted. It's no wonder they abandon him in the end. Luke, on the other hand, makes it clear who are genuine disciples and who are not. In the topsy-turvy world of Jesus's kingdom, outsiders become insiders, the poor are powerful, a leper holds the distinction as the greatest Jew who ever lived, and a thief becomes the hero who steals his way into heaven. At the same time, it's easy to see who won't make it to heaven—the very persons you would expect to be there such as those who are blessed: the healthy, the wealthy, the wise. Luke makes it clear what it takes to follow Jesus: be needy. Finally, John tells the story of ideal discipleship. Who were the greatest followers of Jesus? Peter? James? Thomas? It's not who you think. John uses four nameless, faceless persons to reveal the genuine qualities of an authentic disciple: love, faith, humility, and faithfulness. Of the four, the beloved disciple is the best disciple. The surprise comes, however, when the reader is forced to answer the question: "Who is the disciple whom Jesus loves?" The answer: it could be you.

This is what we need. To put it bluntly, we need to go back to the Bible to rediscover what it takes to follow Jesus. To belong to a community of faith requires humility. We must recognize that many believers before us have walked the same narrow path that leads to life. They wrestled with the same questions; they argued over the essentials of genuine Christianity just as we do today. Think about it. There have been thousands of different kinds of Christians who have lived in thousands of different kinds of communities for thousands of years, and it all started with the first followers of Jesus. Church history preserves their legacy. They followed Jesus, then taught others how to follow Jesus, passing down their testimony of how they met the one who changed their lives forever. Their story is our story; the first will be the last. Like those who have gone before, we lead when we follow, we teach when we learn. Let's learn how to follow Jesus according to Matthew, Mark, Luke, and John.

THE GOSPEL
OF MATTHEW

A Training Manual for Discipleship

1

Fit for Faith

Who could move a mountain? Who would love their enemy?

Who could rejoice in pain, and turn the other cheek, and *still*

say, "Surely God is with us today"?

Rich Mullins, *The Jesus Record*

Everyone has a nickname. Sometimes our given names won't do. We call him, "George," or her, "Mary," but for friends who know them best, he's "pudge" and she's "yacker." Most of us earned our nicknames; some of us despise them. Sometimes they don't even fit. But, whatever our feelings, nicknames stick. We can't get rid of them. Despite our protests or boastful claims, we are known by what we are called.

If God had a nickname for you, what would it be? Slacker? Moaner? Gimme? Softy? Peppy? Sunshine? Freight Train? Rock? Can you imagine God saying as you kneel in prayer, "Well now! Look who it is! Here comes 'mopie' to cheer us up today!"? Ouch. The reason I bring up such a painful subject is that it seems to have been Jesus's habit to nickname his friends. He called James and John the "sons of thunder."

He named Simon "the stone." He may have even called Thomas "the twin." He should have nicknamed Judas "the traitor." But to me the most interesting nickname he gave to his disciples was the one found in Matthew's Gospel: Jesus called the twelve "little faith." He pinned the name on them at the very beginning of the story. And, like most of us, they seemed to live up to their name tag. Time after time, page after page, the disciples rarely exhibit what we would call "great faith." Jesus, on the other hand, personifies the greatest faith: faith in God, faith in the kingdom, faith in the power of his word, faith in those who listen well, faith even in his twelve disciples. There's the rub. Jesus, a man full of faith, believes in faithless men. Why? Because, according to Matthew's Gospel, Jesus is the gift of faith for those who believe. Thus the conundrum: the kind of disciple we are depends on the kind of Lord he is. Our discipleship reveals his lordship. We follow a man we cannot see. We are believers.

Every Gospel writer does discipleship differently. For Matthew, disciples are made when Jesus is absent (the reality for every reader of his Gospel). The story begins with the angel's promise that Jesus would be "Immanuel" (a nickname?), meaning "God with us." It ends with the resurrected Messiah's promise: "I am with you always." These bookends of divine presence frame the story of how Jesus made his disciples into faithful followers. As a matter of fact, many scholars have called Matthew's Gospel a "manual for discipleship."[1] The Gospel works like a manual of instruction, showing any reader how to make a disciple by tracking Jesus's training of the twelve. In his presence, the disciples learn about discipleship. In his absence, the twelve *become* disciples. The reader marks the progress and learns how to make disciples, just like Jesus did. Consequently, the student becomes the teacher, disciples become disciplers, and the Great Commission is fulfilled in the *absence* of Jesus who promises: "I am with you always." Matthew tells the story of Immanuel: God is with us when disciples make disciples.

Matthew's Gospel has a strange ending. He never tells us what happened to Jesus after the resurrection. Instead, he describes how Jesus gathered his disciples on a mountain and gave them authority to make disciples. The end. There is no story of Jesus being caught up in the clouds. There is no account of what will happen to the twelve once they follow their Lord's command. There is no promise of a "comforter" who will guide them in all truth. Nothing. The scene ends with Jesus promising his disciples that he would be with them to the end of the world. So, there are two pressing realities bearing down on any reader at this point, two obvious conclusions that anyone could draw: Jesus is not here and the world has not come to an end. What did Jesus mean? How is Jesus present when it's obvious that he's absent? Where did he go? Matthew doesn't feel obliged to end his Gospel by answering the question. The ascension, at this point, wouldn't make sense. Can you see the mixed message? Even as Jesus is departing from them, carried away into the heavens, he shouts down to his faithful followers: "I'll never leave you;

In his presence,

the disciples learn about discipleship.

In his absence, the twelve become disciples.

I'll be with you from now on!" Instead, Matthew leaves the question of Jesus's presence/absence to the mind of every reader.

How am I supposed to follow Jesus when he isn't here? Matthew's Gospel is the answer to the question. It seems that, as disciples make disciples, Jesus *is present* to the end of the age. Because, as any reader of Matthew's Gospel can infer, the twelve made disciples, who made disciples, and so on, and so on, resulting in the Gospel I hold in my hands—a Gospel that makes disciples even after the twelve are no longer present. This, I believe, is the literary effect of Matthew's Gospel. On first read, Matthew's Gospel evokes faith. Then, the ending makes the new disciple reread the story to learn how to make disciples. Finally, the irony comes home. As it is in the case of any reader, so it was in the case of the twelve: disciples are made when Jesus is absent, and in the making of a disciple, Jesus is present—even to the end of the age. Thus the saying of Jesus found only in Matthew comes true: "It is enough for the disciple that he become like his teacher" (Matt. 10:25). In other words, Matthew's Gospel makes a disciple much like Jesus did for the twelve. Jesus is present when we read the story. We hear from him, we listen to the stories as if he were discipling us. Then, putting the gospel aside, reality dawns on us: he's not here, coaching us every step of the way. We wonder what Jesus would say to us given this situation or that problem. We've read the story. Now, how do we live it? The test of our devotion comes when Jesus is absent—same as the twelve.

Have you ever noticed that, when you read Matthew's Gospel, Jesus seems to be talking directly to you? Throughout the narrative, the scene is repeated: Jesus gathers the twelve to teach them about the reign of God. As a reader, you're eavesdropping on special instructions given to the twelve for *their* mission to the "lost sheep of Israel." Then, without warning, Jesus talks over their heads and begins to speak about circumstances beyond the experiences of the twelve: "But whenever they persecute you in one city, flee to the next; for truly I say to you, *you will not finish going through the cities of Israel until the Son of Man comes*" (Matt. 10:23). "Wait a minute," you think to yourself, "the twelve didn't visit *every city of Israel* on that mission." Who is Jesus talking to? Later, Jesus teaches the twelve about recovering "lost sheep" and speaks of a time when he *won't* be with them: "For where two or three have gathered together in My name, I am there in their midst" (18:20). Disturbing words, no doubt, for the twelve—comfort for those of us who know the reality of his absence all too well. In Matthew's Gospel, there are several places where Jesus talks past the twelve and their world, and speaks of the future—a future when he would be gone, a future beyond the twelve, a future where disciples would gather in his name without him, a future where disciples are made by disciples—our future. So, it shouldn't surprise us that, according to Matthew, Jesus's last words were "Make disciples of all peoples, baptizing them in the name of the Father and the Son and the Holy Spirit, teaching them to keep everything I commanded you; and, look at it like this! I am with you every day, even to the end of the age" (my translation). That's the one promise every follower of Jesus wants to believe. He is here. Jesus is Immanuel.

Between a Rock and a Hard Place: Test #1

Jesus left his disciples by themselves on several occasions to test them. Why he left them alone is obvious: he was preparing them for his exit. There are four places in Matthew's Gospel where Jesus is "absent" from the twelve: the stilling of the storm (8:23–27); walking on the water (14:22–33); the failed exorcism (17:14–20); the trial and crucifixion of Jesus (26:56–27:66). The first two stories are paired together by a boat. In Matthew's Gospel, the boat is where Jesus makes disciples. Why? When he first called them to follow him, Jesus claimed that he would make them "fishers of men" (4:19). *In a boat* Jesus turned fishermen into disciples by teaching them a lesson about faith. Once they learned they could trust Jesus for who he is (faith), then they would learn how to follow him (faithfulness) for what he was destined to be. This is how disciples become disciplers: once a disciple learns who Jesus is, then he discovers what he will become. In the process, a mystery is revealed and a transformation occurs: fishermen fish, disciples disciple—what they do is who they are *and* what Jesus did for them is what they will be. Ironically, all of this happens in a boat.

The reader of Matthew's Gospel gets to see how Jesus did it. Essentially, the making of a disciple is a story about two rocks: Jesus and Peter. In his sermon, Jesus claimed that anyone who "hears these words of Mine and acts on them, may be compared to a wise man who built his house on the rock" (7:24). The moron, on the other hand, builds his house without regard to the importance of a firm foundation. In that case, when the wind blows and the waves crash against the fool's house, it falls down (v. 27). These words fall on deaf ears today since we do not face the same constraints as ancient builders. We can put a house just about anywhere we want it. All that is required is to dig for footings, pour concrete, and a foundation is made by man. In Jesus's day, one had to find a foundation before a house could be built. Location was determined by discovery. This is what the disciples had to learn. As a reader, we watch the scenario unfold right before our eyes. Will the twelve discover the rock and withstand the beating of the wind and the waves? Or, will all fall down? Will Simon walk on a firm foundation, or will Peter sink like a rock (get the pun)? The answer? All it takes is faith. The problem? These men are known by the nickname "little faith." This doesn't look good for the home team.

The first time Jesus called the disciples "little faith," he was teaching them about worry and doubt. Unbelievers, he taught them, worry about the necessities of life: food and drink, clothing and protection, life and death. Believers, however, trust in a God who knows how to take care of his own. "But if God clothes the grass of the field with flowers, which is here today and gone tomorrow, will he not do much more for you, little faith?" (6:30, my translation). This comes in the middle of the famous "Sermon on the Mount." These are a few of the words that Jesus expected his disciples to build their lives upon—like a rock. So that, when life rains down hard on the faithful, when the storms of pain blow against the shelter of our souls, the believer stands rock solid. Trusting in the loving care of our heavenly Father reveals that we are his children. To doubt God is to act like a fool—an unbeliever who thinks that everything depends on himself. "The Gentiles eagerly seek all these things; for your heavenly Father knows that you need all these things" (v. 32). To worry about life, then, is to act like an unbeliever. Indeed, doubting God is the opposite of faith—a notorious problem for those who claim to follow Jesus.

Worry seems to plague those who have the most to lose. What if I lose my job? What if I lose the affection of my spouse? What if I lose my health? What if I lost my house, my pension, my family? What if I lost everything? I am ashamed to admit it, but at least once a fortnight I run worst-case scenarios through my head, working out contingency plans: "If I lost my job, then we would have to sell this, and then we would be able to keep our house this long until our savings would run out, in the meanwhile I would have to find a job—any job—and then I might have to move, leaving my family behind so that the kids wouldn't have to move to another school. . . ." Of course, recently many Americans have lived the nightmare of losing it all. It's been a cold, sullen reminder to all of us that life is fragile. Certainly, we have much to worry about. Yet, I didn't know what worry was until I became a father. It's one thing to stew over my own affairs. It's quite something else to fret over the welfare of our children. From their first steps to the first time I watched the tail lights of their car leave our driveway without me, anxiety has become a way of life. Sometimes I lie awake at night contemplating what could have happened in light of the day's events. "If my wife hadn't stepped out to help Grace get out of the van at school, then the other car whipping by our van wouldn't have seen her, then Sheri wouldn't have yelled at the car, then Grace . . ." I can stew for hours. How foolish. If God knows what we need before we need it, then he is our provider. If God takes care of fields and flowers, birds and grass, then he is our protector. Fools think they are their own providers. Morons build their houses on the shifting sand of their own sensibilities. This is why they worry. The wise, on the other hand, have faith in God. This is the first lesson disciples must learn; they are believers.

In Matthew's Gospel, it didn't take Jesus much time to find the wise man. As soon as he finished his sermon, he went to Capernaum and met a man of great faith. He wasn't one of the twelve, nor was he in the company following Jesus down the mountain. This man wasn't even a Jew. Jesus found great faith in a Roman soldier. The centurion approached Jesus with news of a sick servant. Jesus, breaking the purity code, offered to go to the man's house to heal the boy. The soldier's response is classic (words that *any* disciple of Jesus should say): "Lord, I am not worthy for You to come under my roof, but *just say the word*, and my servant will be healed" (8:8). Jesus was astonished. He hadn't found faith like that among any of the Jews—not even his own disciples. Notice the soldier's resolve: all he needed to hear from Jesus were words. That's *exactly* how Jesus characterized the wise man who builds his house upon the rock: "whoever hears these words of mine and acts upon them." The rest of chapter eight, however, tells the opposite story: when disciples hear the words of Jesus and fail to act upon them because they have "little faith."

"The foxes have holes and the birds of the air have nests, but the Son of Man has nowhere to lay His head" (v. 20). Was Jesus bragging or complaining? Was he looking for empathy or making a declaration of freedom? For disciples who tend to worry about the necessities of life, these are ominous words, providing little comfort. In fact, to most of his auditors, Jesus's warning would have sounded more like resignation—even a contradiction of what he had claimed before—especially when, in the next episode, he fell asleep in a boat (he literally had nowhere to lay his head). Jesus found rest anywhere. Who needs a home? I cannot help but wonder if the other "disciple" asked permission to bury his father to see how far Jesus would go with his "no worries" agenda. Jesus responded bluntly: "Follow Me, and allow the dead to bury their own dead" (v. 22). What is the implication of these rather harsh words, other than the fact that Jesus demanded complete allegiance—even above family obligations? Those who refuse to follow Jesus are dead; those who follow him have life—they have nothing to worry about. With these simple lessons about faith and discipleship ringing in the ears of the twelve, Jesus "got into the boat, [and] His disciples *followed Him*" (v. 23).

Matthew tells us that Jesus was oblivious to the great storm that swept over the sea. He was asleep. His disciples, on the other hand, panicked. To us, a boat trip in the midst of a raging storm would be scary enough. Low-pressure systems can wreak havoc for those who travel on terra aqua. The people of New Testament times, however, knew nothing of low-pressure systems and trough lines that produce squalls (the technical jargon of modern prognosticators). Jews in Jesus's day—as well as other first-century Mediterraneans—believed that divine powers controlled nature. They even had one word for wind and spirit: *pneuma* in Greek (or *ruach* in Aramaic). Spiritual beings controlled the elements. The oceans and seas—the chaos of primeval powers—were the abode of evil. (This is why the demons that possessed the Gadarene demoniac caused the herd of swine to rush into the sea; vv. 31–33.) So, when the twelve were overwhelmed by the storm, they recognized that the powers were trying to destroy them. What was *unbelievable* to them, no doubt, was that Jesus could sleep through all of this. That's what faith looks like: finding rest in the middle of a storm.

In Matthew's version of the stilling of the storm, the disciples awaken Jesus with the words, "Save us, Lord; we are perishing!" (v. 25). To me, this looks like an accurate assessment of their situation. A boat that is taking in water in the middle of a terrible storm is doomed. Their request "save us, Lord" makes perfect sense. That this was not the way Jesus felt about the situation is obvious. Jesus was angry, chiding them for waking him up: "Why are you acting like cowards, little faith?" Why is Jesus upset with the twelve? There are a number of reasons. First, he was sleeping. Peaceful sleep in the middle of the storm models the faith of one who rests in the knowledge of a kind, heavenly Father (cf. 6:8, 32). Anyone awakened unnecessarily from deep sleep would be perturbed. Can't a guy get a little shut-eye around here? Secondly, remember what Jesus said to the disciple who wanted to bury his father? Those who don't follow Jesus are dead. The implication, then, was that those who follow him have life. The disciples, on the heels of what looks like a legitimate request ("Save us, Lord"), declare: "we are *perishing*." With Jesus asleep in the boat, the disciples were convinced that their welfare was in jeopardy. Certain death was imminent. The only thing to do, to their way of thinking, was to wake up Jesus with the prayer: Save us, Lord! This, I believe, offended Jesus. What may look like an act of faith—asking for Jesus's help—was, in reality, an act of cowardice. Fear and doubt—that which makes cowards of us all—are polar opposites of faith. Thus, the nickname Jesus gave to the twelve is evermore applicable: "Why are you timid, *little faith*?" Ironically, his rebuke comes during the storm, when lessons of faith are learned.

I'm not sure that I counted the cost when I began to follow Jesus. For the most part, my "prayer" for salvation sounded much like the disciples' cry of desperation: Save me, Lord, or else I will perish in hell! The good news is, as it is with any who call upon his name, he heard my prayer and saved me from the torment of my soul. Since then I have never doubted that I meant it or that he heard me. And yet, there have been times when I have cried the same prayer, for different reasons, and found a different result. This confuses me. On a number of occasions I have repeated the prayer, "Save me, Lord; I'm dying down here!" and nothing happens. The winds still blow, the storms persist, my boat sinks. Sometimes I don't think I'm going to make it. I'm afraid that life's disappointments will drown out my devotion. "Why doesn't he answer me?" I wonder. My request is legitimate. This is life and death. Doubt creeps in like a stowaway. The powers, it seems, are overwhelming me. Evil and suffering persist unchecked. "Why does he let things like this happen? Why doesn't he do something? Is he numb to my pain, my sorrow, my worries? Doesn't he understand? Doesn't he see the problem?" Other Christians have been in the same boat. They know the anguish of a soul tormented by loneliness. Has Jesus forgotten what it is like down here? He promised us he would never leave us or forsake us. Where is he now? There's no relief in sight, no break in the weather; death keeps pounding away, stealing my confidence, feeding my fear. I want to run, but where can I go? I'm trapped in the boat of faith. Jesus is with me, I believe. But sometimes it feels like he's asleep at the wheel. "Wake up! Wake up! Can't you see that I'm dying? Save me, Lord; I'm perishing!" Then, in the midst of the storm, I hear his voice: "Why are you afraid, little faith?"

This is why I'm afraid. If God's eye is on the sparrow, then why do babies die? If God clothes the grass of the field with flowers, then why do the elderly die of exposure during harsh winters? If trusting in Jesus is no guarantee that life will get better, then why follow him into the boat? If he promises us that he will always be with us, then why does it seem like we're alone when we need him the most? Most of the time, I can't help but cry out in desperation: *"Save us, Lord; we are perishing!"* And what is heaven's reply? The winds do not stop. The waves wash over us. Our lifeboat is sinking. The storms rage. This is the time for faith.

Since Jesus rebuked the twelve before he rebuked the storm, then what should the disciples have asked for? Their timid cry disappointed Jesus. It reminded him of their "little faith." By contrast, what would the "great faith" of a disciple look like? In this situation, what were the twelve disciples supposed to do? The careful reader of Matthew's Gospel already knows. Doubters worry about things they can't control; believers trust in God. Only a fool would believe that bad times never come. The wise man, on the other hand, builds his life on the words of Jesus, knowing that hard times are inevitable. God cares, Jesus taught us. That kind of faith withstands the winds and the sea. The man of great faith knows the power of his master's word. "Just say the word, and my servant will be healed," the Roman centurion exclaimed. Why worry? The master speaks and the heavens obey. Therefore, what the twelve should have said was "Speak Lord; we are listening!" His words are life. His words are rock solid. His words calm troubled waters. Disciples of great faith know these things. The twelve, on the other hand, marveled at the power of his words: "What kind of a man is this, that even the winds and the sea obey Him?" (8:27). They didn't seem to know who was in the boat with them.

It all comes down to this: I can't cross the sea without Jesus. As long as he is in the boat with me, everything will be alright. That is what I count on. That is what I've built my house on. This is what I believe. Jesus, Lord of heaven and earth, can speak the word and make the pain go away. To unbelievers this kind of faith looks pretty foolish. They like to point out the obvious: storms are bad things. Yet, even while the hard winds blow and waves of disappointment crash against our lives, we persist in our belief that God cares for us. Why? Because disciples know that we learn to believe when God is the only one we can trust. Lessons on faith always come when a boat is sinking. No matter what happens, we know that he is with us. And, at any time, in any place, he can speak the word. Howling winds are reduced to a pleasant breeze. Angry waters give way to serenity. He can calm and quiet my soul with a single word. Storms squeeze faith out of the disciple. The testing of our faith can be a good thing. Besides, faith is what separates believers from unbelievers. This is good news. Jesus makes believers out of us—especially those who follow him into a boat.

Walking by Faith, Not by Sight: Test #2

After Jesus stopped the storm, the twelve asked a question that no one seemed able to answer: "Who is this?" Many tried. Different persons had different answers. John the Baptizer had his doubts about Jesus's identity: "Are You the Expected One, or shall we look for someone else?" (11:3). The multitude reluctantly admitted the possibility of Jesus's messianic potential: "This man cannot be the Son of David, can he?" (12:23). The Pharisees argued he was "Beelzebul," the lord of demons (12:24). Jesus's hometown would claim nothing more than that he was

Disciples know that we learn to believe

when God is the only one we can trust.

Lessons on faith always come when a boat

is sinking. No matter what happens,

we know that he is with us.

"the carpenter's son" (13:55). Herod Antipas thought that he was John the Baptizer *redivivus*. Amazingly, Jesus never tried to set the record straight regarding his identity. Instead, he constantly teased his listeners with hints of his significance: "something greater than the temple is here" (12:6), "something greater than Jonah is here" (v. 41), "something greater than Solomon is here" (v. 42). The secret of his identity, it seems, was hidden to the eyes of those who saw him. It's no wonder that, in the midst of the story of everyone's struggle to figure out who Jesus was, Matthew strings together in chapter 13 a number of parables that share the common theme of things that are hidden from view: seeds sown, leavening dough, treasures in fields, costly pearl, fish in the sea, treasures of a scribe. Ironically, Jesus used parables to teach about the hidden truths of God: "I will open My mouth in parables; I will utter things hidden since the foundation of the world" (v. 35; here Matthew quotes Ps. 78:2). Indeed, the parables tended to conceal more than they revealed. It's hard to see what Jesus meant (13:36).

It comes as no surprise, then, that Jesus screamed out (in frustration?): "Nobody understands me. Nobody knows who I am, except you, Father!"

(my paraphrase of 11:27). Not the religious leaders, not the crowds, not twelve disciples, not even John the Baptizer—no one got it. A solitary life can turn into loneliness when no one understands. Jesus, on the other hand, exclaimed: "I praise You, Father, Lord of heaven and earth, that You have hidden *these things* from the wise and intelligent and have revealed them to infants" (v. 25). For him this was reason enough to surround himself with those who would understand. Jesus was out to make disciples who would get it. "Come to Me, all who are weary and heavy-laden, and I will give you rest. Take My yoke upon you and learn from Me,[2] for I am gentle and humble in heart, and you will find rest for your souls. For My yoke is easy and My burden is light" (vv. 28–30). These words echo throughout the stories that follow, resonating in the second test of the faith(fulness) of the twelve—a test of discipleship that comes, once again, while they are in a boat.

For Matthew, there is an intrinsic link between the miracles of Jesus and his identity. Matthew seemed to emphasize that where faith abounded, miracles abounded all the more. Unbelief stifled the miraculous as well as the ability to see the significance of Jesus. Ironically, faith produced miracles, and miracles hindered faith. Notice how often in Matthew's Gospel Jesus emphasized that it was the faith of the penitent that made the miraculous happen (8:13; 9:22; 9:29; 15:28). And, for those who witnessed these things, notice how often miracles tended to obscure their perception of Jesus—it made things worse (11:2, 3, 20; 13:54, 58; 14:2). For Matthew, then, Jesus's miracles were not performed in order to get people to believe—to see who he really is (that's John's technique). Miracles were performed *because* people believed, that is, they saw who he really was. This is the essence of faith: disciples know who Jesus is. The last time the twelve got into a boat, they were asking the question: "Who is this?" This time, they will answer it for themselves.

Do you have a favorite miracle of Jesus? Most of us prefer those miracles that feature Jesus's compassion for the needy, or his victory over the enemies of disease and death. My favorite is recorded only by John—the raising of Lazarus. To me this is the most fantastic miracle of them all. There are a couple of miracles, however, that I don't care for. I realize it sounds heretical to admit it. Most of Jesus's miracles make sense. He heals to help the weak, he stills the storm to protect his disciples, he raises the dead to bring hope to those who mourn, he feeds the hungry so that they won't starve. These miracles I like. He doesn't perform them for dramatic effect. We would never expect to hear him announce triumphantly, "Ta da!" after one of his miracles. No. Jesus was no showman. This is why certain miracles bother me. Like, when he changed water into wine. Running out of wine is no crisis. Or, when he paid a temple tax by having Peter catch a fish with a coin in its mouth. (I've never heard a sermon relating the implications of this miracle to tithing!) My least favorite of all, however, is when Jesus walked on the water. Given the circumstances, this miracle is a bit over the top. There was no crisis.

The disciples were not in any danger. As the story goes, the only problem was that the twelve couldn't cross the sea in their boat because of stiff winds. That's it. This is a story about tough sailing. Granted, it was in the middle of the night. The twelve were having a hard time making any progress. Eventually, they became frightened. But, it wasn't the prevailing winds or the darkness of night that gripped their hearts with fear. It was *Jesus walking on the water* that scared them out of their wits. They didn't believe that they were in any danger *until he showed up* walking on the water. Why did he do it? Why all the fuss? Since the twelve weren't in any danger, why did Jesus come to them walking on the water? Was this an act of divine bravado? "Look at me, I can walk on water!" What's going on here?

Before he performed this fanciful miracle, Jesus had just learned of the death of John the Baptizer. At that moment, Jesus tried to get away from everyone (14:13). Why did he want to be alone? What was on his mind as he sought solitude? We don't know for sure, but it seems rather obvious that Jesus needed time alone to grieve over John's death. And, like all of us, when someone close to us dies, we invariably begin to think about our own death. That's what I think Jesus was thinking about: his own death. Unlike John, Jesus was not regarded as an honorable prophet. We know that from the previous story. Unlike John, Jesus would not receive an honorable death—death by crucifixion was a cursed death according to the law. And, unlike John, Jesus would not receive an honorable burial from his followers. In the end, they forsook him. As a matter of fact, if it were up to the twelve, Jesus wouldn't have received a proper burial. Whether or not Jesus knew these things *at this point*, we can never tell. He eventually predicted all three happenings: that he would be rejected by his own people, that he would die a dishonorable death, and that his disciples would scatter like sheep without a shepherd. He knew he was going to leave them, eventually. Would the twelve be ready for his absence? A prophet greater than John was present! Did the twelve know that? John's death made him realize that it was time for another test.

Jesus wanted to be by himself. The crowds wouldn't let him. They persisted in following him by land as he navigated across the sea by boat. Once he arrived on land, he spent the rest of the day healing the sick; Matthew tells us that Jesus felt sorry for them (14:13–14). Once night fell, the twelve were ready for a break. Once again, the disciples assess the situation accurately. The hour is late, there is no food, the crowd must be sent home to fend for themselves. Jesus's reply sounds like he knew that the twelve were up to something: "They do not need to go away; you give them something to eat!" (v. 16). Indeed, the disciples had procured enough food for themselves: five loaves of bread and two fish. If they were to break out the meal intended only for them, a hungry mob could turn into a nasty riot. Their request to send the crowds away was a matter of self-preservation. This didn't square with Jesus. He was training the twelve to take his place once he was gone. The last thing he probably wanted to do was to minister to the needs of the masses; he needed time to grieve. Obviously, food wasn't on his mind at all. Those who mourn never feel like eating. Yet, his disciples were hungry; the crowd was hungry. Selflessly Jesus fed the crowd and made the disciples help. Later, he would have his time alone, and so would the twelve.

"Immediately He made the disciples get into the boat and go ahead of Him to the other side, while He sent the crowds away" (v. 22). Eventually, the disciples got their wish; Jesus dismissed the crowd. This time, however, he made the twelve get in the boat without him, and sent them away, too. At this point, if I were one of the disciples, I would have been a bit reluctant to climb into the boat with orders to cross the sea *without Jesus*. Unbeknownst to the twelve, Jesus was sending them on a training exercise: to navigate difficult waters without him. Standing on the shore and facing the breeze, Jesus knew the winds were against them. That was the point. The question that still needed answering was whether the twelve would recognize their need of him in troubled waters. Would Jesus, with his promise of meeting them "on the other side," be a source of comfort in difficult times? Or, would the promise of his coming haunt them like a ghost from the past? The overtones of this story operate on so many levels. Some interpreters find the salvation story in this episode, "I was sinking deep in sin, far from the peaceful shore" (read the old-time gospel hymn, "Love Lifted Me"). Others see the language of "crossing over" as a reference to the believer's death—Peter's tract across the waters pictures the journey of every believer who walks through the valley of the shadows of death. I hear echoes of Psalm 69:

> Save me, O God,
>   For the waters have threatened my life.
> I have sunk in deep mire, and there is no foothold;
>   I have come into deep waters, and a flood overflows me.
> I am weary with my crying; my throat is parched;
>   *My eyes fail while I wait for my God.*
>
> verses 1–3

This is a story about faith and resilience in the wake of the promise of Jesus's return.

The most common prayer of the early church was a simple Aramaic phrase: maranatha ("Come, Lord"). After two thousand years, we don't pray that way anymore. It seems as though the mockers have gotten the best of us: "Where is the promise of his coming?" Their question goads believers into all kinds of contrivances. Some of us persist in "setting the date." Impatient with waiting, we try to bring solace to the church by assuring ourselves that we have inside information, predicting the year, month, even day of Christ's return. Tired of rowing the boat against contrary winds, we grit our apocalyptic teeth and hold out for the last day when God finally gives the wicked their due. Yet, prophets come and go, life carries on, and no one seems to know when. Embarrassed by our gullibility, scholars come forth to declare that Jesus didn't mean it. We've all misunderstood him: the twelve, the early church, the Gospel writers, preachers and teachers—all of us have put words into his mouth, foolishly expecting a "second coming." It's taken two thousand years, but experts have finally come forth to dispel this childish "chicken-little" notion of the end of the world. We'll all be better off if we accept the obvious: Jesus isn't coming back. We will go to him, but he will not come to us.

> *If absence makes the heart grow fonder,*
> *then two thousand years should make*
> *the church desperate for Jesus.*

If absence makes the heart grow fonder, then two thousand years should make the church desperate for Jesus. Even though date-setters make us look foolish, even though better minds have given up hoping for a fairy-tale ending, I shall persist in praying, "Maranatha." Sometimes it's the only prayer I know. While we strain against the oars, trying to do what Jesus told us to do, the echoes of a promise still ring in our ears, a haunting refrain that never ends. So, we pray, "Lord, come. We need you now more than ever. Sometimes we're not sure if we're going to make it. It's getting hard down here. Please, come." Even though it seems like a ghost of a chance, I pray, "Maranatha." Even though I can't see how it could happen, I pray, "Maranatha." My eyes fail while I wait for my God. I wish I heard more disciples praying, "Maranatha."

When the disciples saw Jesus walking on the water they mistook him for a ghost. They were having a hard time getting across the sea "for the wind was contrary" (Matt. 14:24). Unexpected as it was, seeing a phantom in the winds of a chaotic sea made sense to these fishermen. This was no hallucination. They believed that spirits and powers manipulated the elements. Having one of those spirits come after them spelled certain doom. So, "they cried out in fear" (v. 26). Their eyes failed them; they mistook Jesus for a phantom. Jesus tried to put their minds at ease. "Take courage, it is I; do not be afraid" (v. 27). The last time the twelve were in a boat, troubled by bad seas, their cowardice prevented them from trusting Jesus. Jesus, in the midst of the storm, chided the disciples for their lack of faith. This time, things were different. The twelve were not in danger. Jesus was not with them in the boat. In the midst of the storm, a word of encouragement comes rather than a lesson on faith. Jesus assumes that their lack of courage was due to their inability to see him for who he really is.

Notice the progression: (1) take courage, because (2) I'm here: therefore, (3) don't be afraid. The problem is as it was before: the twelve aren't sure who they're dealing with. Peter: "Lord, *if it is You*, command me to come to You on the water" (v. 28). How's that for a bold assertion, a confident profession of faith! Peter's request is not based on a wholehearted endorsement of the phantom's claim. His notion, to go out walking on the water, looks more like a test to unmask the ghost's deception than a declaration of unfettered faith. Remember, at this point, they don't think it's Jesus. How could they? They were surprised that he could rebuke the powers that govern the wind and the seas. If they *did* believe it was Jesus—without a doubt—then Peter should have said: "Lord, command the winds and the sea to be still!" Instead, Peter puts forward a preposterous idea: have a *real* man walk on water—for everyone knows that only *ghosts* can.

Imagine Peter's surprise when the phantom says, "Come on!" To me, therefore, the most hilarious words in the whole Gospel are "And Peter got out of the boat, and walked on the water and came toward Jesus" (v. 29). There was no good reason for Peter to abandon ship. It wasn't sinking. Why did he do it? Literally, Peter was testing the waters—to see if the voice in the wind was Jesus. He thought he saw a ghost. He heard the word. Would he trust his ears or his eyes? Stepping out of the boat and sinking would verify what he thought he saw—a ghost trying to coax him out to drown. Walking on the water—the impossible—would prove the word true. Both actions would require some faith, because nobody gets out of a boat unless it's sinking. This is why I never understood why Jesus rebuked Peter for sinking. At least he had enough faith to try! What about the eleven who stayed in the dry boat? This never made sense to

me. What Jesus should have said was "Attaboy Peter! At least you gave
it a shot." If Peter sank because of his little faith, then the men in the
boat deserved the harsher rebuke for having no faith at all.

Yet Peter's experience was based on sights and sounds. He walked
because he believed what his ears heard; and he sank because of what
his eyes saw. But I don't believe Jesus chastised Peter because his feet
failed him. True, the story does say that after Peter took notice of the
wind, and fear overwhelmed him, then he began to sink. In this respect,
"Lord, save me!" is a legitimate request. But that's the point I want to
contend with. Once Jesus grabbed Peter and lifted him out of the water,
he said, "O little faith, why did you doubt?" The question I would ask
is, What did Peter doubt? That he could walk on water? No, he already
proved that he could. The winds were just as fearsome before he got
out of the boat as when he walked on water. Why was Jesus upset with
Peter? What was Peter doubting?

Think about it. Peter had walked some distance away from the boat.
It wasn't until after Peter cried out for help that Jesus "stretched out His
hand and took hold of him" (v. 31). What does that imply? Peter was
close to Jesus. All Jesus had to do was "stretch out his hand," no more
than a couple feet away, to grab Peter. So here's the picture. Peter walks
toward Jesus—so close that, from the perspective of those who stayed
in the boat, they appear to be standing side by side—close enough that
now Peter can *see that it was Jesus*. Then, Peter takes his eyes off Jesus
and takes in the unreal: now there are *two* men standing on water. He
begins to sink. He's going down. Jesus is right there with him. Peter
calls out in fear, "Lord, save me!" He has no doubts now. He knows
it's Jesus. And yet, the irony is this: having recognized Jesus, his feet
fail him and he sinks. Jesus can't believe it. "O little faith, why did you
doubt?" Doubt what? Doubt that Jesus would save you, Peter. He was
standing right there. He saw you go down. All he had to do was reach
out and grab you. Why did you think you had to ask him for help? Did
you think he wouldn't save you unless you cried out in fear? Did you
doubt his care for you? Did you honestly believe that Jesus would have
let you drown? Didn't Jesus say a few days before, "What man is there
among you who has a sheep, and if it falls into a pit on the Sabbath, will
he not take hold of it and lift it out?" (12:11). Are you not more valuable
than sheep, little faith?

I shared my take on this story a few months ago at a retreat and one
of the participants remarked: "Of course! That makes sense. If a father
is teaching his son how to swim, and the son begins to flail about in the
water, wouldn't the father, who is right there with him, be a bit insulted
if the son believes he has to call out to his dad to save him?" Exactly.
This was a training session. Jesus was out to teach his disciples that,

even in his absence, he would care for them no matter what. All they had to do was believe what he said: "Come to Me, all who are weary and heavy-laden, and I will give you rest. Take My yoke upon you and learn from Me, for I am gentle and humble in heart, and you will find rest for your souls. For My yoke is easy and My burden is light" (11:28–30). Light enough to walk on water. Enough rest to persevere against difficult winds. Anybody tired of the fight? Anybody weary of trying to do what Jesus commanded? Are you looking for a little rest, for a little solace? Come to Jesus. Walk on the waters of your battle. Have no doubts when the fight overwhelms you. "But I'm sinking, Lord! I don't know how long I can stand this!" He knows. He's right there with you. You know that, because you've heard his voice. You know it's true because you've seen him with eyes of faith. You don't have to cry out in desperation. He cares for you. Believe it. For, like Peter, we walk by faith and not by sight.

"You never forget burying your first baby." That's what the funeral director said to me while we were waiting for the family to gather around the little casket at the cemetery. He's right. I still carry that memory with me. Her name was Abby. She was born into the arms of a loving couple and a big brother—a little boy who was very animated in his excitement over the new arrival. The celebration didn't last long. On the day that she was born it was discovered that Abby's heart wasn't right. She was rushed to the children's hospital that specialized in helping children with heart problems. Even that expression bothers me. For everyone knows that hearts only develop problems over time. We prayed night and day for that little girl. I don't think I've prayed any harder or any longer than I did for her. After nearly a three-month battle, she died.

I've been told that the worst pain in the world is when parents have to bury their child. The young couple faced their heartache with more courage and strength than I thought possible. They endured the three-month ordeal of hoping against hope that medical odds were wrong. They believed in a God who can bring death to life. They trusted him despite the outcome. Even after they faced the horrible feeling of coming home to an empty nursery, explaining to a little boy that the sister he so looked forward to cuddling wouldn't come home, they kept saying that they still believed that God is good. To this day they don't know that I was devastated. My faith hung in the balance. I questioned the goodness of God as I considered their pain. I dreaded the funeral. But they—to my eyes—they got out of the boat and walked on water. As far as I know, they never cried out in faithless desperation, they never questioned God's care for their little girl. The pain was deep, their grief as stiff as contrary winds. But they persisted in their belief that God was still on their side.

A few months later, Abby's mom showed me a picture they planned to dedicate to the church in Abby's memory. It pictures a little girl wearing

Sunday dress looking out the window of her bedroom in great expectation of someone's arrival. We hung the picture in the children's building. "This gives us comfort, pastor," the couple explained. "We know that Abby waits for us with Jesus." What took me by surprise wasn't their words of profound conviction, or their desire to memorialize their daughter. What amazed me was that Abby's mom and dad said these things with a smile—always with a smile. I was looking on from the safety of my boat of faith. I sometimes wondered if the winds and the waves would be too much for them. I wouldn't have blamed them if their sorrow had washed over them, making them drown in doubt and despair. Instead, they kept on walking. And I couldn't believe my eyes.

"When they got into the boat, the wind stopped. And those who were in the boat worshiped Him, saying, 'You are certainly God's Son!'" (14:32–33). The twelve have come a long way. Jesus called them, promising that he would make them his disciples—fishers of men. After the first test in the boat, they could only ask, "Who is this?" It took another test in a boat to make them see: "You are *certainly* God's Son!" No ifs, ands, or

Faithfulness is revealed by what disciples do,

not by what they say.

This is the making of a disciple, part two.

buts. This they knew for certain. It took Peter's leap of faith *and* Jesus's rescue of a drowning man to prove to the disciples that Jesus was no phantom. Once he was in the boat, everything turned out alright. The wind stopped, Peter was safe and sound, and they all reached the other side. It took a while, but now the twelve recognized Jesus for who he is. Contrasted with the faith of those who waited for them on the shore, however, the perceptiveness of the twelve looks pretty pathetic. Notice how the narrator characterizes the sequence of events shortly after Jesus's finale of making disciples in a boat. Once the people on the shore waiting for Jesus recognized him, they brought all who were sick and begged Jesus to allow them to touch his tunic. For "as many as touched it were cured" (v. 36). They made quick work of their faith. No reticence, no hesitation, no doubt—the men of Gennesaret recognized Jesus and counted on the miraculous. Their need of him revealed their faith in him. This was the very lesson Jesus tried to teach the twelve.

It took two boat trips and several chapters of a Gospel to get there, but they finally arrived: the twelve believed in Jesus. Those whom he nicknamed "little faith" had been borne along by faith to become disciples of Jesus. Now another test remains: would these twelve who have faith be found faithful? Having faith is only half of the story. Jesus will test their knowledge with a simple question: "Who am I?" And, precisely on cue, Peter will give the correct answer: "You are the Christ, the Son of the living God" (16:16). End of story, right? Wrong. It's one thing to say the right words, it's quite something else to do the right thing. Faithfulness is revealed by what disciples do, not by what they say. This is the making of a disciple, part two.

2

Fitted for a Crown

We have neither humility enough to be faithful, nor faith enough to be humble.

George MacDonald, *The Miracles of Our Lord*

When it comes to rewards, Jesus seemed to give mixed signals. Sometimes he led people to believe that everyone in his kingdom would get the same reward. The parable of the day laborers proves the point (Matt. 20:1–16). Whether a man works all day or merely the last hour, all receive the same wage. Elsewhere, Jesus taught that the faithful would receive greater rewards than the faithless: "Take away the talent from him, and give it to the one who has the ten talents. For to everyone who has, more shall be given, and he will have an abundance; but from the one who does not have, even what he does have shall be taken away" (25:28–29). It's no wonder, then, that the twelve competed for the approval of Jesus.

Sometimes it was Peter making boastful claims over the rest (26:33). Once James and John staked their rightful claim to the most desired positions of power in Jesus's government (20:21–23). At one point, the disciples hoped Jesus would settle the issue for them: "Who then is greatest in the kingdom of heaven?" (18:1). Even though he promised the twelve that each one would equally inherit thrones in the kingdom come (19:28), they persisted in their contest for favor. Jesus even seemed to show favorites, fueling the flames of jealousy and contempt among his disciples. Twice Jesus took three of the twelve aside for special treatment. Peter, James, and John—the same three most vocal in their quest for recognition—were privy to the greatest high and lowest low in the life of Jesus. They witnessed both the glory and the agony of Jesus: the transfiguration on the mountain and his prayer in the public park called Gethsemane. Ironically, these are the only other times Jesus was separated from his disciples before the end. His absence was more apparent for nine than three. Nevertheless, in both instances, his absence was a test of his disciples' faithfulness.

The first episode, glory on the mountain, marks the beginning of this new phase of training. The agony in Gethsemane, at the other end of the story, was Jesus's last chance to teach the twelve the final lesson before he was taken away. Once again, Jesus knew that his imminent departure would result in a considerable test of his disciples' allegiance. At first, he was trying to teach the twelve who he was—to have faith in him. The last half of Matthew's Gospel, framed by these two stories, traces Jesus's attempt to train the twelve for the greater and even more important test of their faithfulness. Both training stories are paired together by Jesus taking Peter, James, and John with him—away from the rest of the disciples. And, in both cases, the three and the nine would learn what it takes to be a faithful follower of Jesus in his absence. For, as everyone knows, it's not what you do in the presence of one whom you hope to impress that matters. Loyalty is best seen when no one is looking. "For the Son of Man is going to come in the glory of His Father with His angels, and will then repay every man *according to his deeds*" (16:27).

Did Jesus play favorites? Did he encourage the disciples to compete for his affection in order to get them to be more devoted to him? Did he prize Peter, James, and John above the rest of the disciples? That's the way the twelve saw it. But, that's not what Jesus was doing. When the twelve put their question to their master, Jesus spoke of the last being first, driving home the point with a startling illustration: his choice disciple would be like a child (18:1–4). When James and John jockeyed for favorable positions in the kingdom, Jesus talked about greatness found in a slave, not a lord (20:26–27). Therefore, Jesus didn't take Peter, James, and John with him to witness the transfiguration or to pray with him because they were more important than the rest. These three weren't necessarily Jesus's "best friends." Instead, Jesus kept them close at hand for remedial work—they needed special attention because they didn't understand what he was trying to teach them.[1] Think about it. Since Jesus had been trying to drill the concept into their heads that greatness is leastness, and that the last will be first, then Peter, James, or John shouldn't have been flattered by Jesus's invitation to be first among the twelve. Instead, they should have been offended by his offer. He takes the least and makes them the greatest—that's how Jesus makes faithful disciples. But of course, the chosen three didn't see it that way. That's because they *didn't* understand. Boy, are they going to learn a lesson they'll never forget. And that's the point.

Seeing but Not Hearing: Test #3

It took a while but Jesus finally succeeded. He taught the disciples to see him as he is: the Christ, the Son of God. This revelation confirmed the work of God. That's what Jesus meant when he affirmed Peter's declaration: "Blessed are you, Simon Barjona, because flesh and blood did not reveal this to you, but My Father who is in heaven" (Matt. 16:17). Jesus students received no outside help. Peter passed the midterm exam on his own. It was a two-part essay. Question #1 was easy to answer: "Who do people say that the Son of Man is?" (v. 13). The disciples passed along the scuttlebutt to Jesus: "Some say John the Baptist; and others, Elijah; but still others, Jeremiah, or one of the prophets" (v. 14). No doubt, Jesus himself had heard many of these things. Misunderstanding abounded as he tried to reveal his identity to those who had eyes of faith to see. But then, Jesus asked the question that mattered the most: "But who do you say that I am?" (v. 15). At this point, Peter blurted out the right answer. It's what the disciples had learned to be true—especially after Jesus walked on water: "You are certainly God's Son!" (14:33). Yet, Peter was singled out for recognition. Jesus maintained that God had revealed this to Peter—no disciple, no man, not even Jesus told Peter who he was—"flesh and blood did not reveal this to you." Peter displayed divine insight. Therefore, in Jesus's eyes Peter was worthy of honor: to be the rock foundation of Jesus's church, *and* to receive "the keys of the kingdom of heaven." Like a wise man, Jesus discovered a rock to build his house upon, knowing that no storm, not even "the gates of Hades" would overpower it (16:18).

Peter must have felt pretty good about himself. Jesus promised him unparalleled power. He alone could unleash the power of the kingdom of heaven on earth. The keeper of the keys could unlock any prison on earth, releasing those bound by spiritual powers. And, whatever Peter bound on earth would be bound in heaven. He could stop any evil power, he could correct any injustice, he could push back the darkness. These keys would have come in handy earlier. Think of what Peter could have done when the disciples faced the powers of heaven and earth in storms on the sea. Later, the nine could have used the kingdom keys to release the boy imprisoned by evil spirits. Peter had the power. Imagine, therefore, what must have been going through his mind when Jesus began to prepare his disciples for the doomsday scenario: "From that time Jesus began to show His disciples that He must go to Jerusalem, and suffer many things from the elders and chief priests and scribes, and be killed, and be raised up on the third day" (v. 21). One minute Jesus is celebrating Peter's confession. The next moment he speaks of a cruel death, stripped of all power and honor. Peter wouldn't hear of it; rattling his keys like a saber he declares: "God forbid it, Lord! This shall never happen to You" (v. 22).

How quickly Peter went from being the spokesman of God to becoming Satan incarnate. That's what happens when power comes to those who aren't used to it. It goes straight to their heads. The language Matthew used to describe the heated exchange between Jesus and Peter is unsettling to readers who would expect a more irenic dialogue between the Master and his "best friend." First, Peter is said to have "rebuked" Jesus—the same word Matthew used to describe how Jesus quieted the storm (8:26). Peter *rebuked* Jesus! Can you imagine? What was he thinking? Then, as if that weren't enough to shock any reader, Jesus spared no feelings in his riposte and called his "rock" the devil. "You are a stumbling block to Me; for you are not setting your mind on God's interests, but man's" (16:23). The rock was turning into a stone of offense—a stumbling block. Jesus claimed that Peter heard the words of God. Then, Peter speaks the words of Satan. What happened?

I see Peter brandishing the keys of the kingdom like a weapon. He's just been told that whatever he binds on earth will be bound in heaven. Then, he hears Jesus announce that he is resigned to what the future holds for him, that is, to be delivered to the powers to be killed. Against this hostility, Peter decided to use his newly acquired keys to keep Jesus safe. The "rock" has spoken. His words are strong. With an oath, Peter swears that Jesus will not befall such an evil fate. He won't let it happen. After all, he has the keys.

Students often surprise their teachers. At times they appear so perceptive, so intelligent—as if all the work a teacher puts into her class is paying off. Then, without warning, and much to the disappointment of their mentor, students can be so dumb. It's an ugly scene. The teacher explodes in disbelief, the prized pupil is crowned with a dunce cap, and the class endures another speech about "hard work" and "paying attention" and "having so much to learn with so little time." Due to Peter's faux pas, Jesus had to start over by re-issuing the call to follow him. "Then Jesus said to *His disciples*, 'If anyone wishes to come after Me . . .'" (v. 24). How would those words fall on the ears of the twelve? I can imagine the disciples' confusion: "What does he mean, 'if anyone wants to follow me'? What does he think we've been doing all this time? We left everything. We have been following you, Jesus. Who are you talking to?" But of course, if they listened closely, they would hear why Jesus seems to be starting over with them. The stakes have been raised. They're entering a new path, taking a different road. I believe Jesus felt obliged to set before the twelve what would lie ahead. From this point forward, his destiny would be theirs. There could be no hesitation. He had to warn them from the beginning, as he did the first time he called them. Following Jesus would be costly. Only this time, it would mean his death and theirs. "So," Jesus was essentially saying, "if you're going to follow me from here on out, bring your own cross. We're headed for Jerusalem."

Life must be lost before it can be found. Messianic suffering must precede messianic glory. Only those who give what they have will get what they don't have. In the natural order of things, death comes after life. In the kingdom of God, death must precede life, since power over death can only come by dying. The agony and glory of Jesus will teach them that (v. 28). Until then, the disciples must learn to listen to Jesus in order to see the glory of his kingdom. Their faithfulness will ensure their reward. "For the Son of Man is going to come in the glory of His Father with His angels, and will then repay every man *according to his deeds*" (v. 27). Up to this point, the disciples have learned what to say ("You're the Christ, the Son of God!"). From now on they will learn what to do, because the kind of Messiah Jesus came to be reveals the kind of disciple they must be: faithful to the end.

Jesus lived a crucified life long before he died. Before he came to Jerusalem to meet his fate, Jesus had been toting his cross around, inviting others to join him in his death march to glory. Paul wrote: "The world has been crucified to me, and I to the world" (Gal. 6:14). He understood what the good news of Jesus required of him. Following Jesus meant being conformed to the "fellowship of His sufferings" (Phil. 3:10) and "carrying about in the body the dying of Jesus" (2 Cor. 4:10). Seeing such a death lived out before the world is a constant reminder of where we come from and where we're headed: a cross defines our lives.

Many exemplars have preserved the picture perfect. One of these portraits inspires me every time I think of her: Charlotte Diggs Moon. To me, she portrays what Jesus tried to teach the twelve about faithfulness, about dying to live, about bearing a cross and finding glory. In this case, the cross upon which Lottie Moon died was the plight of the Chinese people. Leaving behind a comfortable life in America, Lottie committed herself to bringing the good news of Jesus Christ to a people she had only read about. A diminutive girl, she quickly fit in, adopting the way of the Chinese people, living on scraps of food, and teaching girls to read and write. She spent her life and her living in a little town literally halfway around the world, sharing her faith and pouring out her soul. After forty years of hard work, she died of malnutrition on Christmas Eve, 1912. She was buried close to her hometown in Virginia. Her headstone reads: FAITHFUL UNTO DEATH.

All I can think about is what she gave up. She was a well-educated woman (an uncommon grace in her day), prepared for a comfortable life of teaching in the South. She was engaged to a prominent minister and scholar. She belonged to a family of great means and much love. But, she left it all to find the fellowship of Jesus' sufferings. What drives a woman like this? Why are these stories replicated, over and over again, throughout the history of the church? Antony of Egypt, Benedict of Nursia, Francis of Assisi, Albert Schweitzer, Dietrich Bonhoeffer, Jim Elliot, Mother Teresa, Henri Nouwen. If it's true that the glory of Christ's kingdom far outshines the sacrifice of any dedicated servant of the Lord (Easter!), then a glimpse of heaven is all we need to carry the cross upon which we shall die. Death

Jesus lived a crucified life long before he died.

has already been decided for us. Losing our lives, then, is no sacrifice since they are spent for Christ. His death is the only death that wasn't in vain. His life is the only life that makes sense. What else is there?

All of us want our lives to count for something. The only way we can find meaning for living is in dying. We get when we give; we find when we lose. Time slips away, one way or another. We can't preserve time like beans in a mason jar. We weren't made to have to live with regrets, either. We have to make a choice; we have to do something. Like loose change, the days burn holes in our pockets. How shall we spend our time? What shall we do with this commodity called life? Hear the famous words of Jim Elliot: "He is no fool who gives what he cannot keep to gain what he cannot lose." This is the lesson all disciples of Christ must learn, even the twelve.

The twin stories of the transfiguration of Jesus on the top of the mountain and the failed exorcism at the bottom of the mountain are paired together by the failure of Jesus's disciples (Matt. 17:1–20). In both episodes, Jesus's absence provides the extenuating circumstances for their gaff. For Peter, James, and John, they see but they do not hear. For the nine left behind, they speak but they do not heal. Both stories teach the reader what Jesus is trying to teach the twelve about faithful discipleship. And, in both episodes we learn why the disciples fail the test: the fraternal twins of power and pride undo the kingdom work. Only in self-denial and humility does a disciple learn kingdom authority. That's the lesson Jesus was trying to teach Peter when he accused him of yielding to Satan's influence. Now he will teach them all.

Although this is a story about Jesus, the episode of the transfiguration seems to revolve around the chosen three: "he was transfigured *before them*," "Moses and Elijah appeared *to them*," "Peter answered" the voices that were talking to Jesus, the divine voice spoke to the *disciples* not Jesus, "when the disciples heard this, they fell on their faces and were much afraid." The details of the story center on what the disciples saw, what they heard, how they reacted to this sneak preview of Easter morning. The transfiguration was as much for their benefit as it was for Jesus' sake. And yet, the reader is left with the impression that these bystanders seemed to get in the way. Eavesdropping on a private conversation, Peter interrupts the council with an idea of his own. But the building of three holy tabernacles for three holy prophets doesn't go over very well. This is apparent when God interrupts Peter with the warning: "This is My beloved Son, with whom I am well-pleased; listen to Him!" (17:5). God seems angry. But why? The Hebrew Scriptures are filled with stories of honorable hosts extending acts of hospitality to mysterious travelers who visit God's people like angels incognito. Again, Peter's proposal seems appropriate to the occasion. What's the problem?

Pride and power are the problem. Notice the first words that come out of Peter's mouth: "Lord, it is good for us to be here" (v. 4). Why would he say that, unless he believes that Jesus made the right choice in taking only three to the mountaintop? Nearly a week before the event, Jesus predicted that some of his disciples would not die until they saw the glory of the Son of Man "coming in His kingdom" (16:28). Peter, no doubt, believed Jesus's words were coming true. He and the sons of Zebedee were witnesses of these things by Jesus's choice of them. Essentially, Peter was saying to Jesus, "You chose well." Why? Well, Peter holds the keys of the kingdom. He decides to bind on earth what is loosed from heaven. I believe his desire to build three tabernacles was not an impetuous, uncalculated response to an overwhelming experience. Instead, I see Peter trying to make heavenly visitors—bound by honor—to stay with them on mount glory. Jacob wrestled an angel for a blessing. Abraham and Sarah coaxed their divine visitors with a meal and a sacrifice. Peter offers to build a holy shrine for three powerful prophets who wrought every kind of miracle. Think of the power that these three men wielded like swords for God's righteous cause. With a force like this, what foe could prevail? Remember, Peter was the one who said he wouldn't let Jesus die. By impressing Moses and Elijah for Christ's kingdom, victory would be assured. I may be reading between the lines beyond what the lines allow. Certainly, nowhere in the text does Peter seek to employ the prophets for his cause. Peter may have simply wanted to stay on the mountain without facing the valley of Jesus' self-pronounced Via Dolorosa. Nevertheless, the power and glory of what Peter saw made him feel privileged—perhaps like an insider who thinks he knows the mind of his master's plan. But the problem is not what Peter has seen; it's what he hasn't heard. This is why God said, "You're not listening!"

Jesus let these three disciples watch from a distance the glory of his transfiguration. After God rebuked Peter, the chosen three cowered on the ground like frightened animals. Jesus came to them (some distance away?) and had to rouse them with a touch and a command: "Get up and don't be afraid." The pendulum swing of Peter's experience must have left him dazed and confused. Earlier, Jesus crowned Peter with divine honors, bestowing upon him a divine right and claim: God speaks to Peter. Soon afterward, Peter has to hear Jesus say: "Get behind me Satan! You're not seeing things like God sees." On the mount of glory, Peter, James, and John are the chosen companions of Jesus who get to see what no man has seen before: resurrection glory. Then, God has to shout out to the one who is supposed to be able to hear his still, small voice: *"Listen to Jesus!"* The one who seems closest to Jesus is yet so far away. Those who think they are privileged in spiritual things end up doing the wrong things. Many who say the right words at the right time begin to believe in the power of their own words. "Let him who thinks he stands take heed lest he fall," Paul warned the Corinthians. Pride is a deadly poison that always corrupts the powerful. Of all those who claim to follow Jesus, some preachers can be the world's worst when it comes to the problem of pride and power. I should know. I am one.

Jesus knew that he would build his church on persons like Peter. Those who hear God's voice, have unusual spiritual perception, and then are given the responsibility of speaking God's Word—these are the ones who know the power of words and the seduction of pride. It's a pretty heady thing to stand before a congregation and tell people week after week what God thinks. To make matters worse (or better?), there are some congregants who come expecting to hear from God by listening to the preacher. There are moments, as every minister of the gospel knows, when preachers say the right words. They face an impossible task that nobody covets, like speaking words to grieving family and friends during the funeral of a ten-year-old boy who drowned. God somehow uses the messenger to bring hope to a company overwhelmed by disaster. In those moments, when nobody was looking, I would sense the pleasure of God—as if I had a band of heavenly angels fall on my neck and kiss my soul. I knew it wasn't me. Even while I was speaking, I knew that words fell from my lips too easily to be formed by human invention. Before the funeral I had cried out in desperation, "Oh God, help me! What can I say? What can I do?" Then, in the relief of the moment that it was all over, well-wishers would grace my head with garlands of flowery words. Afterwards, reflecting on the praise of listeners, I would toy with the idea that I was "special," or "gifted," or, as one member loved to say, "Pastor, you've got the anointing." It's easy to believe you're chosen above the rest when you speak the words of God.

Pride wears an ugly face. Words that were meant to heal lead to harm when offered in condescending tones. It's easy to look down on people from a pulpit. Most preachers tend to think that they know God best. They constantly deal with members of their churches who believe the same. This makes for a deadly combination. After a while, the arrogance that often comes with influence and the opportunity to declare, "thus saith the Lord" Sunday after Sunday tempt ministers to think they have all the answers. By nature or by default, preachers are opinionated people. We have been given the keys to the kingdom. Our eyes have seen the coming of the glory of the Lord. We have dreams and visions of what should be. We aspire to be "great men for God" in order to do "great things for God." The problem is, our definition of greatness is not necessarily God's design. We shouldn't be flattered by our high profile positions of influence. We shouldn't let the power of our pulpits rush to our heads like cheap wine. We shouldn't believe that we're uniquely qualified to wield the sword of Christ's kingdom with powerful words. Instead, we should learn a lesson from Peter. We were chosen because we have much to learn. We were called because we have farther to go. It may look like we're getting special treatment. Sometimes ministers see the mysterious things of God. Sometimes we speak the truth when all else are silent. But most of the time, we don't understand and we don't know what to do. Talk less, listen more. Jesus is the beloved Son of God, God's choice servant—no one else. Those who are kept closest to his side need the most help. Sometimes I wish I could learn to keep my mouth shut.

The disciples that were "left behind" should have proved to be more faithful than the three who required constant attention. This is why Jesus seems so disappointed with the mess he found at the foot of the mountain. Imagine his frustration when the father of a lunatic reported

the failure of the nine disciples. He had just given special instructions
to the three regarding what they saw. "Tell the vision to no one until
the Son of Man has risen from the dead" (17:9). This time Peter did
what God told him to do. He listened to Jesus describe, without inter-
rupting, what would happen when they arrived in Jerusalem. Just like
the Baptizer, Jesus would suffer at the hands of the powers—this they
understood (v. 13). Jesus's death was evermore on his mind as he approached the end. But he also spoke of resurrection glory. For the first
time, the three may have known what he was talking about. They got a
glimpse of the future in Jesus's transfiguration—a vision that would stay
with them till Easter. They also learned a lesson for the future (test #4!):
God's plan rarely conforms to human expectations. Elijahs come and
Elijahs go. What they have always been taught is not necessarily what
will always be (vv. 10–12). Most of the time, understanding the ways of

> *Those who are kept closest to his side*
>
> *need the most help.*

God requires hindsight as much as foresight. Jesus tried to prepare them
for what would be; yet even he knew that they wouldn't be able to teach
what they had heard or preach what they had seen until he was gone.
Then they would learn what Jesus came to do. Then they would receive
"all authority" to oppose hostile powers and make disciples throughout
the world. But, were his trainees ready for his departure? He had only
so much time. This troubled him more than anything. That's why he
exploded when he discovered that the nine disciples failed to heal the boy
overcome by evil powers in his absence. "O unbelieving and perverted
generation, how long shall I be with you? How long shall I put up with
you?" Then, he spoke the words that could only be possible for a few
more weeks: "Bring him here to Me" (v. 17).

In the same way he rebuked Peter, Jesus rebuked the demon that
plagued the boy. After the demonstration of his power, the nine asked
Jesus *privately* why they lacked power to do the same (v. 19). They were
ashamed of their impotence, not wanting to discuss such things publicly.
Jesus attributed the disciples' inability to heal the boy to their "little faith."
Then, as the reader would expect, Jesus teaches his followers another
lesson about having faith—a lesson they should have already learned by
now. The surprise comes, however, when Jesus compares great faith to

a mustard seed. What he should have said was, "If you have great faith the size of a mountain then you could say to that mountain, 'Be gone,' and it would crumble before you." After all, if the problem were "little faith," then such a dramatic contrast would be fitting.

The irony in Jesus's analogy is that faith the size of a mustard seed would have dwarfed his disciples' faith at this point. Once again, Jesus drives the point home: leastness is greatness in his kingdom—even when it comes to faith and faithfulness. Little faith is all they have, and eventually, it would be enough to move mountains—especially when a mountain stands between them and the object of their faith. Even in Jesus's absence, the nine believed they could overcome the powers; that's why they didn't wait until Jesus came back. They didn't tell the boy's father, "We're sorry. Jesus isn't here. We better wait till he comes back." As a matter of fact, some may have even considered it bold—an act of arrogance—to attempt such a feat without Jesus. Not the nine. They gave it a go, and they failed. Even they were confused by their inability to cast out the demon. This is why, I believe, Jesus was making light of their predicament. Having faith the size of a mustard seed isn't very much faith in the overall scheme of things. And, that's the point. They had enough faith even with Jesus removed from them a mountain away. His absence was their opportunity for greatness. Yet, all it takes is a little faith to be faithful. "Truly I say to you, unless you are converted and become like children, you will not enter the kingdom of heaven. Whoever then humbles himself as this child, he is the greatest in the kingdom of heaven" (18:3–4). In the kingdom reign of Christ, size doesn't matter. Even a hobbit can bring down a mountain.

Even as I write these words, J. R. R. Tolkien's *The Lord of the Rings: The Two Towers* is attracting moviegoers by the millions. My son and I are purists. We love the books more than the movies. Nevertheless, to see Tolkien's imaginative story come alive before our eyes makes the myth more real. My favorite character in the trilogy is Gollum. His name comes from the horrible sound he makes when he tries to talk, at times swallowing his words with a gulp. To Frodo, the main character of the story, Gollum is a hybrid of the past and the future—a constant reminder of what was and what could be for any hobbit possessed by the obsession for power. For those who are not fans of Tolkien, I don't have the time or space (nor the nerve!) to give a full description of the story. Nevertheless, for all the intricacies of the mythology and the sheer genius that gave birth to Middle-earth, the moral of the story is quite simple: power corrupts. The two hobbits, Frodo and Gollum, know this all too well. They are the smallest of all creatures. Yet, the greatest power forged comes into their hands unexpectedly—a golden ring of absolute dominion. Gollum killed his cousin to possess it. Frodo nearly lost his life trying to destroy it. Their paths cross, their destinies intertwined, when their lust for power gets the better of both of them.

Ironically, in the end, it was their insatiable desire for supremacy that brought about the end of absolute power. It's a pretty ridiculous sight: two little hobbits fighting over the ring that rules them all. Eventually, the struggle ends when the ring is destroyed in the fires that bellow from the Mountain of Doom. In the process, Gollum loses his life, Frodo his ring finger (signet?). The terrible reign of evil is abated. Hostile powers lose their grip over all inhabitants of Middle-earth because two little hobbits were fighting over the ring. Tolkien's message is biblical: the littlest accomplishes great things because of his littleness. Faithfulness is measured by the least of all. Mistaken by others as children, hobbits model greatness.

It's easy for Christians to lose sight of this simple fact. It doesn't matter who you are or what you hope to be. It doesn't matter what you claim to know or who your friends are. Whether you're standing on the mountain of glory, or down in the valley opposing the powers, when it comes to advancing the cause of Christ, all Jesus needs is a man or woman with a little faith. That's all. He can build his house on people

---

Sometimes we forget: Jesus took a little army of twelve men nicknamed "little faith" and brought the kingdom of heaven to earth.

---

like that. Even the gates of hell's fortress of evil will not withstand the force of faithful disciples. Sometimes we forget: Jesus took a little army of twelve men nicknamed "little faith" and brought the kingdom of heaven to earth. This is why he taught us to pray, "Thy kingdom come, Thy will be done, on earth as it is in heaven." What is big in heaven is small on earth. Who can see?

Hearing but Not Seeing: Test #4

This is the last test for the twelve. Up to this point we've watched them learn how to follow Jesus in his absence. The first two lessons taught them how to have faith in Jesus; the last two taught them how to hold on to their faith. At first, the twelve had to learn who Jesus is; ultimately, they needed to learn what he came to do. The reason? By becoming his disciples they discover who they are meant to be and what they are destined to do. So that, in the end, they will carry on in his absence: making disciples of all peoples. But, before that could happen, they needed to learn the most painful lesson of them all. God rarely works things out like we expect. Even though we are told what usually happens to disciples of Christ, it's hard to see God's hand at work. Christians must carry their own cross. We know that. But when that time comes—and it comes to all who follow Jesus—it usually takes us by surprise. This is when we need Jesus the most: when life knocks the breath out of us. Socked in the stomach by unexpected blows, we fall to our knees and wonder, "What happened? Has God abandoned us? Things were going so well." See how quickly it can all fall apart. "Maybe it was all a bad dream," we rationalize. Waking up to the reality of a cruel world is hard enough. Tracing God's finger in the middle of a living nightmare is harder still.

The disciples were asleep when Jesus was betrayed. Jesus, on the other hand, was wide awake with anticipation. Ironically, this episode reads like a photographic negative of the first test, when Jesus slept in a boat while the storm raged around him. During that test, it was the twelve who were overcome by what they saw and woke up Jesus to deal with the powers. This time, Jesus sees the storm that is brewing; he knew what was about to happen. As a matter of fact, from his vantage point in the Garden, he could see the trail of torches that made a path from the high priest's quarters, out of the city, down the valley, and up the Mount of Olives to the park where he and the twelve were staying. Even as he prayed, "not my will but Thine," he could see them coming for him. His disciples, on the other hand, didn't see it coming, even though Jesus warned them countless times. The most recent attempt was when Jesus gathered his disciples around a table to celebrate Passover earlier that evening. By the time he finished talking, however, the twelve didn't feel like eating. Jesus had made his forecast. Before the night was over, he would be betrayed by Judas, denied by Peter, and abandoned by the ten. "You will all fall away because of Me this night, for it is written, 'I will strike down the shepherd, and the sheep of the flock shall be scattered'" (Matt. 26:31). Peter, speaking up over the rest, denied his upcoming denial, "'Even if I have to die with You, I will not deny You.' All the disciples said the same thing too" (v. 35).

Once they came to Gethsemane, the Shepherd kept three sheep close to him while he prayed. Peter, James, and John were separated from the nine to keep Jesus company in the middle of the night.[2] The last time they were on a mountain, Jesus was some distance from the three disciples when they saw Moses and Elijah talking to Jesus. This time Jesus was alone—there were no heavenly visitors, no visions of glory. This time there was nothing to see; yet, once again the disciples were close enough to overhear Jesus's conversation. "My Father, if it is possible, let this cup pass from Me." Obviously, neither the chosen three nor the nine were troubled by Jesus's grief. Vigilance was lost to sleep. Before, a storm in a boat kept them wide-eyed. This time they slept like babies without a care in the world. Then, Jesus woke them up for the last time.

What they saw must have seemed like a bad dream. Judas singled out Jesus for the temple police, who took him into custody without a fight. Even when one of the disciples tried to keep his vow—to die with Jesus by wielding a sword—Jesus rejected the overture: "Put your sword back into its place; for all those who take up the sword shall perish by the sword" (v. 52). Resigned to his fate, Jesus gave in to his enemies. At this, the disciples ran like mice abandoning a sinking ship. To me, the narrator's comments summing up the betrayal of Jesus are among the saddest words in the New Testament: "Then all the disciples left Him and fled" (v. 56).

They betrayed him. The same disciples who claimed that they would die with him abandoned him in his darkest hour. We're so accustomed to the story the tragedy barely affects us anymore. How could someone so powerful be taken without a fight? Why did Judas turn against Jesus? Why would any of his followers betray him? What did Jesus do to deserve such a horrible end? And the question that bothers me the most: Why didn't the twelve see this coming? Why weren't they more prepared for this moment? How could they take their rest at a time like this? Jesus had told them repeatedly what would happen when they came to Jerusalem. They heard what he said. Why didn't they do something about it? Instead, their actions betrayed their shock and dismay. They ran like cowards because they didn't know what was going on. After all Jesus had invested in them, after all he taught them, they still didn't see. The greatest becomes the least so the least can become the greatest. Eventually, they would get it. But at this point in the story, the darkness of the moment swallows the heart of these faithless disciples. They were so much a part of Jesus's life; from this point on they practically disappear from the narrative. They are gone with the night; they left him to die alone. That's what bothers me the most—because it reminds me of me.

I make so many claims. I rely upon my words to convince myself and those who will listen that I mean what I say. I belong to a world of good intentions. Like the twelve, I share table with hungry pilgrims who hope to find forgiveness among traitors—never believing that I could be the one. Like the twelve, I make promises to Christ that I will never turn my back on him, no matter how bad it gets. Like the twelve, I'm not bothered by the things that grieve the heart of Jesus. I take my ease; I sleep well. I'm not sure I have ever been "deeply grieved, to the point of death." Like the twelve, I have forsaken Jesus for the same reason. Deep down, where the human condition rests comfortably, I am a selfish person. I think for myself. I act in my own best interest. My survival supercedes all priorities. When it comes to losing my life, I'd rather keep it. Sacrifice normally comes on my terms. I am more apt to pray, "Not thy will but mine be done." To give in feels like giving up. To be spent for Christ scares me. Letting go is too risky. Of course, Jesus didn't think like me. He did what he taught the twelve to do. He gave away everything he ever had: his possessions, his time, his talent, his love, his friendship, his mercy, his life. His disciples knew that better than anyone. Why couldn't they follow his lead? Why didn't they believe like him? "To save your life you must lose it," he taught them. Why didn't they see it coming? Did anyone get it? Did anyone understand this marvelous, mysterious life of total surrender to God?

She came to bury Jesus while he was still alive. That more than anything else offended the twelve. Jesus had been talking about death for several days. Peter couldn't talk him out of it. Everything Jesus did since he arrived in Jerusalem seemed to provoke it. Jesus had a death wish. The disciples didn't want to believe it. As long as Jesus was alive, their dreams of kingdom glory could come true. If Jesus died, their dreams would die with him. That's why the twelve became so angry with the woman who poured burial spices all over Jesus the day before he died. Burial ointment is wasted on the living. To cover Jesus's body with such costly perfume would mean that all was lost. Obviously, she was resigned to the fact that Jesus would die. To the twelve, she looked like a silly woman who had given up all hope. Besides, even if Jesus were to die, didn't her actions betray her concern: that no one would be there to give Jesus an honorable burial? This offended the disciples. "Why this waste? For this perfume might have been sold for a high price and the money given to the poor" (26:8–9). Smelling like grief, Jesus became a dead man walking.[3] He cast the odor of a living sacrifice. Jesus seemed pleased by the woman's sacrifice: "Why do you bother the woman? For she has done a good deed to Me. For you always have the poor with you; but *you do not always have Me*. For when she poured this perfume on My body, she did it to prepare Me for burial" (vv. 10–12).

According to Jesus, this woman showed great insight. She knew what Jesus came to do. She knew that Jesus would be gone soon. Therefore, she knew what she had to do. Her actions revealed the essence of Jesus's mission—the heart of the gospel message: he died so that we might live.

His sacrifice invites ours. Or, in the words of the apostle Paul, "Though He was rich, yet for your sake He became poor, so that you through His poverty might become rich" (2 Cor. 8:9). Her gospel gift would never be forgotten: "Truly I say to you, wherever this gospel is preached in the whole world, what this woman has done will also be spoken of in memory of her" (Matt. 26:13). What a profound honor, what great insight. How did she know? Why was she able to see what the twelve refused to believe?

In the previous two chapters of Matthew's Gospel, Jesus was preparing his disciples for his departure. The subject of his death led to discussions regarding the end of all things: the end of the temple, the end of wars, the end of persecution, the end of all kingdoms, the end of time. In the middle of all the confusing apocalyptic scenarios, Jesus stressed one thing: be faithful. Some will be fooled, some will lose patience, some will fall away, some will grow complacent—but true disciples remain faithful to the end. It's not how you start, it's how you finish. That's why Jesus centered on judgment day scenarios to teach his disciples the meaning of faithfulness. Three parables in Matthew 25 all carry the same significance: on the last day, faithful disciples will be rewarded. And, what does that faithfulness look like? It looks like five girls who are prepared for their wedding when their hero comes to sweep them off their feet. It looks like two managers who take care of the shop while the owner is away on business. It looks like people who always do the right thing: when they see what others need, they give what they have (like burial spices). The difference between the faithful and the faithless is as different as sheep and goats. The last day will prove it.

Of those three parables, the last probably had the greatest impact on Jesus's listeners. The first two parables speak of business as usual. There is no surprise when five lazy virgins or one lazy steward meet an undesirable end. They get what they deserve. It's the last story, the parable of the sheep and the goats, that packs a punch. Notice how, even in the parable, the main characters (both good and bad) are confused by their lot. They are incredulous to what the King tells them. "I was hungry, and you gave Me something to eat; I was thirsty, and you gave Me something to drink; I was a stranger, and you invited Me in; naked, and you clothed Me; I was sick, and you visited Me; I was in prison, and you came to Me" (Matt. 25:35–36). Notice how the absence of the King is assumed (as well as the absence of the bridegroom and the master of three slaves in the previous two parables). The sheep respond: "When did we see *you* like that?" They can't believe that a King so powerful and glorious would ever stoop so low. How could such a thing happen? "Lord, when did we see You hungry, and feed You, or thirsty, and give You something to drink? When did we see You a stranger, and invite

You in, or naked, and clothe You? When did we see You sick, or in prison, and come to You?" (vv. 37–39). Anyone listening to Jesus would be able to connect the dots. The King disguised as a needy beggar, a poor stranger, a sick invalid, or a shameful prisoner is Jesus. But how could these things be? Jesus restored beggars, helped strangers, healed the sick, and came to set the captives free. Imagine the surprise of his disciples when it begins to dawn on them that Jesus is speaking allegorically about himself. They would have easily identified with the sheep and the goats, shocked by such a reversal of fortune. Up to this point in Matthew's Gospel, the twelve had never seen Jesus weak, sick, frail, imprisoned—becoming the least of all. They could, no doubt, echo the sentiment of the herd that stood before the King on the last day. "When did we see you like this?" Listen to the words of King Jesus: "To the extent that you did it to one of these brothers of Mine, even the least of them, you did it to Me" (v. 40).

There was one little lamb who saw the King dressed like a pauper. She was the one who not only heard the word but could also see the kingdom of heaven. The greatest becomes the least, the King will be stripped of his royal splendor, the life-giver will die, the poor will be the constant reminder of Jesus's absence, and those most faithful to Jesus will abandon him like blind goats. "Lord, when would we ever see *you* so needy?" She understood what Jesus had been trying to teach his followers for days. She got it. She made no claims, never said a word. Her actions, however, spoke volumes. Better to do what you can while you have the chance. That's what faithfulness looks like. Thank you, lady, for pouring it on. He needed it. The twelve, on the other hand, didn't get it. But they will. Before their very eyes, they will see Jesus become the least of these.

Some of the songs we sing in worship bother me. "Lord, I want to know you," or "Open our eyes Lord, we want to see Jesus, to reach out and touch Him, and say that we love Him," or "Oh, how I love Jesus," or "If ever I loved thee, my Jesus 'tis now." It's not the sentiment these songwriters hoped to convey that is troublesome. I don't think we realize what we're singing. We sing of our desire to love Christ, to know him better, to "reach out and touch him," to serve him with all that we are. At times, it feels like our worship is more about convincing ourselves that we love him than expressing the impulse of a heart dedicated to him. Do we really want to "reach out and touch him"? Are we sure of the outcome, of what would happen if he "opened our eyes"? What does it mean for a congregation of people to sing of their desire "to love him more"? How do I love Jesus? Is that possible? As we sing the songs, I can imagine that he is present with us, that he is listening to our love songs. But, is that it? Is that the extent of what it means to serve him, to love him? How am I supposed to love Jesus when he's not here?

I was hungry and you gave Me nothing to eat; I was thirsty, and you gave Me nothing to drink. On the last night of his life, Jesus came to a table prepared for his disciples hungry and thirsty. They would eat the provisions; Jesus would not. The bread was his body, the wine his blood. As a matter of fact, Jesus concluded the meal with a vow: "I will not drink of this fruit of the vine from now on until that day when I drink it new with you in My Father's kingdom" (26:29). The disciples took their fill. Jesus left the table hungry and thirsty. He knew the meal was for them, not him. He had to be the one, the only one, who could provide the nourishment for their souls. He broke the bread of his body; he offered the cup of a new covenant poured out for many. Leaving the table famished, Jesus would be spent for all of us. Looking past the cross, he promised that he would celebrate with us one day—when the new kingdom issues new wine. Until then, our need of bread and drink would be the constant reminder of his absence. Ironically, we continue to eat *his* last supper—a meal he made for us, even the least. He won't eat and drink the last supper until the last day because the first becomes the last in the kingdom of God.

I was a stranger, and you did not invite me in. Gethsemane was the public park outside of Jerusalem used by travelers who had no place to stay. Usually, honorable guests were invited by residents of Jerusalem to celebrate Passover in their homes. Sometimes, large families would require several houses. Limited space meant that pilgrims of low status had to seek shelter elsewhere. Many would spend the night in Gethsemane during the holy week. Evidently, Jesus and his followers were among the company who couldn't find accommodations in Jerusalem; for example, he stayed in Bethany at least one night (26:6). No doubt, Jesus burned many bridges when he "cleansed" the temple a few days before the seder. He had to sneak into Jerusalem, gathering with the twelve at a prearranged location, in order to begin the feast of unleavened bread. After the meal, Jesus and the disciples headed for the park. There must have been several groups of people staying there—Judas had to identify Jesus among the crowd of pilgrims bedding down for the night. Ironically, Judas singled out Jesus for the authorities with a common greeting: the kiss of hospitality. A stranger in Gethsemane, Jesus hoped to find company among his sleepy disciples. Strangely enough, Judas was the only disciple that wasn't asleep that night. In the end, Jesus was abandoned by his friends—a kiss of friendship sealing his fate. Left alone, no one would take him in during the holiday, that is, no one except his enemies. During any trial, friends would line up to vouch for the integrity of the accused. In Jesus's case, no one showed up to defend him. Peter denied him. "False testimony" was used to secure the desired outcome, "that they might put Him to death" (v. 59). The ultimate irony to me is that the blood money returned by the traitor was used by Jesus's enemies to buy a cemetery *for strangers* (27:7). Even Jerusalem rejected Jesus, preferring a man whose name means "son of the father" (Barabbas) to be released to them for the holiday. Jesus, the one and only "Son of the Father," was a stranger to them (v. 22).

I was naked and you did not clothe me. It wasn't enough for Jesus's enemies that he was sentenced to die a cursed death on a cross. They wanted to humiliate him. Matthew is the only Gospel that tells us that, after Jesus was beaten, "they *stripped Him* and put a scarlet robe on Him" (v. 28). The soldiers were mocking him for sport. They dressed him for the part: King of the Jews. He wore a crown. He held a scepter. He was wrapped in royal colors. He even heard cries befitting a king: "Hail, King of the Jews!" (v. 29). But, for all of their jesting, Jesus wore his royal garments well. See how well the crown of thorns fits his noble brow. Notice how, even today, scarlet robes are draped around the shoulders of a cross in regal splendor. Jesus hanging naked on a cross is the premiere symbol of Christian faith. Nevertheless, the fact that he was stripped naked and beaten like an animal makes my blood boil. Where were the twelve? Where were his followers? Where were his friends who swore an oath that they would die with him? They were gone. They should have been there to help him bear the indignity of such cruel treatment. One of his disciples should have stepped forward in protest of their mockery. But that didn't happen. The soldiers even had to find a complete stranger to bear Jesus's cross (v. 32). Curiously, his name was Simon.

I was sick, and in prison, and you did not visit me. Consider the company Jesus kept as he died. Crucified with thieves, mocked by priests, the soldiers fighting over the clothes off his back like dogs scavenging for a meal—it's no wonder Jesus felt abandoned by God. "My God, My God, why have You forsaken Me?" (v. 46). To onlookers, his abject isolation made them think he was calling out to Elijah for help. Since everyone forsook him (even God), Elijah would be Jesus's last chance for companionship—at least one friend to be with him in the end. Instead, he died a lonely man. One would be hard pressed to find a darker moment in the pages of the Bible. Darkness broods over the death of Jesus. The sky grows black, the temple veil is ripped in half, the earth shakes violently, and unclean graves are opened. Divine displeasure is marked by catastrophic events. The only disciples who saw these things were a few women followers (27:55–56). Only one man, a disciple named Joseph, helped the family bury Jesus.

Usually, the size of the funeral revealed the honorable status of the deceased. Friends and relatives would organize a large crowd to join the funeral in order to honor their beloved. It was customary to mourn the passing of a faithful friend for a week—visiting the grave several times a day. Formal grieving for the most honored (a king) could last as long as a month and attract the whole town to the funeral. Since an honorable burial was so important to a community's social welfare, Jewish law required at least one flute player for the processional of the poorest Israelite who died an honorable death. On the other hand, those who died shameful deaths (crucifixion, drowning, burning) were not mourned with any ritual. Ashamed of the deceased, the family buried the corpse as quickly as possible without ceremony. Death was God's last verdict. Shameful persons died cursed deaths by divine decree.

Jesus died a shameful death. There was no funeral. The twelve abandoned him. Only his mother, her friends, and a stranger named Joseph were there to make sure Jesus was buried. No one visited his grave except the temple police, sent by his enemies to guard a dead man imprisoned by a stone door (vv. 62–66). Jesus, the greatest man who ever lived, became the least of all. It happened so quickly. Within one week everything had changed. The city that welcomed him as King, threw him out like a thief. The twelve who promised to die with him, saved their skin by running away. Both Pilate and the chief priest, at one time fearing the crowd in Jerusalem, used the unruly mob to carry out their plan. "'Lord, when did we see You hungry, or thirsty, or a stranger, or naked, or sick, or in prison, and did not take care of You?' Then He answered them, saying, 'Truly I say to you, to the extent that you did not do it to one of the least of these, you did not do it to Me.'"

One of the least of these, indeed. They were hill people. To the rest of the citizens of a small town in northern Arkansas, they were little more than a topic of conversation—a curiosity and an embarrassment. To outsiders, the poor who lived in the woods like vagabonds confirmed the cartoon caricature of Arkansas hillbillies. They lived in shanties, sometimes made of wood, mud, and canvas. They hunted for game, gleaned the land for food. Their kitchen consisted of a pot over an open fire. Their children were dressed in rags. They always kept to themselves. They were rarely seen in public. Some of the hill people, however, would send their kids to school. But their erratic attendance and lack of social skills made it difficult for everyone. The children rarely made any friends. Teachers dreaded having such high-maintenance students, peers found them easy targets for playground humor, and the children rarely paid enough attention to profit from formal education. During the winter months, the locals wondered how the hill people survived the cold. When the children came to school, they always had crusty noses and hacking coughs. Winter coats were a luxury. Strangely enough, even when conscientious people tried to help, offering free clothing or health care, the hill people didn't take kindly to charity. Coats would be lost, doctor's appointments missed, food offered would be food consumed without a "thank you." They didn't see any need for "church," either. After a while, Christians gave up, letting the hill people have what they wanted: to be left alone.

A rumor began to circulate in the community that a baby died. The infant was born in the winter to one of the families that lived in the hills. Some heard that the baby had pneumonia. The baby's older brother had told a friend at school that the infant had died, and that the family planned to have a funeral. A group of Christians approached the family to see if they would have the funeral in their church. The grieving parents refused, deciding to mourn their loss outside, in the woods, near their "home." It was a cold, wet, winter day when a few of the locals negotiated their way through the woods to pay their last respects. It was a good thing that they brought their own umbrellas. When they arrived, they saw the family gathered around a small pine box, standing in the rain. Dressed in their "Sunday best" (which probably came from the goodwill chest), the father, mother, sisters, and brothers stood with heads bowed. It was a pitiful sight. The few who came from town kept warm with winter coats, shielded temporarily from the elements, keeping a respectable distance.

It seemed especially cold that day. For the longest time, they stood there in silence—a silence that was broken by the haunting sounds of rain dripping on their umbrellas. Eventually, someone tried to offer a few words of comfort. As they fumbled through the service, the mother of the boy who had befriended the brother of the baby told me that she kept thinking, "Why did this have to happen? Don't these people have any more sense than to try to take care of a newborn in the dead of winter out in the middle of nowhere? Why didn't they ask for help? They must be shivering with cold right now. They don't even own coats for the winter. Don't they know any better?" Then, as she stood there in judgment of the scene, she felt her son leave her side. He walked up to the family, took his coat off, and wrapped it around the shoulders of a grieving boy. There he stood in the rain with his arm around his friend, standing side by side with a brokenhearted family, gathered around a baby in a pine box. At that moment, the boy's mother—a good Christian woman—wept and said to herself, "That's what Jesus would do."

Do you see? The next time you pass by a homeless man begging for money, look very carefully into his face. Make eye contact. Study his condition. If you look hard enough, you may recognize the one who has become the least of all. The migrant farmer, the old lady with Alzheimer's, foster children, illegal aliens, the man who prays to the wrong god—these people are easily overlooked. After a while, they fade into the background of our everyday routines. We don't see them anymore. We live with them. We breathe the same air; share the same roads; take in the same beautiful, starry nights. But we don't take notice. We live segregated lives. To be reminded of the "have nots" is rather unsettling for the "haves." Sometimes I grow weary of hearing the same old sermons: Christians should help the poor. Sometimes we give. Sometimes we try to do our part. Sometimes we help the needy. But the poor we will always have with us. Why? Because Jesus promised he would never leave us; because Jesus said that the gathering of two or three in his name would remind us of his absence; because Jesus knew that if we

> *Do you see? The next time you pass by*
> *a homeless man begging for money,*
> *look very carefully into his face.*
> *Make eye contact. Study his condition.*
> *If you look hard enough, you may recognize*
> *the one who has become the least of all.*

ever forgot the least of all, we would forget about him. For those of us who long to see Jesus, look around. He's here. He's Immanuel. He's hungry and thirsty, sick and in prison, impoverished and estranged. Those who recognize him among the least of these, see what he meant when he said that the greatest becomes the least and the least becomes the greatest in his kingdom. That's what separates the sheep from the goats. They see. Open our eyes Lord, we want to see Jesus.

The End of the Beginning

He met them on a mountain. Unlike the first time, Jesus preached no sermon. The disciples had already learned what they needed to do. There was no crowd. The whole world would hear the message. Their number was no longer twelve. Jesus sent eleven disciples to make disciples of all nations. Before, Jesus taught with authority. Now Jesus has all authority (28:18). The end of the story reads like the beginning, yet different. This time Jesus does not descend with his disciples to teach, preach, and heal. The disciples must go on without him. This time Jesus is worshiped as the resurrected Christ, but some doubted that it was he (v. 17). This time Jesus spoke of the kingdom of heaven *and* earth (v. 18). This time disciples will make disciples. This time his disciples will be faithful to the end because he will be with them until the last day.

Near the end of his sermon on the mount, Jesus spoke of the end of the ages in different terms. He described what would happen to faithless disciples on the last day. "Not everyone who says to Me, 'Lord, Lord,' will enter the kingdom of heaven, but he who does the will of My Father who is in heaven will enter. Many will say to Me on that day, 'Lord, Lord, did we not prophesy in Your name, and in Your name cast out demons, and in Your name perform many miracles?' And then I will declare to them, 'I never knew you; depart from Me, you who practice lawlessness'" (7:21–23). The last day will reveal two kinds of faithless disciples: those who think they have faith but are not faithful, and those who think they are faithful but have no faith. To be a follower of Jesus, a disciple must have faith in him and be faithful to him. That's what Matthew's Gospel teaches every reader *because* that's what Jesus taught his disciples. We saw it with our own eyes, we heard it with our own ears. Therefore, like the faithful followers who remained at the end of the story, we hear the Great Commission as if Jesus were giving us the same charge. For just as Jesus made disciples out of eleven followers, so also he makes disciples out of us. Because, when disciples disciple, Jesus is present—even to the last day. The student becomes the teacher. The kingdom of heaven is established on earth. Jesus is present in his absence. The end of the story is our beginning.

THE GOSPEL
OF MARK

Farming the Gospel

3

Sowing the Seed

Follow in His footsteps, Go where He has trod, In the world's
great trouble, Risk yourself for God.

Bryan Jeffery Leech, "Let Your Heart Be Broken"

He was one of us. In his mind, he was a farmer, a physician, a
groom, a thief, a son, a prophet, a shepherd. To those who saw
him, he was something more. Some called him "Master." Some called
him "Teacher." Many hoped that he would be their "Messiah." Others
saw him as a fraud, a deceiver, a con man. A voice from the heavens
declared, "This is My beloved Son" (Mark 9:7). Whoever he was, he had
one message. It was a rather simple message. He never strayed from
the point. He seemed obsessed by one goal. He stayed on task. He sang
one song: the reign of God has come. Therefore, with all of the talk of a
kingdom, one would expect the herald to proclaim himself "king." But
he didn't. He kept comparing himself to everyday people. He was a "son
of man." He was a farmer. He was one of us. His name was "Jesus." He
came from Nazareth. And, he shook up the world.

In Mark's Gospel, Jesus appears at the beginning of the story as a man without reputation. There is no royal genealogy. Mark tells no stories of divine birth or miraculous events. No angels announce his arrival. Instead, he comes as one of many pilgrims, led into the desert to be baptized by a prophet named "John." Then, the first indication that this was no ordinary man comes in the form of a heavenly voice and a spiritual dove. God confirms what Mark claimed at the beginning of his Gospel: "The beginning of the gospel of Jesus Christ, the Son of God" (1:1). At his baptism, Jesus was anointed[1] by God's Spirit, he was declared the beloved Son by God's voice (vv. 10–11). Soon, the anointed one announces (to no one in particular): "The time is fulfilled, and the kingdom of God is at hand; repent and believe in the gospel" (v. 15). At this point, the reader of Mark's Gospel has no reason to believe that this is true. One must wait and see whether Jesus lives up to his claim.

Mark has not prepared his readers like other Gospel writers. By the time Jesus is baptized in Matthew's Gospel, you already know that he fulfills all kinds of prophecy, and that he had no earthly father. According to Luke, Jesus was not only born of a virgin, but he was somewhat of a child prodigy, adored by angels. In John, Jesus is the pre-incarnate Word of God made flesh. It comes as no surprise, therefore, when Jesus is able to call disciples to follow him using only the enticing words, "Come, and you will see" (John 1:39). Who wouldn't? But that's not the way it works in Mark's Gospel. From the beginning, Jesus appears only as a man—a man who makes an incredible claim. The rest of the story reveals whether Mark, the heavenly voice, and Jesus were right. Jesus Christ is the Son of God who brought the kingdom of God to earth. That's quite a tall tale. Who would believe it?

We sometimes forget that Mark didn't write his Gospel for us. He wrote it for a group of people who didn't have several hundred years of Christian history behind them to help make sense of his Gospel. They were not familiar with the "Lord's Prayer," had never sung a single verse of "Amazing Grace," nor had ever seen a church building with stained glass and a steeple towering above the rest. To them a Roman cross was not a beautiful religious symbol but a horrible political reality. God as Trinity would have been a novel idea. Mark's readers/auditors didn't know the "whole" story. They couldn't compare Mark's story with Matthew, Luke, or John. As a matter of fact, Mark was probably the first Christian to try to put on paper the gospel that had been preached for a generation. Therefore, when we as twenty-first-century readers pick up the second Gospel of the New Testament, we fill in "the gaps" of Mark's story with a reservoir of knowledge unavailable to first-century readers. Scholars remind us of these things. If we want to read, or hear, Mark's Gospel as if it were written for us, then we need to try to set aside our preconceptions and listen to the story for its own sake, on its own terms. Such a "fresh" reading will open our eyes to Mark's unique creativity. As Christians, we believe God inspired Mark to tell the gospel story. Others followed his example. We have four Gospels. But Mark was the first.

Imagine your first impression of Jesus if you were a first-century Mediterranean hearing Mark's Gospel for the first time. More than likely you would "hear" the Gospel because most people were illiterate. Reading and writing weren't necessary—it was an aural culture. So Mark wrote his Gospel with listeners in mind. He knew that people would "hear" the story. What would they see with their mind's eye? Jesus was a Jew with extraordinary powers. A voice from heaven declares his special status: he is a beloved Son of God. He is endowed with divine powers meant for good. After surviving a brief battle in the desert with Satan, Jesus boasts, "It's time for the reign of God." Then, after collecting a few followers, Jesus heads for a Galilean fishing village to take his message

To them a Roman cross was not a beautiful religious symbol but a horrible political reality.

on the road. At the synagogue in Capernaum, Jesus's listeners marvel over his teaching: he teaches with authority—not like the professional teachers called "scribes." In the middle of the lesson, a man with an "unclean spirit" (opposite of Jesus's heavenly Spirit) interrupts the meeting and cries out, "What business do we have with each other, Jesus of Nazareth? Have You come to destroy us? I know who You are—the Holy One of God!" (1:24). Jesus commands the demon(s) to leave. By Jesus's word, the man is thrown into convulsions and exorcized of the unclean spirit to the amazement of the assembly.

After this wild episode, things get stranger still. Jesus draws demons like moths to a flame. He didn't go looking for them; they come from everywhere. Some cause fevers, some sickness, some infirmities—they all seek Jesus: "And He healed many who were ill with various diseases, and cast out many demons; and He was not permitting the demons to speak, because they knew who He was" (v. 34). Were they looking for help or coming to do battle? It's difficult to know. One thing's for sure: Jesus displayed unusual power over evil spirits. From the very beginning of Mark's Gospel, this story looks like the clash of the Titans: the Son of

God versus the sons of Satan. Jesus comes to push back the darkness. Evil's reign is abated, for a while.

It didn't take long for the crowds to get out of hand. Picture the kinds of people that hovered around Jesus: diseased, crippled, blind, demonized. In those days there were no hospitals. Certainly, Jesus's clientele would belong in one. Desperate for a cure they would always swarm the house where he was staying. In Mark's Gospel the crowds that followed Jesus were more of a nuisance than a blessing. At times, Jesus's disciples acted more like bodyguards than apprentices (3:9–10). Once the crowd was so thick there wasn't enough elbowroom to eat (v. 20). Numbers grew so fast that Jesus had to escape their notice by hiding in the desert. When the disciples came to fetch Jesus and bring him back to the miserable mob, he said, "Let us go somewhere else" (1:38 [my paraphrase]). Thus, Mark summarized Jesus's twofold ministry in terms of announcing the kingdom of God and casting out demons (v. 39). Of course, Jesus taught. Yes, he healed the sick. But as far as Mark is concerned, the main task of Jesus's kingdom work was exorcisms. Whenever he entered a new town, proclaiming the advent of the kingdom of God, demons came after him.

This made perfect sense to Mark's auditors. If Jesus were a true son of God, the evil powers would marshal forces and attack. Have you ever noticed how many episodes in the first five chapters of Mark's Gospel feature demons? They're everywhere. Why? Because human misery was mostly explained by the pervasive presence of evil powers. If a woman had a fever, it was due to an evil spirit oppressing her body. If a boy was rolling around on the ground, foaming at the mouth, his wrenched body contorted due to horrible seizures, then it was believed that evil forces were at work, torturing his soul. Nature's powers were divine, yet unpredictable—just like God. Sometimes the wrath of God was too easily seen in horrible plagues and devastating storms. This is how the ancients made sense of their world. For Mark's Gospel, then, Jesus must be the son of man who proves he's the Son of God by overpowering evil and suffering. To his enemies, Jesus's power over demons proved the opposite: the evil spirits obeyed him because he was their master, the Lord of demons. The scribes could not deny the power Jesus had over demons. They questioned the source of his power: "He is possessed by Beelzebul. . . . He casts out the demons by the ruler of the demons" (3:22).

Today, those who dabble in the strange world of the occult are often dismissed as dangerous and eccentric. The Romans shared the same sentiment. They were suspicious of the Magi, the wise men who could read the stars and manipulate the powers. Magicians were revered by some as masters of the elements; feared by most because of their ability to curse enemies with spells of disease and death. At the same time, magicians were hired to pronounce incantations guaranteeing long life and success. Amulets, magical charms, were sold to those who lived in fear of evil powers. They were worn around the neck, sown into garments, protecting the most important zones of the human body: head, chest, loins, feet, and hands. Charm bracelets were not fashion accessories. Jewelry was the primitive version of a bulletproof vest. Therefore, the merchandising of magical powers meant big business for those who perfected their craft (see Acts 19:19, 24). That's what makes Mark's story so unique. Jesus didn't act like your typical magician. He not only worked his magic for free, he failed to use conventional methods to manipulate the powers. He sold no amulets; he cast no spells. There were no secret incantations, no esoteric babblings. Jesus commanded the evil spirits with words that everyone understood. The Galileans called it "teaching with authority." No doubt his methods were unconventional in so many ways.

That would be the theme of Jesus's work according to Mark: unconventional. Jesus was a dangerous man, a "rebel" with a cause. He not only took on the evil powers of the spirit world, he challenged the earthly institutions of power as well. He pronounced forgiveness of sins *outside* the temple to people who could never enter the temple (Lev. 21:18–20). He broke Sabbath regulations, ate with unclean people, and touched lepers. It's no wonder the religious authorities (read, "power brokers for God") believed that Jesus was Satan incarnate. Even his own family thought he had lost his mind (Mark 3:21). Jesus flew in the face of conventional wisdom, acting as if the reign of God had come—challenging all authority, suspending all rules. Think about it. If God reigns supreme, then everything changes: the sick are blessed, the evil spirits are vanquished, sins are forgiven, and every day becomes a Sabbath day. Rest has finally come to the house of God, where everyone is family (vv. 31–35). This is what Jesus meant when he said that it was time for the kingdom of God. Jesus was taking back what God had made. The world was no longer the domain of darkness. Jesus was God's thief, plundering the strong man's house (v. 27).

Given our proclivities for orderliness and propriety, I think most of us would have been embarrassed by Jesus. We live by codes of conduct. We believe in making good impressions. We study the habits of successful persons in order to promote admirable behavior. We reward efficiency. We establish institutions to preserve legacies. We prefer handsome leaders. We want to hear what we already believe. Family obligations have been enshrined as the highest good. We promote nationalism by extolling the virtue of those who have made "the greatest sacrifice," dying for their country. We always try to put presumptuous people in their place. No one likes a loud mouth. We maintain that all of us should try to get along with one another. The American work ethic is upheld to ensure that people get what they deserve. And, we believe that religious convictions are private matters. Zealots are bad news; to be passionate for a cause is to be a menace to society. What we want, more than anything, is peace and quiet.

Jesus was loud and disturbing. Sometimes he didn't measure his words, using crass illustrations when speaking of holy realities (7:18–19). On certain occasions he could be reckless in word and deed (11:12–17). He despised respectful greetings. He disowned his family, he offended his friends, gave in to his enemies, and scandalized rebels. Jesus made trouble wherever he went. It's not a pretty picture for us to behold. It's hard, indeed, for most believers to swallow. We want our Jesus to be the calm, dignified man we have created in our own image. The handsome man in our paintings, the wise sage promoted in our films—this is the Jesus we admire. But Mark's story won't let us get away with it. Philip Yancey hammers the point home when he reminds us how Jesus defies our sensibilities:

> Two words one could never think of applying to the Jesus of the Gospels: boring and predictable. How is it, then, that the church has tamed such a character—has, in Dorothy Sayers' words, "very efficiently pared the claws of the Lion of Judah, certified Him as a fitting household pet for pale curates and pious old ladies"?[2]

Honestly, I've giggled to myself when I have considered the question asked by the faddish bracelet WWJD: "What would Jesus do?" "He would probably make us all mad," I mutter to myself. I hope he has forgiven

The more I read Mark's Gospel, the more I am convinced that Jesus would have been a difficult man "to get along with."

us for trying to make him a Baptist, or a Presbyterian, or a Methodist, or a Catholic. The more I read Mark's Gospel, the more I am convinced that Jesus would have been a difficult man "to get along with." He would never ask our opinion. He would always expect us to do what he told us to do—no questions asked. He would demand our undying loyalty, all of our time, every bit of energy we could muster to effect the kingdom of God. And, he would act as if it would take every single one of us to do it. Most of Jesus's listeners liked what they heard and believed what they saw. Do we?

Jesus was God's farmer, sowing the seed of the kingdom into the hearts of all people. Up to this point, Mark's Gospel has made a pretty good case for Jesus as the Christ, the Son of God. Jesus is an unusual man with extraordinary abilities. He has done well: overcoming evil with good, exciting the masses—he is powerful and popular. For Mark's audience, however, it remains to be seen whether the strong man's house will *fall* and if the gospel seed will *fall* on fertile soil.

Risky Business

Jesus decided to expand his kingdom effort. He chose twelve disciples and gave them the same task: to announce the reign of God and to cast out demons (3:13–15). At the beginning of *their* kingdom work, Jesus tells a parable that's supposed to make sense to them and only them. It's a story about a farmer sowing seed. He broadcasts his keep on the ground that to any other person looks like farmable soil. But, to the eye of the experienced farmer, not all soils are the same. He looks past the current situation and sees what will be, keeping his eyes on the harvest to come—the endgame of all farmers. Although all dirt has the same appearance in the beginning, the farmer knows that not all soils produce. Some seed falls along the path. Some seed falls on shallow soil—a fact that no one would know except the farmer who has worked these fields before. Some seed falls on ground that will eventually yield weeds; but that won't be known until it's too late. Finally, some seed falls on good soil—ground that produces the desired result: it will yield more seed for sowing (4:3–9). After hearing the parable, the disciples asked Jesus what the story meant. He was astonished by their question. "Do you not understand this parable? How will you understand all the parables?" (v. 13). Jesus couldn't believe that his disciples didn't understand what he was saying. He expected the crowds to miss the point because they were outsiders (see vv. 11–12). Besides, the parable wasn't for them; it was for those who had ears to hear, like the disciples. To him, the parable of the farmer was key to unlocking the mystery of the kingdom. If his disciples didn't get this, they wouldn't understand anything.

Why was this parable so important to Jesus? No other parable seemed to be as crucial to Jesus's teaching. When the disciples were confused over the meaning of other parables, for example, what defiles a man

(7:14–23), Jesus didn't say, "Look! You've got to understand this teaching before you can understand anything else." On the other hand, the parable of the farmer and the four kinds of soil was paradigmatic for his ministry—a model of what was and what will be. Mark, therefore, used the parable as a literary road map for his Gospel. This parable was supposed to explain everything. Consequently, Jesus's challenge to the twelve becomes a challenge to any "hearer" of Mark's Gospel: "He who has ears to hear, let him hear." Do we hear what Jesus was trying to say? If we don't get this, we won't understand Mark's Gospel.

The four kinds of soils sum up the four kinds of receptions to Jesus when he announced the kingdom of God.[3] Mark shows his listeners how Jesus encountered these four kinds of people as he broadcast the seed of his gospel message for all. Not everyone took it well. As any reader can see, some of Jesus's listeners were hard-headed and hard-hearted, like the beaten down path the farmer uses to traverse the fields. Jesus never seemed to get through to them—Satan made sure of that. Others liked what Jesus was saying and welcomed his message from the start. Their shallow reasons for following Jesus, however, became all too evident when times got tough. Their devotion quickly fades when difficulties beat down on them like the summer sun. It can get pretty hot following Jesus. Some listeners wanted to hear what Jesus was saying. But they are more careful in how they attend to the kingdom. Discretion is the word. They know that blind devotion can lead to impetuous decisions. There are other matters that weigh on the soul: providing for family, fulfilling obligations, maintaining comfort. One must act responsibly when it comes to following Jesus. According to Jesus, however, these concerns—the cares of the world—choke the kingdom work. Divided allegiances prevent maturation. Crops fail when weeds steal nourishment from the heart of the soil. Only one kind of soil, the good dirt, produces the intended result for the farmer. Good soil brings rewards to the hard-working farmer. Seed sown in good soil produces more seed.

Jesus chose a provocative analogy to explain his kingdom work. As any Galilean would know, farming is a risky business. Crop failure is the risk all farmers have to take. They know they have to spend in order to receive, give in order to get, sow in order to harvest. But the risk of vain labor hangs over the head of every worker. It is worth noting that, in his little parable, there are some risks that Galilean farmers would face that Jesus didn't include, for example, war or drought—the occasional hazards of farming in Galilee. Instead, Jesus centered on the more common threats to a successful harvest: the condition of the soil, and the risk of planting a summer crop. Most Galilean farmers relied upon a winter crop to feed their families. Winter rains would saturate the soil, ensuring germination of seed sown in late autumn. Spring rains would bring the crops to maturity; the harvest would come in May. Occasionally, Galilean farmers would put in a summer crop for autumn harvest. This was a riskier venture since the farmer faced the prospect of intermittent showers, the hot summer sun, and weeds that thrive in such conditions. Obviously, Jesus was not referring to the more common, winter crop when describing the work of the kingdom—the sun was never a threat. Instead, he chose to compare his work to the farmer who sows a summer crop that would often result in vain labor. The surprise of the story, of course, is that this risky summer crop produces a harvest better than the best winter crop. Most farmers expected a yield of seed per grain numbering around tenfold. An unusually generous harvest would result in a twentyfold yield. The Roman historian Pliny reports that, for areas similar to Galilee, a truly exceptional harvest would produce a thirtyfold yield.[4] The yield of Jesus' summer crop is miraculous: "thirty, sixty, and a hundredfold." The risk was worth the result. This is the way Jesus saw the kingdom work. It was a risky business that would produce miraculous results.

Jesus was a generous farmer. He wasn't stingy with gospel seed. He acted as if divine resources were in endless supply; he threw seed everywhere, regardless of the condition of the soil. We miss that part of the parable. When we farm the fields of God's kingdom, we are far more selective, far more efficient with our seed. We live in a world accustomed to quotas, production goals, outcomes assessed, limited overhead, profit margins, and insurance. Quantifying our success, we strive for the best results, the right outcome with minimal risk. We want to play it safe by analyzing "prospects" for the kingdom, categorizing people who "might be receptive to the gospel." Judging by appearances, we find good soil and carefully plant a single seed into the heart of a listener, trusting that God will make the little plant grow.

This is our strategy. Find the good soil, plant a single seed, wait for the results. To do otherwise would be a waste of precious resources. Besides, it's hard enough to get farmers to join the labor. We have to make it as comfortable as possible for novices. We want to ensure a positive experience for our Future Farmers of America (FFA). This requires matching the condition of the soil to the experience of the farmer. It's all pretty technical stuff. Databases and surveys help our FFA develop geographical strategies: people who live together should farm together. Socioeconomic strata must be studied in order to line up a farmer's background to the soil he is working. We wouldn't want to match an inexperienced planter with a hard-pan field. Educated people relate better to intellectuals; blue-collar farmers know how to work poor soil. Methodology is also very important. Farmers must be trained in order to maximize effort. We have to make sure the farmer plants the single seed the right way. What if he makes a mistake, plants the seed too deep or too shallow? What if he—God forbid—tries to farm the *wrong kind* of soil?

I think we've missed the point. For all of our evangelism training and church growth strategies, we're not bringing in a very good harvest. The American church is too obsessed with our own definitions of success to see what we're missing. Fear of failure drives our desire to control conditions for optimum planting. We believe in targeting our resources—time, money, personnel—to make sure the "right soil" gets the "right treatment" in order to guarantee the "right result." When something goes wrong, that is, no one "gets saved," we pore over the data to look for flaws in strategy, methodology, presentation, and training. We act as if our success is dependent upon our abilities. After all, if we've matched the right farmer with the right soil at the right time, shouldn't we get the proper result? Here's the truth of the matter: No Christian can do a *bad* job of sharing their faith. Success for the farmer of Christ's kingdom is not measured by effectiveness. The only way a farmer can fail—the only way he is responsible for the harvest—is if no seed is sown. There is no wasted effort, no poor presentation of the gospel, no guaranteed methodology, no perfected strategies for evange-

Jesus was a generous farmer.

He wasn't stingy with gospel seed.

He acted as if divine resources were in

endless supply; he threw seed everywhere,

regardless of the condition of the soil.

lism. There can be no wasted seed. The point of the parable is *not* for farmers to try to decide the difference between soil that deserves the seed and soils that do not. Remember, from the beginning all soils look the same to the inexperienced farmer; who can tell?

The point of the parable is this: *sow the seed*. Sow it on all kinds of soil. Sow it often. Sow it when most farmers think it's a waste of time. Be bold. Let it fly. Sow the summer crop. Broadcast the gospel of Jesus into the hearts of all people. Throw it on the hard-hearted. Cast seed upon the soil of the wealthy, the criminal, the pagan, the capitalist, the religious, the good prospect, the bad prospect, no prospect. Sow the seed. Then the miraculous harvest will come. Look what happened when *one* farmer reached into his bag, grabbed a handful of gospel, and threw it out to anyone who would listen.

Jesus assumed that his disciples would understand the point of the parable since they had seen—some of them from the very beginning—what the work of the kingdom would require. They were witnesses of these

> *For all of our evangelism training and church growth strategies, we're not bringing in a very good harvest. The American church is too obsessed with our own definitions of success to see what we're missing.*

things. They should have recognized the different soils upon which Jesus had cast the seed of his gospel. Like birds, demons had made every attempt to pluck the seed from the hearts of Jesus's listeners; evil spirits always seemed to show up when Jesus was preaching. Crowds of people followed Jesus, impressed by his marvelous deeds. Jesus, on the other hand, was not flattered by their "joyful reception." He constantly tried to get away from the multitudes that hounded him every step of the way. According to Jesus, they had eyes but they couldn't see what he was doing; they had ears but they didn't understand (4:12). Popularity is a fickle thing. Pharisees appeared to question everything Jesus did: eating with sinners, refusing to fast, working on the Sabbath. These concerns were irrelevant to Jesus. The cares of this world seemed trivial to the farmer sowing the seed of God's reign on earth, where sinners are forgiven (2:1–12), and outcasts celebrate God's blessings (vv. 15–22), and the Sabbath proves to be a day of rest and restoration (2:23–3:5).

By this point in Mark's Gospel, Jesus thought that he had already sown the gospel seed on all four soils—especially the good soil, the disciples. Having received the word, they were ready to produce fruit—at least, that was Jesus's expectation. He would soon send them out to do the same work of planting and harvesting: announcing the kingdom and casting out demons (6:7–13). That's why he told the parable. Advancing the reign of God would be just as risky for them as it was for him. It also explains why he was so disappointed in his disciples' ignorance. They were acting more like the soil that was hard and rocky than the good soil that would produce more seed. Farming in God's field yields surprising results—even for Jesus.

"Err on the side of caution." That's the motto of my generation. Boomers believe in keeping options open, managing risk, taking measured chances, covering all the bases. When we were rebels, even our "protests" were calculated and organized, safe demonstrations of our malcontent (sit-ins!). Learning our lessons from the sixties, we've come to the conclusion that it is possible to take some things too far. This is why the "millennials" scare us. With them, everything is supposed to be taken to the "extreme"—extreme sports, extreme racing, extreme biking, extreme skiing, extreme music (what's all the screaming about?). Bored with living, this batch of humans wants to feel something *constantly*. So, they push the envelope of normality in hopes of exposing raw emotion, unfettered feelings, the gasping-for-air thrills that come with living without limits. To those of us who prefer the predictable, unnecessary risk-taking smacks of immaturity—especially when these young believers bring their "no fear" attitude into the church. Their reckless behavior borders on the profane (visit the Cornerstone Festival in Bushnell, Illinois, and see for yourself). Yet, to them, playing it safe is ungodly. Avoiding surprises preserves hypocrisy.

Ours is a God of mystery and wonder. And, since God must be mysterious to be God, then disciples of Jesus must learn what it means to be vulnerable in their discovery of him. Jesus is not a proposition. Careful, well-reasoned arguments cannot make anyone experience God. Slam-dancing in the presence of God is real joy. Music is a servant of the soul and master of the body. Worship is timeless when all things are sacred. Curiosity is a gift from God, not the impulse of a rebel heart. Indeed, every heart has an open door. Since Jesus takes all comers, it takes all kinds to do the kingdom work of God. Following Jesus, therefore, cannot be anything else but risky business.

Even though I prefer my stodgy brand of Christianity, I find the extreme winds blowing through the fields of God's kingdom both refreshing and unnerving. But isn't that the way it's supposed to be with God? We are taught to fear God because he is mysterious, unpredictable, and invitingly dangerous. God defies our reasoning. Even metaphors fail us when we contemplate God. His thoughts are not our thoughts. His ways are not our ways. He is illogical, unreasonable, and unimaginable. I think the millennials are on to something. They want to be dangerous in their faith, guzzling the grace of God as if it were their last drink of redemption. They want to revel in the mysteries of God's power because he is a passionate lover. They want to be surprised by God. They want a full-throttle, audio-induced, visually-stimulated, cunningly-devised, open-ended, in-over-their-heads, goose-pimpled relationship with God. And, it seems to me, whether they liked it or not, that's exactly what the twelve got from Jesus: an invitation to risk it all for God. What a wild and bumpy ride! The surprising part of Mark's story is discovering who held on to the end.

Before the parable of the farmer and the soils, the disciples of Jesus appear as benign characters in Mark's Gospel, contributing little to the story. After Jesus scolds his disciples for their imperceptiveness, the twelve are thrust into the limelight of Mark's narrative focus. Now the reader's attention is directed to the twelve disciples. Since they don't understand the parable, we are left to wonder: what kind of soil were they? Before chapter four, the disciples did what was expected of them. They dropped what they were doing and followed Jesus (1:16–20; 2:13–14). They found Jesus when people needed help (1:35–39). They went where Jesus went and did what Jesus told them to do (3:7–9). They didn't say much. After chapter four, in light of Jesus's (and the readers') discovery that the disciples don't understand the parable of the farmer and the soils, the behavior of the twelve disciples takes center stage. Time after time, the disciples reveal how ignorant they really are, which also begs the question: did Jesus find good soil in which to sow his gospel

I think the millennials are on to something. They want to be dangerous in their faith, guzzling the grace of God as if it were their last drink of redemption.

seed? At times they seem to fit every category. Sometimes the disciples can't get it through their thick skulls what Jesus is trying to teach them (8:17–18). Although they were the first to receive the gospel seed of Jesus's kingdom gladly, in the end, they abandoned Jesus. Persecuted, they denied him and ran away. Several times the disciples appear distracted by the worries of the world (4:38), the deceitfulness of riches (6:37), and the desires for other things (9:34). Sometimes they get the job done (6:12–13). What adds to the drama of Mark's Gospel is that the success of the kingdom rests on the shoulders of Jesus's followers. Yet, he sowed the seed on *all* kinds of soil. What the reader is trying to figure out is where the harvest will come from.

It takes all kinds to do the kingdom work. Jesus knew that. You would have expected him to be more selective—to share the gospel with only those who would understand. Instead, he persisted in broadcasting the seed on all kinds of hearts. To those who monitor success in terms of risk management, this approach appears rather foolish. After all, think of all the wasted seed. Imagine how silly the parable sounded to Galilean farmers. Why would anyone waste so much seed on such a risky summer crop? In the face of overwhelming failure, how could Jesus's kingdom work succeed? Indeed, once the reader has finished the story—the crowds turn on Jesus, the disciples betray Jesus, the rulers crucify Jesus, the women who visit the empty tomb keep the discovery to themselves—it might be easy to conclude that Jesus failed in his mission.[5] In other words, the optimistic farmer of Jesus's parable underestimated the risk of sowing seed for a summer crop, working a shallow field filled with weeds. Is that it? Is Mark's story no more than a splendid tragedy telling the sad tale of a magnificent farmer's crop failure? Didn't Jesus prove to be the Son of God who established God's reign on earth? What happened to the disciples? Didn't Jesus do some good? Wasn't there someone in the crowd who understood the mystery of the kingdom of God? Did Jesus find anyone with ears to hear? What about his dream of divine reign? Did it come to pass? Didn't he make a difference? Or do we all live in a field of nothing more than weeds and fruitless deeds—a vain labor?

This is the effect of Mark's Gospel. It makes the reader/auditor question whether Jesus ever found good soil for his gospel seed. We identify with Jesus because the threat of a vain labor hangs over all of our heads like a curse. "Cursed is the ground because of you; In toil you will eat of it All the days of your life. Both thorns and thistles it shall grow for you; And you will eat the plants of the field; By the sweat of your face You will eat bread, Till you return to the ground, Because from it you were taken; For you are dust, And to dust you shall return" (Gen. 3:17b–19). This is why the ending of Mark's Gospel puzzles the reader. The only way Jesus could have been considered successful would be if his followers carried on with his mission: sowing the gospel seed, that is, broadcasting the news of Jesus's kingdom reign. And yet, notice what happens. The few women who came to the place where Jesus was buried were intent on finishing the job of preserving the body with burial spices. There was only one problem: who would move the stone door so that they could get to the corpse? When they arrive they discovered an empty tomb and a "young man" sitting by the stone door. Curiously, the narrator tells us that he was wearing a white robe. Shocked by the scene, the women are overwhelmed by what the stranger tells them: "Do not be amazed; you are looking for Jesus the Nazarene, who has been crucified. He has risen; He is not here; behold, here is the place where they laid Him. But go, tell His disciples and Peter, 'He is going ahead of you to Galilee; there you will see Him, just as He told you'" (Mark 16:6–7).

Do the women do what they are told? Will the disciples get the news of Easter morning? Mark's ending leaves much in doubt: "They went out and fled from the tomb, for trembling and astonishment had gripped them; and *they said nothing to anyone*, for they were afraid" (v. 8). Boom. That's the end of the story. Mark's Gospel ends in silence and fear. It leaves the reader with so many questions, so much speculation. Who was the mysterious stranger sitting by the tomb? Was he an angel? Could it have been Jesus? What is the significance of meeting in Galilee? Does it mean that the disciples have to go back to the beginning, to start all over again? Is it true that the women told no one what they saw and heard? If that were the case, then how does Mark know what happened? They must have told somebody. Did the disciples eventually prove to be good soil? Didn't Jesus eventually get his miraculous harvest? In a roundabout way it *could* be; for here I am, having ears to hear the Gospel according to Mark.

Following Twelve Disciples

Mark makes you wonder about the discipleship of the twelve. Looking back over the entire story, they seem to fit all four soils. For example, there are several episodes where evil powers seem to abort Jesus's teaching of the twelve about the reign of God. The most obvious attempt came when Satan tried to steal the seed Jesus had just planted into the hearts of his disciples when he predicted his death and resurrection. There was no parable, no room for misunderstanding; this teaching came in plain words (8:32). Peter knew very well what Jesus was saying, so he "rebuked" Jesus (again, the same word that is used to describe how Jesus "talked" to demons). Unlike Matthew's Gospel, the reader doesn't get to hear exactly what Peter said. Jesus's rebuke of Peter, on the other hand, comes through loud and clear. "Get behind Me, Satan; for you are not setting your mind on God's interests, but man's" (v. 33). Interestingly enough, this entire conversation happened "on the way" (v. 27). When Jesus explained the parable of the farmer and the soils, he described the seed that falls on the first soil in the same terms. "These are the ones who are beside the road [the same word for "way"] where the word is sown; and when they hear, immediately Satan comes and takes away the word which has been sown in them" (4:15). Proof of

84

their ignorance (and Satan's effectiveness?) came the second time Jesus warned his disciples about his imminent death and promised resurrection. Mark notes: "But they did not understand this statement, and they were afraid to ask Him" (9:32). Subsequently, Jesus tried several times to get the twelve to accept God's kingdom agenda. His death and resurrection would deal the crushing blow in defeat of Satan's kingdom. But they couldn't hear what Jesus was saying.

The seed that fell upon the rocky ground proves fruitless when the summer sun scorches the stalk "because it had no root" (4:6). Even though the soil received the word "with joy," it withered because it "had no depth" (vv. 5, 16). Describing the growth as "temporary," the plants that sprang up so quickly fade "when affliction or persecution arises because of the word, immediately they *fall away*" (v. 17). You couldn't find a better description of the twelve disciples in Mark's Gospel. The disciples picture the soil that receives the gospel with joy, dropping their nets (impetuously?) to follow Jesus without question. Soon it becomes apparent how shallow they are in their understanding of the kingdom. *Constantly* the narrator informs the reader of the disciples' difficulty:

"Do you not understand this parable?" (4:13)

"He was explaining everything privately to His own disciples." (4:34)

"For they had not gained any insight from the incident of the loaves, but their heart was hardened." (6:52)

"Are you so lacking in understanding also?" (7:18)

"Do you not yet see or understand? Do you have a hardened heart?" (8:17)

"Do you not yet understand?" (8:21)

"They seized upon that statement, discussing with one another what rising from the dead meant." (9:10)

"Why could we not drive it out?" (9:28)

"But they did not understand this statement, and they were afraid to ask Him." (9:32)

"The disciples rebuked them. But when Jesus saw this, He was indignant." (10:13–14)

"And they were scolding her. But Jesus said, 'Let her alone; why do you bother her?'" (14:5–6)

Indeed, the twelve are dim-witted and hard-hearted. Of course, Jesus knew what he was getting. He even nicknamed the leader of the bunch "Rocky"—the soil that has no depth. What makes the echo of the parable even more resonant is when Jesus anticipates the failure of the twelve. The narrator has Jesus using the same Greek word[6] that was used in the parable of the soils: "You will all *fall away*, because it is written, 'I will strike down the Shepherd, and the sheep shall be scattered'" (14:27; see 4:17). Peter (Rocky) protests using the same language: "Even though all may *fall away*, yet I will not" (v. 29). The picture, then, is complete when Peter denies Jesus, Judas betrays Jesus, and the rest scatter like dandelions.

Several times throughout Mark's Gospel the twelve are worried about their own welfare (4:38; 6:35–38; 8:14–16; 10:28, 37). Jesus had warned them that the "worries of the world, and the deceitfulness of riches, and the desires for other things" would choke the word like weeds (4:19). Notice how, unlike Matthew and Luke, there is no speech in Mark given by Jesus to get his disciples to "count the cost." Mark does not have the parable of the foolish builder or the wise king (Luke 14:28–32). Nowhere in Mark's Gospel does Jesus require *his followers* to give up everything, as he does in Luke: "So then, no one of you can be My disciple who does not give up all his own possessions" (Luke 14:33). Instead, the twelve disciples seem to be confused by what Jesus requires.

After the wealthy man refuses to sell all his possessions and give the profits to the poor, Jesus declared: "How hard it will be for those who are wealthy to enter the kingdom of God!" (Mark 10:23). The disciples were in disbelief. They couldn't accept what Jesus was saying. This caused Jesus to restate his observation dogmatically: rich people won't make it (vv. 24–25). "Then who can be saved?" The disciples' question reveals their bias. They think wealth is a sign of divine favor—that God rewards those with whom he is well pleased. At first, Jesus seems to confirm their convictions. After Peter points out the obvious, "Behold, we have left everything and followed You," Jesus promises that all losses will be recompensed (vv. 28–30). But listen carefully to his words: "There is no one who has left house or brothers or sisters or mother or father or children or farms, for My sake and for the gospel's sake, but that he will receive a hundred times as much now in the present age, houses and brothers and sisters and mothers and children and farms, *along with persecutions*; and in the age to come, eternal life" (vv. 29–30). I can imagine the disciples' confusion. As Jesus was cataloguing the multiple rewards for those who have lost everything for his cause, he sneaks in the phrase, "along with persecutions." It's one thing to get back a hundredfold houses, farms, and family; it's quite something else to be promised the reward of persecution times one hundred. Indeed, when it comes to the gospel of Christ's kingdom, persecution supercedes the cares of the world.

Don't tell missionaries they are making a huge sacrifice to spread the gospel to the ends of the earth. They will take exception to it. We think we're paying them a compliment. They hear implicit criticism in our voice: "I can't believe you live in a house without running water." Or, "How do your children endure such Spartan conditions? Don't they complain?" Or, "So, your kids attend a boarding school in another country. Don't you miss them? Isn't it dangerous?" Or, "It must be hard on you, what with being so far away from your elderly parents back home." When we say such things, it sounds as if we're questioning the wisdom of their decision to follow Christ—that God's call on their lives means jeopardizing their family's welfare. And yet, imagine what they're thinking, home on furlough, trying to deal with a culture they left behind. If I were them, I'd be thinking to myself: "No more dangerous than living in a country where drive-by shootings, abuse of children, murder of the elderly, and raping of women are common stories on the nightly news." As a matter of fact, they're probably glad they don't have to bring their children up in a world of pornography, date rape, booze parties, crack houses, child prostitution, and all the other vices that go along with materialistic excess. What's a life without air-conditioning? Comfort is a relative thing. To them, it's no sacrifice at all to serve God in another country. They say it is a privilege to do what God has called them to do. Perhaps they see what the American church refuses to admit: the cares of the world choke the seed of the gospel.

Did the twelve understand what Jesus was driving at, that is, his kingdom rewards cannot compare to the "rewards" of this world: houses, land, family? Did they agree that the loss of all things is a good thing—that being last is first and being first is last (10:31)? Or, did they think that Jesus was promising some quid pro quo arrangement for devoted followers? Did Peter think that since he had given up houses, business, and family to follow Jesus that he would get a sizeable reward in the kingdom of God—like a huge palace, lands to govern, and a royal family? Visions of personal fiefs and kingdom glory danced in the disciples' heads. How do I know? Read the very next story (vv. 35–45). If this were not so tragic it would be amusing.

Jesus spent most of his last days with the disciples trying to get them to understand the purpose of his mission. Only moments before James and John approached Jesus with an outrageous request, Jesus told the twelve what was going to happen in Jerusalem. Rather than receive a kingdom befitting a king, he would be humiliated, beaten, and killed. Evidently, some of the Passover pilgrims headed for the holy city anticipated the same scenario. Mark records that some of "those who followed were fearful" (v. 32). Their worst fears should have been confirmed by Jesus's ominous prediction: "Behold, we are going up to Jerusalem, and the Son of Man will be delivered to the chief priests and the scribes; and they will condemn Him to death, and will deliver Him to the Gentiles. And they will mock Him and spit upon Him, and scourge Him, and kill Him" (vv. 33–34). The awkward silence that followed such a pessimistic picture of things to come was broken by the audacious request of James and John. What were they thinking? Did they even hear what Jesus had just told them? He's talking about humility and they're dreaming of glory. He's predicting a cross, they're fitting themselves for a crown. He will occupy the seat of accusation, they plan to hold the seat of honor. He will become the least, they hope to be the greatest.

Previously, Jesus had promised his followers that they could ask for anything in his name. James and John took him at his word: "Teacher, we want You to do for us whatever we ask of You" (v. 35). Look carefully at Jesus's response, "What do you want Me to do for you?" (v. 36). What do they want from Jesus? They want to hear guarantees about the rewards they will receive in the kingdom come: "Grant that we may sit, one on Your right and one on Your left, in Your glory" (v. 37). How presumptuous! What arrogance! Jesus reminds them of what lies ahead, that they are following him—that they will go where he goes. "Are you able to drink the cup that I drink?" (v. 38). Thinking that he must be talking about the banquet of heavenly reward, the two replied impetuously, "We are able" (v. 39). Of course, we know that Jesus is talking about the cup of suffering. We know that all disciples *will* follow Jesus—that before a crown of glory, we must wear a crown of thorns—that we must be crucified with Christ.[7] By predicting his passion, Jesus reveals the path of every disciple: "You *will* drink the cup." Then he added, " 'But to sit on My right or on My left, this is not Mine to give; but it is for those for whom it has been prepared.' Hearing this, the ten began to feel indignant with James and John" (vv. 40–41). They were angry that James and John got to Jesus first.

Few things are more sickening than watching disciples fight for positions of power in Christendom. It is such an ugly scene. Jealousies fuel rivalries between those who have power and those who want power. Is there power in the church? Only a fool could ignore the politics of power in churches and denominations. Typically, we fight over control, over resources, over agenda, over money. Isn't it amazing how quickly things can change? A small band of like-minded believers meet together to start a little church and dream of making a difference in their community. Then, with time, new members mean more resources, and more resources mean more opportunity, and before long funds are raised and a beautiful building is erected in the middle of the neighborhood. Soon, personnel and property become battlegrounds for the once irenic congregation that used to meet in a warehouse. Or, a few churches band together to form an organization to channel efforts for the kingdom and what usually happens? Annual meetings require voting members to elect officers, form committees, appease constituents, and ignore the disenfranchised. The consolidation of power eats away at the heart of the gospel. Losers are supposed to win. The last are supposed to be first. The least are supposed to have the greatest positions.

Just once, I would love to see *one follower of Jesus* give in to those who are trying to control committees, churches, denominations, or organizations via power politics (yes, I said it, *give in*). Usually those left out of the loop carp about their plight. But, didn't Jesus say that if someone asks for our coat, we're supposed to give him our shirt as well? So what if "your side" lost the election. Shouldn't we sacrifice our preferences over trivial matters for the sake of the community? Shouldn't we give the power-hungry Christians among us what they want? What if the losers gave up fighting over scraps? The only kingdom worth having is the one worth dying for—the kingdom of God! And, here's an even more radical concept: what if the winners gave the losers what they want? There can be no power struggle if there's nothing to control. That makes no sense to "leaders" seeking recognition. Yet, it makes all the sense in the world to servants who know the *power* of giving in—it's called "sacrifice." There's only one Lord among the servants, and he sacrificed everything for us. We rule when we die. That's what Jesus was trying to teach James and John.

We forget from whence we came. Like James and John we've forgotten where grace found us. Remember who you were *before* Christ? Sinner. What were the sons of thunder before Jesus found them? Fishermen. Neither is material worthy of the ruling class. How many times did these poor fishermen dream of being in power? Did they ever think, while mending their nets after a particularly bad catch, "I wish I were king. What I could do if I were 'king for a day'! I'd get rid of these gut-wrenching taxes. I'd live in a beautiful mansion instead of a shanty. I'd eat the finest foods instead of this stinking, pickled fish. I'd be the most powerful man in the world, venerated by every subject, worthy of every honor." Oppressed people often fantasize about absolute power. As they marched for Jerusalem, then, such dreams must have seemed like they were becoming reality for the twelve. It made perfect sense: the least were going to become the greatest. Fishermen would reign in Jerusalem. Yet, the path to power would take a devastating turn for the worse. The glory of Christ's kingdom would be found on a cross. "For even the Son of Man did not come to be served, but to serve, and to give His life a ransom for many" (10:45). The last thing on the minds of the twelve was that slavery would be (or even could be) God's reward for those who followed Jesus. That certainly wasn't a very appetizing carrot to dangle in front of any disciple. Who would follow Jesus for that? Only a loser who has everything to gain—a sinner saved by grace.

In the very next story, Jesus found the loser—a man who had to beg for daily provisions (vv. 46–52). The intended contrast between these two stories is obvious. We move in the narrative from two disciples contemplating greatness to a blind beggar who epitomizes the least of these. The parade of pilgrims created a circus environment for the citizens of Jericho. Traveling from the north country, the people heading for Jerusalem to celebrate Passover would join other caravans in the Jordan valley, follow the river to Jericho, and then pass through the ancient city for their final ascent to Zion. Thousands of people would pack the streets of Jericho, singing and dancing along the way, anticipating the celebration of the most favored festival of the year. This year's crowd was larger than usual. Messianic expectations were high. Jesus's entry into Jerusalem would be a spectacular event. Palm branches would be used to orchestrate his arrival as the conquering Son of David. As the people sang the familiar songs of their deliverance, even as the disciples were making their own plans to rule in the kingdom to come, Jesus's thoughts revealed a messianic mission of another purpose: "For even the Son of Man did not come to be served, but to serve, and to give His life a ransom for many" (v. 45).

About that time, rising above the songs of messianic praise, a desperate cry for help was heard. Bartimaeus, realizing his only hope was passing by, screamed at the top of his lungs, "Jesus, Son of David, have mercy on me!" (v. 47). The pilgrims tried to silence the beggar; "many were *sternly* telling him to be quiet." How dare he interrupt the Passover procession of a king. But the obnoxious man persisted with his annoying plea for mercy. Jesus stopped the parade, called for the beggar to be brought to him, and then asked Bartimaeus *exactly* the same question he asked James and John—word for word—"What do you want Me to do for you?" (v. 51). The beggar's response not only reveals the simplicity of his need, but also the rich soil of a fertile heart: "Master, I want to see." Jesus looked into the dark eyes of a blinded man and asked him the same question he asks every needy, would-be follower: "What do you want me to do for you?" James and John asked for the world. Bartimaeus asked for the very thing sighted people take for granted every day: "I want to see." Ironically, this is the simple request of any disciple of Jesus who would follow him. Blinded by life, we were all once begging for the mercy of God by the side of the road. "And Jesus said to him, 'Go; your faith has made you well.' Immediately he regained his sight and began following Him on the road" (v. 52). Here Jesus's response surprises me. What he should have said was, "Look what I've done for you. Now, what will you do for me?" Instead, Jesus healed a blind man and said, "Go your own way." But that's *not* what disciples do.

See what grace does to a blind man? Jesus made no assumptions since all men and women freely receive the grace of God. "Go your own way," he said. I think he meant it. Jesus makes no arrangements with his disciples. There will be no prenuptial agreement with the Bride of Christ. We are beggars. What can we offer? What can we do? Like a blind man receiving his sight, all disciples follow Jesus *along the way*. Where else can they go? Bowled over by pure mercy, losers cannot help but follow Jesus. They follow him to Jerusalem. They follow him to a cross. They follow a king destined to wear a crown of thorns.

In Mark's Gospel, the failure of the twelve to follow Jesus to the end makes the reader wonder: "Did the farmer of God's kingdom find good soil for his seed?" Certainly, those who followed Jesus from the beginning should qualify. And many times the twelve disciples seem to fit the bill. They were successful in their mission to extend the kingdom of God to other villages (6:7–13). The seed that was sown in their hearts yielded a harvest for Christ: "They went out and preached that men should repent. And they were casting out many demons and were anointing with oil many sick people and healing them" (vv. 12–13). Yet, at times, the twelve acted like the other three soils. Does Mark intend for his readers to question the devotion of the twelve apostles, doubting their credibility? Does Mark's Gospel make us want to size up other Christians whose dedication to God is questionable? Or does the literary effect of Mark's Gospel make any reader/auditor question his or her *own* discipleship, identifying with the vacillation of the twelve? How many Christians can say that, at one time or another, they have never been hard-headed and hard-hearted when it comes to hearing the Word of God? I think I'm all four soils—some parts of the gospel I like, some parts I ignore.

Mark's Gospel could be used to judge our commitment to Christ, as well as the commitment of other disciples. Both reading strategies are plausible. But I don't think that's what Mark was after. After hearing the story, the auditor can't help but ask the question: what does good soil look like? In fact, Jesus's anticipation of the miraculous harvest makes the reader face the question head-on. Did Jesus receive his harvest: some thirty, some sixty, some a hundredfold? Of course, to us this is a ridiculous question. After two thousand years of Christian history, we can answer without hesitation: Yes, even a thousandfold! But this was not the case for Mark's audience, when Christianity was a brand-new force in the fierce marketplace of competing religions. Any first-century reader would walk away from Mark's story puzzling over the question: "Did Jesus's risky crop bring in the harvest?"

4

Finding Good Soil

If I am sure of anything I am sure that His teaching was never meant to confirm my congenital preference for safe investments and limited liabilities.

C. S. Lewis, *The Four Loves*

Jesus was relentless in his pursuit of the kingdom of God. Nothing and no one could stop him. From the very beginning of Mark's Gospel, Jesus faced fierce opposition. The powers confronted him. The crowds overwhelmed him. The disciples frustrated him. The needy hounded him. The scribes attacked him. The leaders crucified him. Despite all the adversity, Jesus persisted in his belief that the reign of God had come. And, at times, it looked like he single-handedly brought in the kingdom. He exorcized demons. He fed thousands. He trained twelve followers. He healed the sick. He silenced his critics. He defied death. All the while, he kept farming the gospel seed out to anyone who would listen. This was his purpose; this was his mission: finding good soil. Even though crowds flocked to him by the thousands, Jesus would tell his disciples, "Let's get out of here and go somewhere else so that I can announce the good news: this is what I came to do" (1:38; my paraphrase). At a break-neck pace, Jesus was going to see it through. All he needed was for a few seed to find fertile hearts. Then he would bring in the harvest of God.

Jesus was a busy worker. Farming is hard labor. Have you ever noticed how much Jesus accomplished in one day according to Mark? Take "a day in the life of Jesus" in Mark's Gospel. Study how Jesus acts like a man possessed—a man with so little time and so much to do. One of Mark's favorite expressions to transition from one episode to the next is "and immediately." Count how many times Jesus rushes from one scene to the next, cramming more in a day than most could accomplish in a week. In Jesus's kingdom effort there was no rest for the weary. It's no wonder that, collapsing from exhaustion, Jesus had no problem sleeping through a storm in a boat in the middle of the night. As long as there was sun to burn, there was work to be done. Farmers only have so much time to put in their crops. Indeed, Jesus wasted no time getting the word out. He knew that the significance of his mission would be measured by the success of his labor. The only thing that matters to any farmer is the harvest. And before a farmer can gather a good harvest, he must sow seed on good soil before it's too late. Having read Mark's Gospel, looking over Jesus's life and work, one cannot help but ask: Did God's farmer find good dirt in time? The three soils resulting in crop failure are easy enough to spot. But what about the good earth? Mark's story makes the reader puzzle over the possibilities.

"And some fell along the way . . ."

Jesus's first convert after the parable of the soils has much in common with the last disciple he made before he died. They both match the description of the first soil. Consider the story of the man possessed by legions of demons (5:1–20). In this case, evil fowl have come to roost in the soul of a man who epitomizes uncleanness: he is possessed by unclean spirits and he lives with unclean corpses. What chance does the gospel seed have here? Fast forward to the end of the Gospel. Heading for Jerusalem, Jesus sowed seed "along the way" and found a follower in a blind man begging beside the road (10:46–52). The three Greek words that translate "along the way" are found in only two places: 4:4 (describing the soil) and 10:46 (describing the beggar). For Mark's Gospel, then, both a demon-possessed man and a blind beggar make for good planting. From the very beginning to the very end, Jesus would broadcast the gospel on every kind of soil, hoping that it would take root and bear fruit. Who would have thought that a beggar and a demoniac would prove to be good soil? Only a farmer who believes in a miraculous harvest.

Chapter divisions disrupt the flow of a good story. This is what happens when modern readers finish "chapter 4" of Mark's Gospel without regard for the "beginning" of chapter 5.[1] Actually, these two stories, the calming of the storm and the exorcism of the demoniac from Gerasa, are meant to be read together in order to tell a bigger story. Jesus has just finished telling the twelve that they were special compared to the crowd. It was Jesus's intent to stump outsiders with parables—mysterious stories that occluded the meaning of his teaching. The twelve, on the other hand, were given insight to the parables because Jesus "was explaining everything privately" (4:34). It seemed that the "good soil" needed a little help receiving the implanted word. That the twelve *didn't understand* the mystery of the kingdom of God is evident in the next story. After Jesus worked the miracle of calming wind and waves, the disciples replied, "Who then is this, that even the wind and the sea obey Him?" (v. 41). Then, in the very next episode, even as the disciples were scratching their heads over Jesus's identity, a demoniac comes crying out of the tombs: "What business do we have with each other, Jesus, Son of the Most High God?" (5:7). The man troubled by legions of demons has no trouble identifying Jesus. What Jesus came to do, on the other hand, remained a mystery—both for the demoniac and the twelve.

Ironically, the kingdom rule of God would mean the subjugation of evil powers called "Legion." This hoard of demons used the familiar designation of the principal military division of Roman Imperial forces. A legion of Roman soldiers, numbering from 2,500 to 6,000 men, would pour into occupied territories to secure Rome's domination of imperial subjects. As a matter of fact, for first-century Mediterraneans, "legions" carried the same significance as the terms we use to quantify eternality, "begillions" (who can count past zillion?). "How many grains of sand are there on the seashore?" A first-century subject of the Roman Empire would say, "legions." Therefore, when the man identified the demons within as "legion," images of unending Roman dominance and oppression came to mind. Indeed, a man ravaged by demons, who lived with dead people, who could not be chained, who cut himself with sharp rocks—a bloody mess of a man who wailed night and day in misery—pictured Roman cruelty to a tee. This is why "Legion" begs not to be sent out of the country (v. 10). They occupied Gerasa, one of the cities of the Decapolis (a constellation of ten Greek cities ruled by Rome). Once the unclean spirits were cast into the "herd" of unclean swine, "Legion" drowned in the sea (reminiscent of the Red Sea?).[2] When those tending to the pigs reported what had happened, the people of Gerasa shooed Jesus away (vv. 14–17).

Troubled, no doubt, by their loss and Jesus's peculiar abilities, the townsfolk saw Jesus as a threat rather than a hope. Lost in all of the confusion was the fact that Jesus *had done them a favor.* The mad man who had caused such grief and trouble for their town, scaring off no telling how many travelers, would no longer be their menace. When the people of Gerasa came to Jesus, they "observed the man who had been demon-possessed sitting down, clothed and in his right mind, the very man who had had the 'legion'" (v. 15). The unwanted occupation of their territory was gone. They should have celebrated the demise of "legion." They preferred, however, to send Jesus back where he came from.

Why did Jesus come to the outskirts of Gerasa, anyway? Did he have plans to announce the reign of God's kingdom there? If so, it would have been the first time he left Jewish country to bring the Good News to Gentiles. On the Jewish side of the lake, crowds begged him to stay. On the Gentile side, the crowd begged him to leave. At first glance, it may have seemed like a wasted trip. But then again, Jesus found good soil for his gospel seed. The man who used to live with dead people wanted to follow Jesus. As Jesus and the twelve were getting back into the boat, the ex-demoniac asked to join their company. Jesus had other ideas. "Go home to your people and report to them what great things the Lord has done for you, and how He had mercy on you" (v. 19). It turns out that this man who used to live with the unclean (corpses) will return to live with the unclean (Gentiles). The man who used to cry out on the mountains night and day about his miserable existence will proclaim the Good News of God's kingdom reign in the cities: "And he went away and began to proclaim in Decapolis what great things Jesus had done for him; and everyone was amazed" (v. 20). Marveled indeed! As long as he was around, who could deny the power of Christ's kingdom? They could send Jesus away but *he* would be their constant reminder that Rome was not the only power in town. One man takes the Good News to ten cities. That sounds like a miraculous harvest to me.

"Don't call me legion anymore." Before he met Jesus, the demoniac bore the name of his captors. It took legions of evil powers to bring this man to the edge of destruction. As he returned to his own country, the man from Gerasa would be an everlasting testimony to the power of *one* man, Jesus. This more than anything else confounds unbelievers. Sinners are transformed by the power of one man. To me, the surest sign that Jesus reigns now is the changed life of any pagan. Pick one: drug addict, alcoholic, pedophile, adulterer, homosexual, thief, liar, abuser, snob, racist, materialist. Evil powers can make a mess of anyone's life. And yet, any pagan can become a kindhearted, gentle-spirited, gen-erous, devoted, reliable, purified human being by the power of Jesus

Christ. How else can it be explained? The power of Christ's kingdom will overpower any power opposed to the power of God—*any power*, whether spiritual, physical, angelic, demonic, political, social, personal, corporate, medical, or psychological. Believers are living monuments to the power of Christ's mercy. Unbelievers may dismiss Jesus. They may deny the relevance of our faith. They may question the benefits of our ways. They can even deny the existence of God. But they have to deal with us. Whether they like it or not, we are here to stay. We're not going away. We cannot help but tell what great things Jesus has done for us. Like the demoniac from Gerasa, we are known by a new name. Don't call me "legion" anymore. I belong to another. He changed me. As long as we're around, no one can deny the power of Jesus.

Jesus told the man exorcised of legions of demons to tell everyone "what great things the Lord has done for you, and how *He had mercy on you*" (5:19). The only other place in Mark's Gospel where "mercy" is mentioned is in the story of blind Bartimaeus (10:46–52). As Jesus was leaving Jericho for Jerusalem on Palm Sunday, he overheard the cry of a blind man begging for mercy (vv. 47–48). The people of Gerasa tried to bind the demoniac with chains. The pilgrims on the road to Jerusalem preparing for Passover tried to gag the blind man's mouth.

> *To me, the surest sign that Jesus reigns now is the changed life of any pagan.*

The demoniac cried out, "Jesus, Son of the Most High God." Bartimaeus screamed out, "Jesus, Son of David." The demoniac wanted to follow Jesus, but he was sent back to his own people. Jesus told the blind man, "go *your own way*," but he ended up following Jesus "on the road" (v. 52). Both of these stories reveal how the soil that receives the seed of Christ's kingdom along the way can turn into good soil; it's only by the mercy of God. To people's way of thinking back then, a man plagued by demons or blindness is getting what he deserves. These afflictions are the just punishments of God. Consequently, the cursed are easily ignored, cast to the side of the road. They are helpless and hopeless. To the blessed of God, a demoniac and a blind man are nuisances. To Jesus, these men would become undeniable demonstrations of the power of God's mercy. That's what changes the hard ground that marks the path of a farmer sowing seed into good soil—mercy.

Grace gives us what we don't deserve; mercy keeps us from getting what we do deserve. This is good news: no one lies beyond the voice of the one announcing good news. Anyone can have ears to hear. This is why Jesus believed in the miraculous harvest. His mercy changes everything. No prejudice can stop the irrepressible mercy of God. A demoniac from Gerasa and a blind man named Bartimaeus knew that better than anyone.

Labels. We all use them. Labels are handy tags that we slap on the people we don't want to deal with. Rather than struggle with the arguments of those who don't think like us, we dismiss their opinions by assigning them to the pre-assigned categories of our experience. She's liberal, he's narrow-minded, she's trouble, he's paranoid, she's a Bible-thumper, he's a reprobate, they're all just a bunch of hypocrites. Labels help us stay in control of a chaotic world. Tags are easier to read than people. But the truth is this: life is more complicated than the stereotypes we create. You can call me something you understand but it doesn't change who I am. The most original person who ever lived was the most misunderstood. Jesus defied explanation. They called him everything in the book, trying to dismiss his claims, trying to ignore his influence, trying to silence his voice. His critics labeled him a fraud, a madman, a rebel, a criminal, a drunkard, a fool. It's no wonder he was sympathetic to the marginalized. They lived with labels, too. But Jesus made sure that, in his kingdom, labels would never stick. He changed a demoniac into a preacher. He blessed a cursed man. The mercy man was crucified as a blasphemer. Easter proves how wrong people can be. Lies are temporal; truth is eternal. It doesn't matter what people call you. The truth of who you are is what Jesus has done for you.

"And some fell on the shallow . . ."

Children are simple. Motives are never questioned. Feelings are never hidden. What they say is what they mean. What they need is never in doubt. They believe what they are told. Curiosity comes naturally. Every question has an answer. And all stories are real. Although they are incredibly demanding, they are easily ignored. They embody the future but have no sense of the past. They celebrate the simplest of things and overlook the greatest of mistakes. They can show great resolve, yet cry so easily. They have to give in all the time, but they rarely give up on anything. Children need help but always learn how to survive. They want everything but require very little. What they see is all that matters. They love to make believe. They accept things as they are. Children are simple people.

Jesus prized children. To him, they were the best example of what he was trying to teach twelve men. Children pictured what a disciple is supposed to be: "Truly I say to you, whoever does not receive the kingdom of God like a child will not enter it at all" (10:15). *And*, children represented what Christ came to be: "Whoever receives one child like this in My name receives Me" (9:37). Therefore, Jesus reserved his severest warning for those who would scandalize children: "Whoever causes one of these little ones who believe to stumble, it would be better for him if, with a heavy millstone hung around his neck, he had been cast into the sea" (v. 42). The word translated "stumble" is the same word that is used to describe what happens to the seed that falls on the second soil: "They have no firm root in themselves, but are only temporary; then, when affliction or persecution arises because of the word, immediately they *fall away* [or stumble]" (4:17). Crowds may come and go. The twelve, as Jesus predicted, would eventually "fall away" (same word). But Jesus sanctioned children, protecting them when he issued his ominous threat: don't bruise their souls, or you'll go to hell. Due to special dispensations, children should never fall away. Indeed, according to Jesus, they are good soil for the gospel seed of the kingdom.

What was Jesus's tone when he said, "Permit the children to come to Me" (10:14)? I always pictured an irenic voice uttering these beautiful words. Yet that was not the case. Jesus was angry when he said these words. Of course, he wasn't mad at the children or the parents who wanted his blessing. It was his imperceptive disciples that made him angry. Once again, the twelve had missed the message. Just before they left Galilee, Jesus used a child to model the kind of disciple that he was looking for (9:37). "If anyone wants to be first, he shall be last of all and servant of all" (v. 35). These words fit a child better than anyone in the first century. Even though children were desirable signs of God's blessing, they ranked the lowest in the honor pyramid. Even slaves could boss children around. As a matter of fact, that's exactly what the twelve were doing before Jesus corrected their mistake. Acting like stewards (serving Jesus?), the disciples were taking control of the situation, "rebuking" the children and their parents for disturbing Jesus. Before, when Jesus gave the twelve the object lesson about being last, the twelve tried "to *hinder*" a man from doing kingdom work because "he was not following us" (v. 38). Their behavior prompted Jesus's warning about causing "little ones . . . to stumble" (v. 42). This time, the disciples tried to prevent children from bothering Jesus. "Do not *hinder* them; for the kingdom of God belongs to such as these" (10:14). It seems that the twelve believed they could spot the difference between good and bad soil. Of all people, children would make for poor sowing.

Consider Jesus's description of the second soil. It is shallow. It receives the seed "with joy." The plant springs up quickly but has no roots. It has a brief life span. Like the summer sun scorching the plant, hard times sap its strength. It withers away, yielding no fruit (future seed). Like a plant trying to survive the summer crop, the odds were stacked against children in the first-century world. It is estimated that only one out of five children would reach the age of thirty. Disease, war, hunger, and evil powers seemed to target children. The children that appear in Mark's Gospel confirm this observation. "Little ones" were easy prey in a harsh world. Who could build a lasting kingdom on children?

As soon as a twelve-year-old girl died, the mourners who were waiting for death started the funeral since children rarely recovered from serious illness (5:38). When a Gentile woman begged Jesus to heal her "little daughter" who suffered from an unclean spirit, he said: "Let the children be satisfied first, for it is not good to take the children's bread and throw it to the dogs" (7:27). Why? Because children get the leftovers as it is; adults received first portions. In a world of limited goods, children ate scraps since nourishment for adults was more important to maintain a family's livelihood. But, as the woman reminded Jesus, children were never selfish with their measly portions. They often fed scavengers hiding under the table (v. 28). Even the little they had they would give away. Jesus rewarded her insight (lost on the twelve!) by healing her daughter (v. 30). Later, Jesus had to exorcise a demon that kept trying to destroy a boy via suicide (9:22). The boy had suffered from the malady "since childhood" (v. 21). When the demon left his body, the boy fell dead. And, as he did before with the little girl, Jesus took the child by the hand and raised him up (v. 27). That a child could be tormented by demons, thrown into fire and water, seems nearly impossible to us. To our way of thinking, children are sacred space, innocent souls, quarantined from evil powers. But to Mark's audience, children were the most vulnerable to disease, demons, and death. This is why parents wanted Jesus to bless their children. They knew he was a holy man who had great power over evil. His touch would ensure protection, leading to a long life. To the disciples, however, this was a waste of time.

"And He took them in His arms and began blessing them, laying His hands on them" (10:16). In Mark's story, Jesus blessed two things: food and children—nothing else. Ironically, the food he blessed would serve as a memorial of his life and work: "Take it; this is My body" (14:22). Bread is consumed. Wine serves its purpose. And yet, these perishables would prove to be everlasting reminders to Jesus's followers of his life's work. Jesus also taught the twelve that receiving a child in "his name" would be the same as "receiv[ing] Me" (9:37). Children are temporary. They either become adults or meet, to our reckoning, an untimely death.

And yet, Jesus declared that children would forever demonstrate what it means to be a disciple of his. Indeed, what Jesus blessed, food and children, became an everlasting reminder of his kingdom's work. We baptize children; we celebrate the Lord's table with bread. Jesus found living memorials in things that don't last: children, food, drink, and words.

The orality of his mission still takes me by surprise. Wasn't it a risky venture to rely upon people's ears to preserve his legacy? If I were Jesus, I would have made sure that someone would write down such profound words. "Blessed are the pure in heart, for they shall see God. Oooh, that's good. Somebody get that down for me." Or, I should expect the Great Commission to go something like: "Go ye therefore into all the world and write gospels. Publish whatsoever I have taught you. And lo, my words will be with you always, even to the end of the world." Of course, the people of his world were much better equipped to remember what they heard than we are. Being illiterate, the average Galilean had a great capacity to recall lengthy discourse. In fact, rabbinical students in Jesus's day were not only required to memorize the Torah (that's Genesis through Deuteronomy), they also committed to memory four hundred

> *Jesus found living memorials in things that don't last: children, food, drink, and words.*

years of rabbinical teaching! Still, Jesus relied upon spoken words to produce the kingdom of God. What an amazingly ambitious agenda. Spoken words are temporary things. Once they leave your mouth, words are gone with the wind. Even though Jesus realized his words were falling on shallow soil, he persisted in sowing the gospel seed. Knowing they wouldn't last, Jesus still believed in the power of his words. And why shouldn't he? He spoke to friends, enemies, demons, God, Satan, wind, water, corpses, trees, cities, ears, eyes, hands, disease. When he spoke, things happened. This is why God's farmer relied upon the spoken word to plant the Good News of God's kingdom into the hearts of his listeners. Words vanish as soon as they are created. Who can trace the vapor trail of their power? Who could find permanence in things that don't last? Only a man who knows the temporary can make an eternal difference: "Heaven and earth will pass away, but My words will not pass away" (Mark 13:31).

Remember what Jesus said about the second soil? "When affliction or persecution arises because of the word, immediately they fall away" (4:17). Here's the surprising part of the whole story of Mark's Gospel. The only characters that *didn't fall away* were children. The disciples abandoned Jesus when he was arrested. At least the women followed Jesus to the cross, ensuring a proper burial. And yet, when they were told of his resurrection, they ran away in fear, telling no one the good news. Mysteriously, two boys appear in the story of Jesus's passion, one at the beginning and one at the end, signaling to Mark's readers that Jesus did find good soil in the midst of affliction and persecution. Their appearance is brief, more provocative than telling. After Jesus was arrested, when "all left Him and fled," a certain "young man" (teenager)[3] persisted in following Jesus, "wearing nothing but a linen sheet" (14:51). Was this all he had to wear, a poor boy poorly clothed? Whatever the significance, he risked his life to be with Jesus. At this point in the narrative, he was the *only person* following Jesus. Everyone else had "fallen away." Jump to the end of the story. A "young man" wearing a white robe tells the women at Jesus's tomb the good news: "He has risen" (16:6). This boy *was the first* to announce the good news.[4]

We often say that Jesus appeared first to Mary. According to Mark's Gospel, the first person to witness Easter morning was a "young man . . . wearing a white robe" (v. 5).[5] He was the last to follow Jesus and the first to preach the gospel. This mysterious young man pictured childlike obedience for Mark's readers. Grown men abandoned Jesus, terrified for their lives. Women left the tomb in fear, "for trembling and astonishment had gripped them; and they said nothing to anyone" (v. 8). It took a boy to finish what Jesus started. Now we know why he said, "Permit the children to come to me." Children are good soil for the kingdom. Vacation Bible School workers, Sunday School teachers, and nursery workers know that very well.

I had decided to teach the preschoolers during our annual Vacation Bible School (VBS) when my wife asked incredulously, "Do you know what you're doing?" Even though I had never attempted such a feat, I figured a seminary graduate possessed every skill necessary to teach Bible stories to children. "Of course. How hard can it be?" "Tell me what you're planning to do for the craft." "Well," I said without hesitation, "we're going to make felt bookmarks that look like little mice. See, here's all that we need: material, yarn, glue, scissors, even bee-bees for the eyes." "You're kidding," she said. I could tell by her tone that I had forgotten something. "You mean you're going to put scissors into the hands of four-year-olds and hope for the best?" Suddenly it dawned on me that, perhaps, I wasn't cut out for the job. This observation became even more apparent when I finished telling the Bible story during the first day of VBS.

The kids had just come in from playing when I sat them down and told the story about how Jesus taught his disciples to pray. I had the flannel board, the cutout Bible characters, and the story ready to go. I had their undivided attention. And, to my surprise, it came off without a hitch. When it was over, a little girl raised her hand. I was expecting the usual, "When are we going to get our snack?" Instead, she surprised me with the question, "If Jesus was God, who did he pray to?" "Uhhh, ummm. Well, now that's a very good question. Let's see." I was out of my league. What could I say? What great, theological answer did I have for the christological implications of Jesus's prayer life? I gathered every bit of wisdom available to me and said, "Who wants punch and cookies?" The class squealed with approval, a little girl's question was diverted, and a seminary graduate learned why teaching children about Jesus is so rewarding. It's because they ask complicated questions and are satisfied with simple answers. It's because what they like best about Vacation Bible School *is* the punch and cookies, and the games, and the crafts, and the Bible stories. It's because a little girl may never remember the inability of a teacher to answer her question, but will probably never forget how much her teachers loved her. It's because believers have so little time to teach children—they grow up so fast. It's because children automatically love Jesus. It's because all of us were once children, when the Bible was our special book, and God was mysterious, and the song, "Jesus loves the little children," said it all. Blessed are the shallow, for the gospel is sown deep into their hearts.

"And some fell among thorns . . ."

Weeds are the perennial pests of all farmers. Remove one and three show up to take its place. No one has to plant weeds. They always seem to do better than what the farmer is trying to grow. And to make matters worse, weeds thrive under the harshest conditions. They spring up despite drought. They tower over garden plants when the summer sun is unrelenting. Thorny plants steal nourishment, choking stalks intended to produce grain. Even hobby farmers know, left unchecked, weeds can take over the soil. Farmers expect certain losses when it comes to sowing seed. They won't fuss over the few grains that fall along the way. Abundant sowing means that some seed eventually spills on the hard ground. Farmers learn to live with shallow soil. No Galilean could move the massive rocks that lie buried beneath the surface. Every year certain plants fail to mature in the same area because the farmer knows he can do nothing about the "dead spots" caused by unseen boulders. But weeds! Weeds spoil soil in obvious ways. Unsightly, they mar the ground like a curse. Farming turns into vain labor when all that is produced are thorns and thistles (Gen. 3:17–18). A man's hard work may come to naught simply because of weeds. Thorns and thistles are unwanted intruders that drain the land. They are the enemy of all farmers planting for the harvest.

In the first century, Jews believed that they were under the curse of God since Rome occupied the Promised Land. When Jesus was about ten years old, Judea was placed under direct Roman rulership. As an imperial province, Judea was governed by Roman procurators, like Pontius Pilate. Jerusalem, the capital of Judea, was the political hotspot for Roman governors charged with keeping the peace. Messianic pretenders and social revolutionaries would always come to the holy city to make their case. Invariably, these insurrectionists would meet the immovable object of Roman will and find the end of Roman justice on a Roman cross. When Jesus made his "triumphal entry" on Palm Sunday into Jerusalem, the staged event was supposed to signal to the governing powers, Jewish and Roman, that the King had come to claim the kingdom. Therefore, it shouldn't surprise us that the last chapters of Mark's Gospel revolve around Jesus's encounters with the authorities—first Jewish, then Roman. This was inevitable since Jesus presented himself as the Son of David. It was also inevitable that the story would end with Jesus hanging on a Roman cross, crucified with two other insurrectionists (15:7, 27). Remember, for Mark's Gospel, this is the first (and only) time Jesus comes to Jerusalem. Hailed as the heir of David's throne, Jesus would be crucified as "King of the Jews." Welcomed into the city as a king, he would be thrown out of Jerusalem as a fraud. To use an inadequate analogy, the audacity of Jesus's visit to Jerusalem might be compared to a truck driver who organizes a convoy to Washington DC, declaring upon his arrival that he's the president of the United States. It would be only a matter of time before the circus would be shut down.

Of the three undesirable soils of the parable, only the third soil is explicitly described as being "unfruitful" (4:19). It is quite apparent that all three soils result in crop failure. Seed that falls along the way is gobbled up by birds. Shallow soil gives some indication of potential, yet the growth it produces cannot survive summer months. Plants sharing soil with thorns and thistles, on the other hand, have a chance. But notice how Jesus characterized the weed-infested soil as ground that "*becomes* unfruitful." The "worries of the world, the deceit of riches, and the lust for other things" choke the Good News of the kingdom of God. That description of the untimely end of the seed cast upon the third soil reads like a script for the events that transpired once Jesus came to Jerusalem. Power, money, and greed were the unyielding forces that brought about Jesus's demise. As he had done throughout Galilee, Jesus broadcast his gospel seed in Jerusalem. He announced the reign of God and confronted the powers. Jesus declared the temple "unfruitful," and Roman soldiers crowned him "King of the Jews" with thorns. This time, however, the powers overcome Jesus. Jerusalem proves to be unfruitful soil for the gospel. And, once again, the reader wonders: "Did Jesus find good soil among the weeds? Or, did God's farmer fail to bring in the harvest of God's reign at the most crucial time?"

In Mark 11–15 Jesus took on the powers that rule Jerusalem. First, he challenged the religious authorities by "cleansing" the temple. Then, after his arrest, he refused the benefit of Roman law—he chose a trial without defense. In both cases, Jesus's actions reveal a cavalier attitude to those claiming to be in control. The trustees of the Jewish temple questioned Jesus's "authority" to drive out the merchants (11:28). Ironically, it was Jesus's claim to authority that led to his death: "[The high priest asked Jesus] 'Are You the Christ, the Son of the Blessed One?' And Jesus said, 'I am' . . . . And Pilate questioned Him, 'Are You the King of the Jews?' And answering He said to him, 'It is as you say'" (14:61–62; 15:2). He didn't cower in their presence. Both rulers (high priest and governor) couldn't believe Jesus's lack of fear and silent confidence (14:60; 15:4). In fact, Jesus acted as if he were their superior, claiming that both institutions of power would eventually fall because of his kingdom. He predicted the destruction of the temple—not one stone will be left upon another—*and* the coming of his kingdom reign over the whole earth—no room for Rome (Mark 13)! The high priest ripped his clothes, the procurator sent Jesus to the cross, and neither ruler seemed to get through to Jesus that his aspirations for God's kingdom would soon be crushed. A sealed tomb sealed his fate. To both the Jews and the Romans, Jesus got what he deserved. Nobody opposes the powers that be and lives to tell about it.

Of all the places for Jesus to sow his kingdom message, Jerusalem was the most daring field of them all. If I had been a witness to the events that transpired during the "passion week," I would have thought to myself, "What is he trying to do? Is he wanting to get himself killed?" Talk of the reign of God without the ruling class only invites the exercise of their power. It didn't take long—merely five days—for the high priest and the procurator to put down the Jesus movement. Dozens of times before, Jesus had offended synagogue rulers, Pharisees, scribes, even a tetrarch, but he always seemed to escape their hands. They gathered stones; he walked away unharmed. He goaded them; they threatened him. His bravado seemed to excite the masses, but the crowds never got out of hand. There were no riots. Nobody got hurt. No fireworks, until he came to Jerusalem.

It all started when Jesus took the accolades of a few citizens too far. After he was welcomed by the crowds with shouts of messianic praise, Jesus brought his business to the temple. Busy with Passover pilgrims, the temple reminded him of a fig tree without figs—green leaves mean life, but fig trees have one purpose: to produce figs. To show his disgust, Jesus "cleansed" the temple of entrepreneurs *and* cursed a fruitless fig tree. The fact that it wasn't even the season for figs (early spring) was immaterial. Jesus was proving a point. By cursing the fig tree (a common prophetic symbol for Israel), Jesus announced the end of the temple: "May no one ever eat fruit from you again" (11:14). The temple was supposed to be a "house of prayer *for all the nations,*" that is, bearing fruit. Instead, the "deceit of riches" (the third soil!) turned it into "a robbers' den" (v. 17). All of these images run together to teach the disciples that the temple was no longer serving its intended purpose. It would be destroyed. Jesus hammered the death knell over and over again—by cleansing the temple, by cursing the fig tree, by predicting its destruction, and by telling a parable, Jesus tolled the end. *"Now learn the parable from the fig tree*: when its branch has already become tender and *puts forth its leaves,* you know that summer is near" (13:28). The fig tree withered and the temple was eventually destroyed by the Romans forty years later. In Jesus's kingdom, there would be no need of a temple for offering sacrifices.

This is why Jesus died. Jesus was arrested, tried, and convicted of blasphemy by the religious leaders because of his temple tantrum. Hostilities directed against God's holy temple were sacrilegious, which is why the chief priest led the Sanhedrin to move quickly to have Jesus arrested. Charges brought against him before the Jewish council centered on his reckless statements about the temple: "We heard Him say, 'I will destroy this temple made with hands, and in three days I will build another made without hands'" (14:58). According to Mark, this was false testimony (vv. 55–57, 59). Jesus never said such a thing. Nevertheless, it does reveal how some Jews interpreted Jesus's actions and words. Unless Jesus was another Jeremiah, what he said about the temple and what he did in the temple were heretical. Without a temple there could be no sacrifices for sin. Wouldn't that be a serious problem? Not according to one scribe who liked what he heard: "Right, Teacher; You have truly stated that He is One, and there is no one else besides Him; and to love Him with all the heart and with all the understanding and with all the strength, and to love one's neighbor as himself, *is much more than all burnt offerings and sacrifices*" (12:32–33). To obey is better than sacrifice. This was Jeremiah's message (Jer. 7:22–23). This is what the prophets had said all along (1 Sam. 15:22). Jesus saw that the man had potential: "You are not far from the kingdom of God" (Mark 12:34). Ironically,

Jesus spent most of his time *in the temple* broadcasting his message to any who had ears to hear (14:49). One man was listening. Perhaps the seed found good soil in the midst of a fruitless field called Jerusalem.

Christians understand very well why Jesus' sacrifice rendered the temple obsolete; the entire New Testament is built on the premise: a new covenant established in his blood is salvation for those who believe. His obedience resulted in a sacred sacrifice. He *was* trying to get himself killed. And we understand why he did it: his mission was to die for the sins of the world. His death overcame the power of sin. His sacrifice ripped the veil in half. Who needs a temple? It's the *other* power Jesus destroyed that we have a hard time denying. Remember, Jesus entered Jerusalem not only to replace the temple, he went there to take on an empire. He was tried as a blasphemer; he was executed as an insurrectionist. He wasn't stoned by religious fanatics. He was crucified by political powers. He threatened a Roman ruler as much as a Jewish priest. The governing powers knew that Jesus was a dangerous man to them as well. He was a political threat as much as a religious threat. Christians love to point out that our faith eclipses "dead religion," but what about decadent politics? If a temple was rendered insignificant because of the death of Jesus, did power politics die with him, too?

"And some fell among thorns. . . ." Mark's account of the crucifixion of Jesus is filled with several puns that highlight the correlation between the third soil and Roman rule. Of course, the interplay is lost to those who don't read or hear Greek. First, the word that Mark used to describe the band of soldiers who crucified Jesus is nearly identical to the word that occurs several times in the parable of the sower and the soils. "Behold, the *sower* [*speiron*] went out *to sow* [*speirai*]" (4:3); "The soldiers took Him away into the palace (that is, the Praetorium), and they called together the whole Roman *cohort* [*speiran*]" (15:16). "Thorns" appears only four times in Mark's Gospel—thrice in the parable (4:7, 18), and once in chapter fifteen: "After twisting a crown of thorns, they put it on Him" (15:17). Finally, the nearly homonymous words *sunepnixan* and *exepneusen* link the dramatic end of the seed "choked" (*sunepnixan*) by the weeds with the death of Jesus: "And Jesus uttered a loud cry, and breathed His last [*exepneusen*]" (15:37). Scholars refer to this auditory device as *stichwort*—a common tool used by speakers and dramatists to link stories in the minds of the listeners. In addition to these auditory links, notice how often the expression, "King of the Jews" appears in Mark's story (vv. 2, 9, 18, 26, 32 [King of Israel]). The irony would be lost on no one. The clash of two kingdoms, Caesar's and God's, came down to a battle between two rulers, Pilate and Jesus. Who won? The gospel seed of the kingdom fell on the thorny soil of Roman rule and what will come of it? The weeds choked the seed to death. Was Jesus's kingdom cause, then, a fruitless effort—a vain labor leading to a cursed death? Do power politics win in the end?

There was something about the way Jesus died that caught the attention of his executioner. Mark teases the reader with the words, "And when the centurion, who was standing right in front of Him, saw the way He breathed His last, he said, 'Truly this man was the Son of God!'" (15:39). The graphic picture of a Roman centurion facing the cross, professing Jesus as God's Son, provides the ultimate ironic twist in Mark's plot. An expert in crucifixion—a man who knew death very well—declared that Jesus was divine when he died. To the Romans, gods revealed their deity by feats of superhuman strength. In this case, a Roman soldier sees a man who succumbs to death and determines that he is a "Son of God." Why? Notice the curious expression, "saw the way He breathed His last." Most victims of crucifixion left this life with a whimper—a last whisper of breath. Men who died on a cross did not suffer fatal wounds. Sometimes the pain would be so great that criminals would plead with their executioners to spear them through, expediting the inevitable. But the Romans were cruel masters. Their victims would hang for days, eventually suffocating due to exhaustion. Every muscle would be seized by convulsions, throwing a man's body into shock. Panting would turn into faint breathing, forcing the executioner to climb a ladder to see if the victim had died. Often it was difficult to determine when death overtook the crucified (see vv. 44–45). As a result, corpses would hang on the cross for hours, sometimes even for days, to ensure death.

Crucifixion was a silent killer. But that's not the way Jesus died. He left this earth with a death-defying scream: "And Jesus uttered a loud cry, and breathed His last" (v. 37). No doubt, the centurion had never seen anything like this; only the gods have power over life and death. No man dies according to the hour of his choosing—especially the crucified. Jesus, on the other hand, chose to die. He had power over death. He decided when life was over. No man could take his life away. He laid it down. And, no one knew that better than the man who crucified Jesus. He saw the way Jesus *expired*. Standing in front of the cross of Jesus, it took a Roman soldier to recognize the Son of God.

The death of Jesus proves that we cannot separate religion and politics. I am opposed to the death penalty because Jesus was a victim of capital punishment. Killing for the truth is no longer an option for those who follow the one who died for the truth. Indeed, the Roman Empire suffered some significant losses to their troops because a number of soldiers defected when they became Christians. Those who heard Mark's Gospel understood the ramifications of a Roman soldier declaring that Jesus is the "Son of God." That was a title reserved for Caesar. They refused to be called "kings"; they despised "kingdoms" since it perpetuated an antiquated notion of royalty. But no Caesar found it difficult to require that "every knee bow, and every tongue confess that Caesar is Lord." They were sons of God. No one could deny their power. Death was the weapon they used to rule their empire. But when Jesus died, he killed death, stripping all powers of their authority. As the centurion realized, not even crucifixion—Caesar's most feared weapon—took the life of Jesus. He laid it down. An irreplaceable temple was destroyed and an irrepressible empire was conquered by a man who died for us. Disciples

All empires lost their battle for sovereignty

at the cross.

of Jesus need no temple. We have no other King. We owe our lives to him. We swear no other allegiance. Jesus stripped all governments, kingdoms, rulers, dictators of their power when he laid down his life for us. All empires lost their battle for sovereignty at the cross. Christian martyrs for two thousand years have proven that there is no power—not even death—that can overcome us. We don't believe in governments. We don't put our faith in politicians. We are citizens of the kingdom of God—a kingdom Jesus started and exists to this day. All hail King Jesus!

This kingdom of God is a new creation that, by its very existence in this fallen world, defies power politics, violence, and death. A cross, a sacrifice, a life surrendered to God—these are the weapons of our warfare. No man, no foe, no power can take our life away. We've already laid it down. His cross marks the spot.

> If we fail to read the New Testament texts on violence through the lens of *new creation*, we will fall into one of two opposing errors: either we will fall into a foolish utopianism that expects an evil world to receive our nice gestures with friendly smiles, or we will despair of the possibility of living under the "unrealistic" standards exemplified by Jesus. But if we do read the texts through the lens of *new creation*, we will see that the church is called to stand as God's sign of promise in a dark world. Once we see that, our way, however difficult, will be clear.[6]

Government cannot be saved. Politics are irredeemable. They are about the business of gaining power and keeping power, regardless of the form of government—democracy, oligarchy, dictatorship, socialist.

Although some forms of government do power better than others (I prefer democracy), the charge leveled against Jesus, "King of the Jews," will forever remind us that Christ's kingdom cannot co-exist with human government. For him, the way God's reign comes to earth is by *giving power away*. The way justice comes to humanity is by *dying* for sinners. The way a citizen of God's kingdom advances the cause of Christ is by sowing the gospel seed on *all people*. No law can change human hearts. No ruler can do the work of God; it's a job for slaves. Jesus will not be king on our terms. His kingdom is mutually exclusive to all other claims to power. His monarchy requires complete submission to his business. He shares his reign with no power of human invention. For Christians, the power of politics was defeated at the cross. Pilate can wash his hands of the matter, but God will have the last word. The glory of Rome has been reduced to rubble—tourist attractions. The glory of Christ's kingdom shines throughout the whole world, forever and ever.

"They yielded a crop and produced thirty, sixty, and a hundredfold"

Now we see the risky crop sown by Jesus. The kingdom of God hinges upon a demoniac, a blind man, children, and a centurion. To be sure, Jesus cast his gospel seed upon all kinds of soil. And, as Mark's story suggests, some seed found good soil. But think of the improbability of a successful harvest. Few children defied the odds of survival in the first-century Mediterranean world. A demoniac hardly makes for a credible witness. Blind men know only how to beg. A soldier knows no mercy. After it was all said and done, according to Mark's Gospel, this was the best Jesus could do. The great harvest of God's kingdom would depend upon the seed sown in the hearts of these few. What a tragedy! What a splendid, marvelous tragedy! Those who heard Mark's Gospel for the first time must have wrestled with the loose ends of Jesus's implausible mission. Tragedies do that to a person. We live the stories we hear, vicariously making the tragic turn of events our problem. "How could it end this way?" we often say to ourselves, mulling over the details of a plot gone wrong. The Romans crucified Jesus because they thought he was an insurrectionist. The Sanhedrin indicted him because he acted like a blasphemer and sounded like a false prophet. Twelve disciples abandoned him because they didn't understand him. Even the few friends that stuck around to the bitter end, ensuring a proper burial, couldn't believe their eyes or their ears when they saw an empty tomb and heard Easter's message: "He is risen!" Unbelievably, they ran away in fear, telling no one the good news. It's not supposed to end like this.

The day I heard that Charles Schultz had died, I began to anticipate what his last contribution to the funny pages would be. It had been reported that Mr. Schultz's health deteriorated quickly during his last days. Having planned for that day, the creator of "Peanuts" fittingly used his final strip to express his appreciation to all of his readers. I was one of those fans who couldn't start my day without reading about Charlie Brown, Snoopy, and Linus. My eye would automatically fall to the same place on the comics page every day—a habit that was broken within a few days. "Peanuts" was gone. What caught me off guard, however, was the strip that appeared in the Sunday comics of our local paper the weekend following the cartoonist's death. It shows Peppermint Patty (one of my favorite characters) standing in the rain with a football in her hands. She's yelling out to her friends who have abandoned her (they

> *No matter how much it is expected,*
>
> *even though we know that the resurrection*
>
> *of Christ makes it all better, death hurts.*

are "off frame"). As I recall, at first she pleads with her companions to finish the game, giving the rationale that rain and football go together. Eventually, her anger gets the best of her as she hurls insults at the traitors, challenging the manhood of her playmates. Nothing works. The third frame shows her standing alone in the rain, a blank expression on her face, in disbelief that the game's over. In the final frame, Peppermint Patty says pitifully, "We never got to say, 'Good game.'" I know this sounds foolish, but I wept when I read the Sunday comics that day. To me, that's what death feels like. It steals away our last chance to say what we always wanted to say. Death never happens at the right time. It always feels like a bad ending to a good story. No matter how much it is expected, even though we know that the resurrection of Christ makes it all better, death hurts.

It gives me comfort knowing that they didn't take Jesus's life away from him. He laid it down. It helps me to know that he saw it coming, even though his enemies thought that they took him by surprise. He knew his disciples would abandon him; but he also counted on a great reunion: "He is going before you into Galilee; there you will see Him, *just as he said*" (16:7). In the aftermath of the terrible events that transpired during the last days of Jesus, Mark's Gospel ends with a simple story about an empty tomb and a promise. Indeed, Easter makes the cross look better. We believe that he is our only hope. No doubt, his resurrection is our comfort. But Mark's Gospel leaves me wanting: "Why did it have to end this way? Why did Jesus have to suffer so? Why did they have to humiliate him? What did he ever do to deserve this? Why does Mark spend so much time on the terrible details of Jesus's death, giving so little attention to the resurrection? Compared to the darkness that broods over the entire passion narrative, Easter's morning light appears more like a glimmer of hope than a radiant confession of what will be. Why don't we get to see Jesus alive and well? Where's the tearful reunion between the resurrected Jesus and his disciples, where Peter is forgiven and the disciples are commissioned? What about the women? Did the news of Easter morning remain their secret? Is this all we have: an empty tomb, a mysterious stranger, and a promise for tomorrow?"

Mark's Gospel makes me mourn over the death of Jesus and wonder, "Why?" Since the first readers of Mark's Gospel didn't know what was supposed to happen after the empty tomb, the pangs of a story without closure would have haunted them more. Mark's Gospel is open-ended. It invites speculation. The Evangelist's purpose, I believe, was to cause auditors/readers to puzzle over the ending, replaying in their minds—over and over again—the tragic story of a man who came to bring the reign of God to earth and met an untimely death. He entered the narrative world of Mark's Gospel as a man without reputation, promising God's powerful reign. His first words were, "The time is fulfilled, and the kingdom of God is at hand" (1:15). He left this earth the victim of Roman supremacy. His last words were, "My God, My God, why have You forsaken Me?" (15:34). What happened in between is the story of a farmer who tried to find good soil for his gospel seed. He believed in the kingdom come, even though he knew that hostile powers would oppose him. He knew that he was sowing a risky crop, yet he believed in a miraculous harvest. His resurrection vindicated his cause; Mark's Gospel carries on the success of his mission. Why? Because everyone who reads it knows that Jesus was more than a man, and everyone who has ears to hear his words knows that he could be the good soil—some thirty, some sixty, some a hundredfold. Jesus finds good soil in the hearts of those who read the Gospel according to Mark.

A demoniac, a blind man, children, and a Roman soldier—these are the kind of people who receive the kingdom of God. People just like you; people just like me. What a marvelous, splendid tragedy that God's farmer chose to sow such a risky crop. To most industrious farmers, such an effort would be foolish, a waste of time. Summer sowing always fails: the days are long and hot, the birds are hungry, weeds grow like weeds, and the autumn harvest seems like an eternity away. Jesus believed that his kingdom, on the other hand, was worth the risk. His generous life, spent for us like seed thrown on the ground, will yield God's miraculous harvest, even in the soul of a man who used to talk like the devil, or a beggar who couldn't see to live, or children who always get in the way, or a murderer who found life in death. Thank you, Jesus, for entrusting people like us—nobodies—with your kingdom. For we can attest that your word is sown deep into our hearts, and more than anything else, we want to be good soil. Your dream is the only dream worth dreaming. Sow the seed!

> We're a beautiful letdown
> painfully uncool
> The church of the drop outs, the losers,
> the sinners, the failures, and the fools.
> What a beautiful letdown
> are we salt in the wound?
> Let us sing one true tune.

THE GOSPEL

OF LUKE

Having Nothing, Giving Everything

5

The Reverse of the Curse

If Jesus has been raised, then the end of the world has begun.

Wolfhart Pannenberg, *Jesus—God and Man*

A fine line divides believing and pretending. Children move easily from belief in Santa Claus and elves to accepting the Christmas story of angels and wise men. To adults, of course, there is a world of difference between the stories of Kris Kringel and Jesus of Nazareth. Nevertheless, we play along with children on "The Night Before Christmas," believing that strange sounds in the night could be evidence of reindeer on the roof. Then, on Christmas morning, we gather in houses of worship to hear Luke's version of the birth of Jesus read in somber tones. The difference between pretending and believing is discernible only to those who know better. Children, on the other hand, see no difference. They pretend because they believe. Although neither can be seen, angels are as real as elves because children are given to the world of make believe. Their fantasy is reality because they don't know the difference between pretending and believing. That's what makes them children; we accept that—this is innocent child's play; it's a natural part of their mental development. Adults who think like children, on the other hand, are considered dangerous. Often, the inability to discern the difference between fantasy and reality is diagnosed as psychosis, a mental illness that can lead to disastrous results. Adults who pretend that make believe is real need help. We rely upon professionals to help these patients recover the real world.

Sometimes it's hard for me to know whether a believer is pretending or relying upon God. Faith can look like make believe. Desperation can make believers out of all of us. What is the difference between a believer who cannot accept the reality of his cancer, pretending that symptoms do not exist, and the concrete faith of a Christian who trusts God despite unfavorable circumstances? Some would say, "The difference lies in whether or not the person refuses medical treatment." Presumption is never an act of faith. Others would point to the end result; the pretender who is healed is the believer who has real faith. Still others might say, "No one can know for sure." Faith is in the eye of the believer.

There were two men in my parish who faced the same dilemma. Both were about the same age (in their forties), both had loving families (wife and children), both were once active members of the church, had dropped out, then returned to regular attendance once they discovered that they were dying of cancer. Both men sought medical treatment, were told that their cancer was aggressive and had already reached advanced stages. Their prognosis would require the heaviest chemotherapy to arrest the menacing cancer. Both men rejected the treatment recommended by their physicians, and chose alternative, unconventional methods of fighting their disease. One man, I'll call him "Mark," believed that God had told him that he would be healed of cancer if he acted in accordance with his faith. Mark came by my office, told me of his plans to obey God's voice, and wanted to give testimony of God's deliverance the following Sunday during the morning worship service. At the end of the service, Mark announced to the congregation that he was going to trust God's promise and walk in his faith, living as if he had already been healed. After a few weeks, Mark excitedly announced to the Sunday morning gathering of worshipers that God had kept his promise, that all the symptoms of the cancer were gone, and that a medical test recently performed had confirmed the miracle. To say the least, the congregation was overjoyed, celebrating the news with praises to the God who heals.

"Tom" temporarily moved to Mexico to undergo an experimental treatment that was reported to have some success against the more aggressive forms of cancer. The treatment was too new and unconventional, and therefore hadn't been approved for use in America. That didn't stop

Tom. As a matter of fact, he believed that conventional methods were untrustworthy, delaying death and bilking patients of their money in the process. The possibility that he could be the beneficiary of a successful, experimental treatment was more appealing to him than becoming another statistic of the well-known, ineffective chemotherapy. Tom decided that there was no shame in trying the unknown. As a matter of fact, he was convinced that God would heal him, and that he would one day be an encouragement to other cancer patients who have to suffer from this horrible disease.

After several months, both men died of cancer. Even as I write these words, I can still see Mark smiling with great enthusiasm, extolling the strength of God's miraculous hand, telling everyone that he had been healed of cancer. I also recall the quiet desperation of Tom's search for the miracle drug that would rid his body of the disease that threatened his life, half-rationalizing and half-apologizing for his reliance upon the unconventional. During their fight, I couldn't help but think, "What if it's true? What if God has healed Mark? What if Tom did find his miracle cure? Wouldn't that be great!" As a believer, I wanted to make believe that everything would be all right. After all, I was their pastor. I had to believe, I wanted to believe, I did believe. Just a few weeks before he died, I called Mark on the phone. He was in a hospital in another state. Even though his body was eaten up with cancer, Mark continued to believe that God healed him. He sounded just as cheery and optimistic as the day he announced his healing to the church. After our conversation, I bowed my head in disbelief. I couldn't tell if I admired him or pitied him. All I could think about was how his wife and family would make it without him. Would they be angry with him? Would they question God? How could Mark persist in his claim that he had been healed when it seemed obvious to everyone else that he was going to die? To many, his faith must have seemed like a charade. Ignore the obvious and maybe the pain will go away. Yet one can only pretend for so long.

That's exactly what a community gathered for worship thought when another man made an even more preposterous claim. According to Luke's Gospel, Jesus announced his messianic mission and launched his kingdom effort from his hometown. After his baptism, he made his way straight to Nazareth, teaching in various synagogues as he journeyed home. Once he arrived, he took center stage during a synagogue service, reading from the scroll of Isaiah:

> The Spirit of the LORD is upon Me,
> Because He anointed Me as Messiah to preach the gospel to the poor,
> He has sent Me as Apostle to announce the release of prisoners,
> And help the blind see again,

To liberate the oppressed,
To proclaim the year of Jubilee.[1]

Anyone sitting in the synagogue that day would have expected hag-
gadah about the coming Messiah, for this was a very familiar messianic
text. One day all Jews would be relieved of their present distress and
despair. One day God would send his Messiah to come to Israel's aid, right
every wrong, redress every injustice, restoring the glory of God's people.
Of all people, the little town of Nazareth needed to hear a sermon like
that—to escape for a moment from the oppressive rule of the Roman
Empire. Besides, everyone enjoys hearing a sermon about heaven. To us,
it would be like hearing a pastor announce that his sermon on a certain
Sunday would come from the Revelation of John—every ear would be
piqued to hear about the end of the world, the judgment of God, and
rewards for the righteous. In certain respects, Jesus didn't disappoint
his auditors. His sermon would be about the Messiah. As he spoke,
however, it became clear to the crowd that Jesus said much more than
anyone would have expected: "Today this Scripture *has been fulfilled* in
your hearing" (Luke 4:21).

Now, it was painfully obvious to everyone in the room (except Jesus)
that Isaiah 61 had *not* already been fulfilled. Rome was still in power.
The majority of the population was still poor. Blind men still begged for
money. Enemies of Herod and the Roman occupation of the Promised
Land were still in prisons. And, all men were debtors to the privileged
and the powerful. Only a fool would claim that Isaiah's dream had become reality in first-century Israel. But Jesus was no fool. He knew what
the crowd was thinking: "No doubt you will quote this proverb to Me,
'Physician, heal yourself! Whatever we heard was done at Capernaum,
do here in your hometown as well'" (v. 23). *If* Isaiah's vision had been
fulfilled, then how could Jesus explain his state, that is, that he was still
a poor man from Nazareth, where rural life was hard and sick people
still needed help? To the synagogue worshipers in Nazareth, Jesus looked
and sounded like the Great Pretender. His faith bordered on lunacy. Then
things got even worse. Jesus went on to claim that Gentiles would listen
to what he had to say since God's prophets are never believed by the ones
to whom they are sent (vv. 24–27). This was more than the Nazarenes
could take: "And all the people in the synagogue were filled with rage as
they heard these things; and they got up and drove Him out of the city,
and led Him to the brow of the hill on which their city had been built,
in order to throw Him down the cliff" (vv. 28–29). Officially shunned by
his hometown, Jesus left Nazareth never to return again.

How could Jesus claim that Isaiah 61:1–2 had already been fulfilled?
Remember, in Luke's Gospel Jesus had performed no miracle to this

point. In other words, he stood before the Nazarene synagogue as a man without a curriculum vitae. Of course, as the story unfolds, Luke chronicles how Jesus made blind men see again, and brought the promise of heavenly rewards for the poor. But that was after his explosive encounter in Nazareth. Perhaps he would have been better received if he had made these claims *after* his public ministry in Galilee—"This Scripture has been fulfilled." Or, maybe it would have been better if Jesus would have said, "This Scripture *will be* fulfilled before your very eyes." In other words, Jesus would be saying, "Hide and watch!" But that's not how it happened. Jesus said, *"Today* this Scripture has been fulfilled in your ears." How can this be?

The key to understanding Luke's Gospel, as well as the way he does discipleship, is the Spirit of God. As a matter of fact, the Holy Spirit appears in Luke's story more than any other Gospel (twenty times!). Jesus believed that Isaiah's promise had already been fulfilled because God's Spirit had already anointed him. That's what made him the Messiah of God. It's more difficult for English readers to recognize the pun that is clearly evident in Isaiah's Hebrew or Luke's Greek. "Messiah" comes from the Hebrew; "Christ" comes from the Greek. Both mean the same thing, "the anointed one." To press the play on words, Jesus claimed Isaiah's promise had been fulfilled in the ears of his listeners when he said, "The Spirit of the Lord is upon Me, because He *messiahed* Me." Jesus was anointed by God's Spirit. That messianic blessing had already happened (3:21–22). This is why he could claim that Isaiah's prophecy had been fulfilled. Jesus saw himself as the embodiment of God's Spirit, the promise of every messianic hope, the reality of every kingdom blessing. Wherever Jesus went, there would be good news because he is the personification of the gospel. Whomever Jesus met, sick, poor, diseased, famished, or oppressed, they would receive God's blessing because Jesus is the Incarnation of Jubilee. No debts! No sickness! No hunger! No crime! No criminals! No more bad news! God's Spirit means God's presence. And, where God is present, there is no injustice.

Throughout Luke's Gospel story, Jesus lived as if the promise of Isaiah's words were reality. Therefore, to his enemies, Jesus was an imposter, pretending as if God's curse on the poor, the blind, the weak, the outcast didn't exist anymore. It was as if Jesus was ignoring the fact that sin has its consequences. For Jesus to subvert the order of God's judgment on the disobedient invited religious and social anarchy. If sinners no longer know their place, then the mingling of unholy and holy will surely bring the curse of God on *all people*. This is why the "righteous"—healthy, wealthy, and wise—were alarmed by Jesus's behavior. "This man receives sinners and eats with them" (15:2), they complained. By his presence, Jesus signaled the reverse of the curse. With the advent of the kingdom of messianic blessing, the worst sinner is greater than the greatest Jew that ever lived: "When all the people and the tax collectors heard this, they acknowledged God's justice" (7:29). On the other hand, those who thought that they were deserving of the blessings of God became targets of Jesus's invectives. He offered blessings to the poor, but woes to the rich; blessings to the hungry, but woes to the well-fed; blessings to the despised, but woes to the honorable (6:20–26). In the topsy-turvey world of Luke's Gospel story, Jesus seemed to get everything backwards. He laughed with the sinners and wept over the righteous (19:9, 41). Since Jesus believed the promises of God, everything changed. As far as he

> *In the topsy-turvey world of Luke's Gospel story, Jesus seemed to get everything backwards. He laughed with the sinners and wept over the righteous.*

was concerned, the Spirit's anointing meant that the Scriptures had already been fulfilled. Crazy to some, confusing to others, Jesus took Isaiah at his word.

Good News for Shepherds and Lepers

"This will be a sign for you: you will find a baby wrapped in cloths and lying in a manger" (2:12). We've heard this story so often, we don't see how sad it is. To modern ears, the birth narrative of Jesus is a quaint, country story about sheep and shepherds, peace and goodwill, angelic hosts and imperial decrees. Today, living nativity scenes that are sponsored by churches during the Christmas holiday season invite collective "oohs" and "aahs" from visitors who admire the endearing sight of a couple huddled in a barn over the Christ child. Christmas crèches somehow become idyllic portraits of a biblical story filled with details that were anything but desirable. Actually, Luke's account of Jesus's birth is a very dark story. A census of the people meant Roman taxes. Caesar's pax Romana cost money, and poor imperial subjects were going to foot the bill whether they liked it or not—another reminder that God's kingdom was more dream than reality. The fact that Joseph couldn't find shelter for Mary in the town of his nativity (read, "hometown") reveals that no family would take him in due to the shameful circumstances of their predicament. The betrothal of a Jewish man and woman lasted a year to insure the purity of the virgin bride. Instead, Mary became pregnant soon after the beginning of this formal engagement, shaming Joseph's family. What Luke doesn't tell us is what he assumed we would already know: Joseph was shunned by his family when he came home with a pregnant fiancée. Neither a guestroom nor a public house (two possible interpretations of "the inn") was made available to the dishonorable couple. Probably born in a stable, Jesus would be cradled by a feeding trough. No Magi. No gifts of gold, frankincense, or myrrh. No midwife. No family celebration. All alone, in the middle of the night, Joseph and Mary welcomed a baby boy into the world. This is a dark story, indeed.

Piercing the darkness of Bethlehem was the angelic announcement of the Messiah's birth. Humble circumstances give way to dramatic events that break through the narrative with divine force. At this point, Luke employs powerful poetry to deliver a theme that will dominate his Gospel: heaven crashes into earth and only the lowly see. Shepherd boys did the work that was left over for them by the strong. Young men were required to take care of the heavier chores of farming. Boys who came of age performed easier tasks like tending sheep, for example, David ("There remains yet the youngest, and behold, he is tending the sheep" [1 Sam. 16:11]). Notice how the angel's directive brought shepherds good news tailored just for them. "For today in the city of David there has been born *for you* a Savior, who is Christ the Lord. This will be a sign for you: you will find a baby wrapped in cloths and lying in a manger" (Luke 2:11–12). All newborns were wrapped in strips of cloth, mummified to keep them warm. There was nothing significant about that. The special sign for the shepherds was that they would find their Messiah in a feeding trough. There is something very appealing about shepherds gathered around a manger to see the Messiah that was born for them, as if they were tending the Lamb of God. Mary, of course, "treasured up all these things, pondering them in her heart," as mothers tend to do. She knew the significance of the moment. Of all people, why were shepherds invited to see her baby? Why not dignitaries, or nobility, or royalty? No doubt, as Mary welcomed these dirty, little boys to her baby's crib, her own words echoed in her ears:

> My soul exalts the Lord,
>   And my spirit has rejoiced in God my Savior.
> For He has had regard for the humble state of His bondslave; . . .

He has brought down rulers from their thrones,
  And has exalted those who were humble.
He has filled the hungry with good things;
  And sent away the rich empty-handed.

Luke 1:46–48, 52–53

Children love to hear the stories of their birth. Occasionally, our family will break out the pictures that preserve the birthday of our children. Most of the time, our daughters are the ones who especially delight in hearing the details of the day they were born. Months before Grace (our youngest) was born, Emma would ask to see her birthday pictures and talk often about how she looked forward to helping Mommy take care of the new baby. We knew that Emma couldn't wait to get her hands on her little sister. Whenever Sheri described the daily routine of infant care (baths, feeding, dressing, cuddling), Emma would shiver with excitement. Just the thought of changing diapers would make her giggle and hold her nose. Waiting for November 21, 1996, was sheer torture for Emma who prayed every night that God would "give us our baby real soon." So it didn't surprise us when Emma's face beamed with pride the first time she held Grace. As she cradled Grace in her arms, Emma surveyed the hospital room, soaking up the admiration of her parents and grandparents. The moment finally came, all eyes were fixed on one scene, and Emma was in her element. That's why her comment later took all of us by surprise.

Everyone that day had their chance to hold the new baby: brother, sister, grandmas and grandpas—even dad was videotaped rocking his new daughter. The hour was late, and grandparents were about to rush the kids home for bed, when Emma hesitated and said, "I want to see Mommy holding the baby. Mommy, you haven't held Grace. I want Mommy to hold Grace." Once Sheri received Grace into her arms, Emma took in the picture of mother and daughter, and with a smile of satisfaction said, "I love you Mommy." The day was complete, the picture perfect, and Emma changed in my eyes from a little girl in kindergarten to the daughter who will always take care of her mother.

"Mary treasured all these things, pondering them in her heart." Jesus grew up hearing stories about his birthday. Traveling for a census, angels visiting shepherds, and good news found in a manger—bending toward nostalgia, the blending of common details and extraordinary events made the story of Jesus's birth evermore endearing to poor people who counted on the mercy of God. Listening to his family relive the circumstances of his birth, Jesus knew what he was born for. Redeemed by poor parents with a turtledove instead of a lamb (2:22–24; Exod. 13:12; Lev. 12:8), Jesus was destined to be good news for those who have nothing. This is why he came home first to Nazareth to announce the gospel of his anointing. He was one of them. That was the point. He knew that Isaiah's vision was coming true because he was heaven's gift of the poor to the poor. The lowly are exalted, the humble honored because the Messiah was born in David's hometown to poor pilgrims from Nazareth. And, as David's heir, Israel's king would be found among shepherd boys. "He was one of us," the shepherds could say. They celebrated the Messiah born for them, the first evangelists (Luke 2:20). Their story of his birth, however, wouldn't be told with descriptions of royal palaces and rich furnishings. Instead, Jesus came into the world under conditions that only a shepherd could appreciate. Indeed, we know that good tidings of great joy come to all people because the gospel came first to boys who tended sheep and found their Messiah in a feeding trough.

Jews in Jesus's day lived in a world of limited goods. This is why Mary believed that the exalting of the humble would mean the humiliation of the rich (1:53). There was only so much food, water, wine, land, sheep, trees, and grain to go around. They believed that the Promised Land was God's gift to take care of *all* of Israel. If someone had more than what they needed, that meant that someone else had less. The only way the poor would get what they needed would be if the rich shared the wealth. Of course, what made the rich wealthy was their ability to keep what they had rather than give it away. "The poor you will always have with you," Jesus told his disciples.[2] He was resigned to the fact that there would always be rich people hoarding wealth and living in excess. So, if Jesus believed that he was offering good news to the poor, what should that gospel look like? Was Jesus proposing a revolution—to take from the rich and give to the poor? He certainly seems to suggest the idea when he told the parable of the sneaky steward (16:1–8). Here is a story about an accountant who reduces the debts owed by the poor to his wealthy master (indirectly robbing from the rich and giving to the poor). Strangely enough, Jesus holds up the cheater as a model of faithfulness when he added the ironic twist, "His master *praised* the unrighteous steward because he had acted shrewdly" (v. 8). Really? Would a rich man who lent money to poor people be pleased with his manager for reducing their indebtedness to him?

There are several parables in Luke's Gospel where Jesus pictures himself as an undesirable. He's the man who "fell among thieves," was stripped, beaten, and left for dead in the parable of the Good Samaritan (10:30–35). He's the dishonorable host who gives a banquet that no one wants to attend (14:16–24). He's the son of the vineyard owner who is killed by the farmers (20:9–15). He may even be the son that was judged by his brother to have wasted his father's inheritance partying with "harlots"—a prodigal son (15:11–32)! Jesus used these unflattering self-portraits to mock his opponents' opinion of him. What made them angry was that Jesus continuously pushed the envelope of inclusiveness. He ate with the wrong kind of people. He praised the wrong kind of people. The heroes of his stories were the wrong kind of people. To the right kind of people—the righteous, honorable, wealthy—Jesus was a dangerous man. He went about forgiving debts that only God could forgive. He empowered the poor by humiliating the rich. He threatened the righteous by accepting sinners. The undesirables flocked to him, inviting Jesus to their homes.

If you want to get in trouble with pious people, all you have to do is show mercy to those who don't deserve it. Obedient sons and daughters want a God who keeps records. We want God to take notice when we do the right thing so that he will be able to bless us with the right thing. Competing for God's favor, righteous people spend time with righteous people to make sure we're doing what is righteous. Try bringing an immoral person into the group—a well-known adulterer, or thief, or alcoholic, or thug—and see what happens. Forgive their debts. Overlook their indiscretions. Give them the benefit of the doubt. Act like they belong to God as much as anyone else. Pretend like their prayers mean as much to God as those of any righteous person. Enjoy their company. Invite them to your home. Make friends with unbelievers and you will invite the suspicions of your righteous comrades. "How could you go into the house of a bunch of smokers? What about the smell? It takes forever to get the stench out of my hair. What do you do over there, anyway?

> *He ate with the wrong kind of people. He praised the wrong kind of people. The heroes of his stories were the wrong kind of people. To the right kind of people—the righteous, honorable, wealthy—Jesus was a dangerous man.*

Do they get drunk while you're there? What if someone sees you with them? Doesn't their teenage girl have a baby? Aren't you afraid that it will send the wrong message to your daughter? Are you going to invite them to church?" Sometimes I've thought to myself, "I wouldn't dare.

I'm afraid of what might happen if they came." We righteous people can be so cruel.

Recently we had an entire family of unbelievers attending our worship services. For several Sundays they came: father, mother, and several children. At first, those of us who sat around them welcomed them. They seemed pleasantly surprised by our generosity of goodwill. But that goodwill didn't last long. It became apparent to everyone that these people didn't know how to act in church. Their children talked incessantly, rarely drawing the attention of their parents. We would barely be into the sermon when their kids started fidgeting, making loud noises as they played with the toys they brought from home. Occasionally the father or mother would look over and investigate the commotion. We all hoped for some reprimand, some attempt at controlling the chaos. Instead, mom and dad would give each other the "aren't they cute" look, and settle in for the rest of the service. As a matter of fact, when they came to church, they acted like they were in their own living room. Their comfort soon turned to unease, however, once other congregants gave the couple the "evil eye." It was only a matter of time before they quit coming and we could return to our routine of nice, quiet worship.

God forgive us. Why aren't we able to extend grace to those who need it the most? Why aren't we able to give a little space, allow a little latitude to those who don't know how to behave? What's wrong with us? The very kind of people who were attracted to Jesus are the same kind of people who can't stand to be around us. We could chalk it up to our piety. "Pagans don't want to spend time with us because they are convicted by their own sinful ways." The problem with that logic is that it conforms to the way the Pharisees thought: birds of a feather flock together. The reason sinners found Jesus to be such good company wasn't because he was a sinner himself. No. The reason undesirables found Jesus irresistible is the same reason we follow him. He always forgives us. His mercy makes us want to live. We always feel clean in his presence. He takes us as we are. All of us crave God's mercy, especially those of us who need it the most. Freely as we receive, we are to freely give. Pious people should never forget that.

To the Pharisees, Jesus acted just like the unrighteous steward, marking down debts, hoping people "will welcome me into their homes" (16:1–8). Indeed they did. Jesus doled out the mercy of God like it was his to give. In turn, sinners and publicans invited him to their table. This is why the master in the parable praised his sneaky steward. Jesus was claiming that God was pleased with his generosity. Being shrewd with the gifts of God make one a faithful servant (v. 10). If a wealthy man, however, has not been faithful in the use of "unrighteous mammon, who will entrust the true riches" to him? Of course, to those who are "lovers of money," this warning went unheeded (v. 14). Wealthy people remain wealthy people because they require debtors to pay what is owed. What they had forgotten, according to Jesus, was this: what they had didn't belong to them. All are stewards of God's riches. God grants riches to the wealthy in order to take care of the needy. And, like the unrighteous steward, Jesus was generous with his master's riches; he gave away God's mercy free. It's the only thing he could do (v. 3); Jesus was "rich" in God's mercy. He had no "mammon" of his own. On the other hand, those who had not been faithful with their wealth would never receive the "true riches" that result in "eternal dwellings" (reading vv. 9 and 11 as parallel statements). Jesus claimed that there would come a time when *the wealthy* would be needy of God's mercy like poor beggars. Hence, the warning: rich people who didn't give away their wealth would never see heaven's reward. This made no sense to those who believed that they could serve God *and* mammon (v. 13). To them, wealth was the undeniable sign of God's favor. To Jesus, it is the needy—not the rich—who are blessed by God. The next parable, the story of the rich man and Lazarus (16:19–31), reveals how these mutually exclusive ideas collide when a rich man wakes up in hell and, ironically, begs for God's mercy.

The shock of this parable is lost on westerners. That's because we fail to recognize that we have more in common with the rich man who lives in opulence than the beggar who dies of malnutrition. Like Jesus's opponents, we believe that God's blessings are evidenced by prosperity. Unwittingly, we share the bias of the Pharisees. We believe that America is a wealthy nation because God has crowned her with favor. And we hold the unspoken conviction that third-world countries experience God's curse of poverty and disease because of their sinful ways. What is evermore troubling to me is how many Christians believe this is true. Ask them/us. Ask the question: "Are you blessed by God?" Then listen to the catalog of blessings: health, wealth, and influence. How many respondents would give the answer Jesus has been arguing for throughout Luke's Gospel? "I'm blessed because I'm poor, hungry, thirsty, and oppressed." To most Americans, being needy is a weakness. To Jesus, being wealthy is a curse. To which most of us would respond, (like Tevye in *Fiddler on the Roof*), "May the Lord smite me with it. And may I never recover!" That casinos prosper in poor counties illustrates the difference better than we would like to admit.

No parable pictures the reverse of the curse more clearly than the story of the rich man and Lazarus. Jesus left his listeners dazed when he described a man blessed by God suffering in hell and a beggar cursed by God taking the seat of honor at Abraham's heavenly banquet. Eternal destinies mirror terrestrial realities. Notice how the rich man's gate kept the beggar away from the banquet table of food.

Covered with sores and in agony, the leper was "longing to be fed with the crumbs" that fell from the rich man's table of plenty. Strategically placed by the trash (where leftovers are cast away and dogs scavenge for food), the leper begged for mercy. Obviously, the rich man ignored the beggar's plight because he died. But all good things must come to an end. Death is no respecter of persons. Rich people die, too. Just

> *To most Americans, being needy is a weakness.*
>
> *To Jesus, being wealthy is a curse.*

as the leper was carried to the gate of the rich man's house, so also he was "carried away by the angels to Abraham's bosom [i.e., leaning on Abraham's chest, reclining at table, in the seat of honor]" (v. 22). The poor man is now blessed by God, sharing the eternal banquet of heaven. The rich man, on the other hand, takes the station of a beggar. This time, he's the one who's far away, longing for the water that drips from the finger of a leper (yuck!). This time, there is a chasm separating the rich man from the beggar—a chasm as wide as the prejudice that prevented the rich man from helping the leper. This time, it is the wealthy man who begs for the mercy of God, in agony over his condition (vv. 23–24).

Notice that the beggar did nothing to enter into his heavenly reward. Jesus puts him there because he is needy. But the wealthy man earned his punishment. Like his brothers, he ignored "Moses and the Prophets" (v. 29), who warned that social injustice would incur the wrath of God. The rich needed to repent of their excess: "If someone goes to them from the dead" the man in hell pleads, "'they will repent!' But he said to him, 'If they do not listen to Moses and the Prophets, they will not be persuaded even if someone rises from the dead'" (vv. 30–31).

Jesus believed that if a man gained the whole world, he would lose his soul (9:25). Therefore, he constantly encouraged his disciples to share. "Sell your possessions and give to charity" (12:33). "Give that which is within as charity, and then all things are clean for you" (11:41). "None of you can be My disciple who does not give up all his own possessions" (14:33). Rich people were in greater danger of missing the kingdom (18:24). This is why Jesus announced good news to the poor. They didn't share the same shortcomings of the wealthy. The poor have nothing to hoard. Wealth, on the other hand, makes the rich more susceptible to

God's unfavorable verdict. They have everything to lose if they don't share the wealth. Only those who give away what they have can expect to escape the wrath of God. Thus the rich man in Jesus's parable goes to hell. He never repented of hoarding wealth by sharing God's blessing with a poor beggar who died like a dog. The punch of the parable, then, is this: the needs of the poor make the rich accountable to God. Believe it or not, this is good news according to Jesus.

In Luke's Gospel two messages come flying at the reader at the same time. First, the poor are citizens of God's kingdom simply because they are poor. All that it takes to follow Jesus is to be needy. That's it. Luke's version of the gospel is really one of the purest forms of grace that you can find in the entire New Testament. The poor, the sick, the oppressed—these are the outsiders who become insiders to God's favor *merely* because they need him. At the same time, Luke's Gospel records the hardest sayings of Jesus. Jesus is more demanding in Luke than any other Gospel. Disciples must give everything. "None of you can be My disciple who does not give up all his own possessions" (14:33). Thus the irony: those who follow Jesus have nothing to give the Lord who demands all. Yet, an observant reader of Luke's Gospel knows why this is so: Jesus required from his followers what they had already given. Luke is careful to note that after Jesus called the fishermen to follow him, that "they *left everything* and followed Him" (5:11). When Levi became Jesus's disciple, "he *left everything* behind, and got up and began to follow Him" (v. 28). In other words, when Jesus told the crowd that anyone who wanted to follow him had to give up one's possessions, he was describing the twelve. Essentially, he was saying, "Do you want to be a disciple of mine? Then get in line; become like the twelve." Jesus had no rich disciples.

So, where does that put me? Compared to the world's poverty, I'm a wealthy man. Does that mean I can't be a disciple of Jesus, according to Luke? Am I bound for hell like the rich man in Jesus's parable? Not necessarily. In Jesus's day, only the dishonest were rich. Jews were not allowed to charge interest for loans (Exod. 22:25). Scales were supposed to be balanced equitably (Amos 8:5). During the sabbatical year property was to be used by the landless for farming (Exod. 23:11). The Jubilee year cancelled all debts, released all slaves, returned all land to ancestral owners (Lev. 25:13–55). Every fifty years Israel was to rediscover the gift of God's Promised Land for *all* people. Obviously, Israel never observed Jubilees; if they had, the prophets wouldn't have had much to say. Instead, they railed against the unjust practices of the rich who foreclosed on debts the poor could never pay. The rich got richer and the poor got poorer. That's how wealthy people remained wealthy: by ignoring the Law and the Prophets. This is why the rich automatically qualified for hell according to Jesus. They disobeyed God. On the other hand, think of what would have happened if Israel had kept the law and listened to the prophets. Their obedience would mean the end of poverty. Jesus knew that better than anyone. This is why he announced the favorable year of the Lord. It was long overdue. It was time for Jubilee!

Today, people can make money without stealing from the poor. We live in a world of unlimited goods, where charging interest is legal and county clerks record metes and bounds of private property. We live in a different world than Bible times. Does that let us off the hook? Not necessarily. Jesus continued to warn his disciples about the power of possessions even though they had already left everything to follow him. At one point he said, "Beware, and be on your guard against every form of greed; for

Whatever happens to us, we don't want to end up poor. Consequently, it's hard to give more than we should and easy to want more than we need.

not even when one has an abundance does his life consist of his possessions" (Luke 12:15). Of course, that statement is diametrically opposed to the American dream. We believe in quality of life. Therefore, to most Americans, life *is* determined by our possessions. Those who have more have better lives. This is why we look with such pity upon the poor. Their lives must be miserable because they don't have what we have. Whatever happens to us, we don't want to end up poor. Consequently, it's hard to give more than we should and easy to want more than we need.

But what if Jesus was right? What if heaven knows no currency? What if earth knows no injustice? What if Jesus was the richest poor man that ever lived? What if the rich gave to the poor because the needy are *blessed* by God? What if those who have nothing gave everything? What if heaven's jubilee came to earth? What if money didn't matter to the rich or the poor? What if we freely gave as we freely received? Then we would discover what Jesus meant when he said, "Blessed are you who are poor, for yours is the kingdom of God" (6:20). Heaven's wealth would be our good fortune on earth, *and* everyone would be needy. The economy of grace would make all of us poor people—needing daily bread as much as needing God daily. Then we would understand why Jesus remained a poor man. Then we would serve God not mammon. Then we would sing Mary's song. Then we would see the kingdom come. "Oh, God I want to live like Isaiah 61 has been fulfilled *today!*" That would be good news. Isaiah would be proud.

Get Out of Jail Free

It's funny how most people didn't take Jesus seriously. His claims of Isaiah's vision becoming reality looked pretty ridiculous to almost everyone: hometown folk, religious leaders, honorable citizens, Galilean onlookers, Judean rulers, and Roman governors. Of course, those who needed a little fantasy in their lives flocked to Jesus—the poor, the diseased, the demoniacs, the outcasts. And, every supplicant got what he was looking for: Jesus fed the poor, healed the sick, exorcised the demon-possessed, and fellowshipped with sinners. That is, all but one. There was one man who didn't get to see Isaiah's prophecy fulfilled. There was one needy man who didn't get his miracle. And, ironically, he was counting on it more than anyone. He was the first to profess faith in Jesus and the first to doubt him. His name was John. He was a prisoner. And he was hoping that Jesus's claims would come true for him, too. He took Jesus at his word: "The Spirit of the Lord is upon Me, because He anointed Me to preach the gospel to the poor, He has sent Me to proclaim release to the captives . . ." (4:18).

John was disappointed in Jesus. It was reported to him that Jesus had "cured many people of diseases and afflictions and evil spirits; and He granted sight to many who were blind" (7:21). The Baptizer, however, was still in prison. In Luke's narrative world, John was locked up by Herod Antipas long before Jesus made his boastful claims in Nazareth (3:20). Therefore, when John sent his disciples to ask Jesus, "Are You the Expected One, or do we look for someone else?" he was essentially saying, "Have you forgotten me?" Since Jesus claimed that he fulfilled Isaiah's promise, and since it was coming true for the poor, the blind, and the oppressed, there was one part of the promise, as far as the Baptizer was concerned, that had been overlooked by Jesus: releasing the prisoners. In other words, I believe John expected Jesus to overpower the prison guards and work a miraculous jailbreak for the Baptizer as another sign of the fulfillment of Isaiah's promise. But that didn't happen. Why not? John had done his part, preparing the way for the Messiah. Now it was time for Jesus to do his part. John knew that Jesus had already spent quite a bit of time taking care of those who were imprisoned by demons and sickness. John thought it was his turn. He couldn't wait any longer. So he sent his disciples to prod Jesus: "Are you going to get me out of here or not?"

Jesus fired back an answer that probably stunned John. Jesus told John's disciples, "Report to John what you have seen and heard: the blind receive sight, the lame walk, the lepers are cleansed, and the deaf hear, the dead are raised up, the poor have the gospel preached to them" (7:22). Essentially, Jesus was telling John's friends, "Tell him that you're seeing Isaiah's promise becoming reality." But notice what Jesus left out of Isaiah's list of messianic blessings. The poor have the gospel, the blind see, the oppressed are liberated, the favorable year of the Lord has come. What's missing? Jesus seems to have left out the part about prisoners being released. Now hear the stinging rebuke: "Blessed is he who does not take offense at Me" (v. 23). Jesus lived out Isaiah's vision on his own terms. The Nazarenes thought Jesus had gone too far. John believed that Jesus wasn't doing enough. Ironically, both took Jesus at his word. The people of Nazareth dismissed him as a pretender—offended by Jesus's claim, they wanted to kill him for what he said. John, on the other hand, believed what Jesus said. When Jesus didn't keep his word, the Baptizer doubted that Jesus was Isaiah's "expected one." Ironically, Jesus never had his doubts about John. And yet, at that very moment, in Jesus's eyes, John became the least of the least in the kingdom of God (v. 28).

Promises are not guarantees. Guarantees come with expiration dates, terms and conditions, exception clauses, and authorized signatures. Guarantees leave nothing in doubt. What is expected is what is delivered. Customers know exactly what they're getting with a guarantee. Guarantees are insurance policies against disappointment. Therefore, customers can demand satisfaction according to their expectations. Promises, on the other hand, are open-ended. They come without terms, conditions, or requirements. Promises never expire. They can be fulfilled over and over again. Promises come without warranty. As a matter of fact, the worth of a promise depends upon the one making the promise. That's why a broken promise hurts. Promises are personal, and they're open to interpretation. When intentions of the promise makers do not meet expectations of the promise takers, the disappointment feels like abandonment. He said one thing, she heard something else. Jilted and jaded, those who count on promises end up giving up hope on promise keepers.

Many of us get mad at God. For those who take him at his word, the promises of God are supposed to be reliable, bedrock truth. But when his promises fail to meet our expectations, we take God to task for not coming through. He let us down. Confusion sets in quickly. From the days of our childhood, we've been trained to think like a consumer. Shocked and bewildered, our American reflexes kick in as we recite the mantra, "The customer is always right!" We're accustomed to having things done our way because we evermore live in a customized world. Technology and marketers make sure of that. We no longer have to "fit in"—to adapt to the world. Now the world must adapt to us. Personal computers and cell phones foster our need for immediate gratification. The Internet brings the entire world to our living rooms. Satellite television teaches us how to cook, golf, fish, restore furniture, add on rooms, restore marriages, exercise, get in touch with our "spirits," and find alternative careers when we choose. Like a personal secretary, caller ID and answering machines eliminate unnecessary conversation. Like a personal valet, the home shopping network displays clothes we might be interested in purchasing. Cyberdocs, cybermail, cyberbosses, cyberchess, cyberchurch—cyberspace has created a ready-made world that fits our needs and conforms to our desires. Each one of us creates the world we live in—cosmos.com.

But what happens when our ready-made world falls apart? What do we do when life doesn't conform to our expectations? How do we handle the reality that God is Creator and we are not? That he fulfills his promises according to his intentions and not ours? That he refuses to be treated like a fertility god, manipulated by our demands, our desires, our plans, our preferences? Do we call God to the witness stand (or, "in the dock" as C. S. Lewis said), put him on trial, making him answer to the charges of unfaithfulness? Or, do we go back to the Bible and remind ourselves that *his* promises are not *our* guarantees. Could we, like the writer of Hebrews, come to the conclusion that even if God's promises don't come true in our lifetime, he will still make good on every promise before the last day (11:13, 39–40)? Is it possible that God's Word is plain enough—that we're the ones that got it wrong?

John died in Herod's prison (Luke 9:9). Luke never informs his readers about the circumstances of the Baptizer's martyrdom. We get that story from Matthew and Mark. Instead, John the Baptizer passes from the narrative world of Luke's Gospel without notice. Why? I can't help but wonder about John. Did he die in despair, believing that he had failed God? Did his doubts persist about Jesus? What about John's disciples? Did they lose faith in John? Did they ever transfer their loyalties to Jesus? If John had done his job right, shouldn't his disciples have followed Jesus? Or, did they, like their leader, become disillusioned with Jesus? Did John and his disciples take Jesus's warning to heart, or did they hold out hope to the very end that Jesus would liberate *all* prisoners? Why didn't Jesus rescue John? Does this mean that Jesus didn't live up to his own claims? Does John's death prove that the Nazarenes were right, that is, that Jesus was a messianic pretender? Or, did Jesus give himself some wiggle room when he said that God had sent him to *"proclaim* release to the captives"? To proclaim release is one thing, liberating prisoners is something else. Did Jesus set prisoners free?

There were three men who shared the same fate. They were going to die because they were criminals of Rome. Curiously, the fate of all three men changed when they met Jesus, another criminal of Rome. One was released from prison, one was promised heaven, and one died in despair. Barabbas did not have to carry a cross for his crimes because Jesus died in his place. John may have had his doubts about Jesus, but there was at least one prisoner who would have to say that Jesus fulfilled Isaiah's promise. Barabbas was released from prison because of Jesus. Imagine the shocked look on the face of the other two prisoners when Barabbas walks out of jail free. "Why him? Why not me?" they must have thought. Indeed, that's exactly what the crucified criminal said when he complained to Jesus, "Are You not the Christ? Save Yourself and us!" (23:39). Jesus had already saved one. Why not the other two? Of course, his request was not offered in sincerity; he was "hurling abuse at Him," according to the narrator. In fact, echoes of the Baptizer's complaint can be heard in the voice of the man on the cross. If Jesus is Isaiah's hope, then that should mean the release of all prisoners, right? Enter the theologian masked as the third criminal:

> "Do you not even fear God, since you are under the same sentence of condemnation? And we indeed are suffering justly, for we are receiving what we deserve for our deeds; but this man has done nothing wrong." And he was saying, "Jesus, remember me when You come in Your kingdom!"
>
> verses 40–42

To me, it's the most beautiful prayer in the entire Bible. "Jesus, remember me when your kingdom comes." At this point, Jesus was in no position to deliver a kingdom. In fact, the man who made this request knew that Jesus was going to die just like him. He knew that men were supposed to suffer for their crimes; insurrectionists were held in prisons until they were crucified. He knew this all too well. What he couldn't understand, however, was why Jesus shared his fate. Jesus had committed no crime worthy of death. I don't know what he was thinking, but it astounds me when I consider the possibilities. Why did he ask Jesus, "Remember me when you come into your kingdom"? Is this the last ditch effort of a desperate man who took a chance on Jesus because he was his last and only hope? Or, did he see the promise of God's kingdom in Jesus? Whether he meant to or not, the crucified man offered profound theology. His story shouts out what Luke has been saying all along. Jesus believed that the poor were blessed by God because *he was poor*. Jesus believed that prisoners would be released from their captivity *because he would be liberated from death's prison*. Jesus fulfilled Isaiah's promise because he *became* Isaiah's promise. Crucified with Christ, the thief on a cross pictures what

Jesus claimed from the beginning: "He has sent me to proclaim release to the captives. . . . Today this Scripture has been fulfilled in your hearing." So, Jesus *proclaimed*, "Truly I say to you, *today* you shall be with Me in Paradise." For a criminal looking for hope of release from the prison of death, this Scripture was fulfilled in his hearing.

While it is true that Barabbas was liberated from Pilate's prison, his freedom is not the one we celebrate. Interestingly enough, we don't prize Barabbas. We should identify with him, though. Jesus took his place. Jesus died for the man who deserved death. That's the way we normally describe the significance of Jesus's death for us. Jesus was crucified for our crimes—just like Barabbas. Yet Barabbas is not our hero. Painters ignore him; stained glass pictures omit him. When it comes to the first person Jesus died for, most of us are probably ambivalent in our feelings toward Barabbas. It's the other prisoner, the man who died like Jesus, the one who found release in the promise of Isaiah—this is the criminal we admire. Why? He said what we all feel. We know we should get what we deserve. We understand that we are all criminals of God's justice. But Jesus took our place. Indeed, one man got out of jail free for the day. The other was liberated forever. Yet, in both respects, Jesus let the prisoners go free. Hallelujah! Hallelujah! Hallelujah! We get out of jail free.

> I have been crucified with Christ; and it is no longer I who live, but Christ lives in me; and the life which I now live in the flesh I live by faith in the Son of God, who loved me and gave Himself up for me.
>
> Galatians 2:20

From shepherd boys gathered around a manger, to a murderer on a cross, Jesus was good news. He was born in a feeding trough; he died like a criminal. From start to finish, Jesus embodied the life of those he came to save: the helpless and the hopeless. This is grace, that Jesus would stoop so low to save the least, the last, and the lost. Isaiah believed the same. If the widow and the orphan are not experiencing the justice of God, then there is no peace. If the poor and the oppressed are left to themselves to find help, then nobody enjoys the presence of God (Isa. 5:7). But, according to Luke, everything changed when Jesus came into the world. This is why angels burst forth with celebration of good news for *all* people. This is why the heavens burst open and God's Spirit fell on Jesus. It was time for the kingdom of God. No one gets what he deserves when God blesses the world. That is good news. To use the language of Paul, the law of sin and death gives way to the law of Christ. There is no more condemnation. The curse has been removed. Evil and suffering have been spent on Christ. Now, sinners can steal their way into paradise. The poor can pretend that they're rich. All are forgiven for no reason. To be needy is to find favor with God. Jesus made Isaiah's promise come alive for his time and for ours.

If Jesus wasn't simply pretending, but he actually believed that these things were true for our times as much as his time, then what would that kingdom look like now? In other words, how would Luke's Gospel read today? Instead of the rich man and Lazarus, Jesus would probably tell the parable of the Christian and the drug addict. Rather than a manger, Jesus would be born in a trailer park. Instead of dying on a cross, he would be sent to the electric chair. He might mount a pulpit in any church and declare that John's Revelation had already been fulfilled. He would probably live like "white trash," not keep a job, expect handouts from the government, and scream about the injustices endured by American Indians. He would find his best disciples among Black Muslims, and Hispanic migrant workers, and Hasidic Jews. He would fast for Lent and celebrate Mardi Gras. He would grant clemency to all criminals. He would disappoint his best friends. He wouldn't have a bank account, life insurance, or a credit history. And, he would be considered a threat to society, accused of intolerance. He would laugh when the stock market fell, weep when he saw pictures of dead soldiers of American enemies, and act completely ambivalent toward rulings of the Supreme Court. He would be accused of not taking the problem of poverty seriously. He would say that God loves San Francisco. And, he would tell stories about Good Politicians and Prodigal Daughters. Jesus would act as if being poor is not all that bad, as if being rich is a terrible curse, and as if the worst sinners make the best Christians. Essentially, he would teach us that nobody deserves the love of God, hell is real, and perspective is reality. Jesus would live as if God's kingdom had come to America. And, to most of us, it would look pretty ridiculous. Few would take him seriously. We would probably dismiss him as a great actor, deserving an "Oscar" for his performance.

This is why I think we misread the Gospel according to Luke. We don't recognize the difference between good acting and good living. As a matter of fact, we would rather celebrate actors who give realistic performances than performers who act out inimitable realities. The imperial cult of America is celebrity worship. Blockbuster films reward talented actors with heavenly accolades—they are called "stars"—because they know how to make fiction look real. The praises of the masses visiting thespian temples bring riches and glory befitting gods. Saturday night at the movies comes closer to weekly worship than any other Sabbath exercise. Then, the annual festival of self-congratulation called the "Academy Awards" causes devotees to gather around televisions to root for their favorite "performances." Money and power, acclaim and awards come to this elite group simply because they know how to pretend. That's it. That's all there is to it. Actors are able to trick audiences into believing that they really are happy, sad, thoughtful, ambivalent, sensitive, and wicked—whatever the part requires. Essentially, the public bestows millions of dollars upon people who are good fakers. And we love them for it. No wonder we are such cynical people. Our greatest heroes are fakes.

To the naked eye, true believers look like actors. It is the great irony of our times that we are immediately suspicious of anyone who tries to live like Jesus. We're taught to look past the façade of faith, knowing that such public pretense masks a private reality too ugly for the world to see. Christians are dismissed from the public arena because everyone knows that no one lives what they say they believe. Christians are known for holding to standards that they don't keep, for talking about faith and relying upon medicine. This is why praying for rain looks foolish. A woman may say that she has "weather faith," asking God to keep a massive ice storm that will cover the entire state from hitting the little town where she has to bury her husband, but all of us "know" that science governs weather predictions. Or, when parents claim that God will heal their child of cerebral palsy, the assumption is made that a new medical procedure has been found that will reverse spasms and involuntary movements. God always seems to heal what cannot be seen. Evil spirits may plague third world countries, but everyone in America knows that demons can't enter our country—they don't make it through customs. Churches have no ministers of exorcism.

Jesus stopped storms, restored a withered hand, and ripped demons out of the souls of men, women, and children because he *believed in God's kingdom*. I want a faith like that. But, I'm too afraid of what people might think if I tried to live out a faith like that. Most believers who take their faith too seriously end up taking themselves too seriously. Yet I love to see my children take their faith too seriously, like when they pray for their sick dog, or trust God for the recovery of a lost toy, or complain to God when it rains. There's something very appealing about a child who pretends that God hears him better if he prays louder.

I'm going to start praying for rain, again. I'm going to trust that God will heal my wife's patient—a little boy who suffers from autism. Without apology, I'm going to tell prisoners they can find freedom in Christ, that a dying man's last breath can get him into heaven, and that demons still devise wicked schemes. I'm going to give more money to the poor because God has canceled all their debts. I'm going to act like all rich people need help, all sinners make great Christians, and the most insignificant person I know is my best friend. These are things that I haven't done lately because I haven't seen the kingdom-reign of God like Jesus did. But now I do thanks to Luke. From now on, I'm going to pretend like the kingdom of God has come because . . . I claim to follow Jesus.

6

Blessed Are the Cursed

His appearance in our midst has made it undeniably clear
that changing the human heart and changing human society
are not separate tasks, but are as interconnected as the two
beams of the cross.

Henri J. M. Nouwen, *The Wounded Healer*

Jesus made disciples out of needy people. That's the way it happened in Luke's Gospel. Jesus helped them; they followed him. In the other Gospels, however, we read a different story—it's difficult to tell why the first disciples of Jesus followed him. In Matthew and Mark, Jesus is a stranger who walks up to some fishermen and says, "Come, follow Me, and I will make you fishers of men." Inexplicably, they take Jesus up on his invitation, leaving their livelihood behind them. They literally dropped what they were doing and followed him, for no apparent reason. In John's Gospel, the first followers of Jesus had a little help. The Baptizer sent a few of his disciples to Jesus with the endorsement,

"Look, the Lamb of God!" It took a couple of times, but John's disciples finally realized that Jesus was the "coming one" of whom John had been preaching. They followed Jesus because John told them to. According to John's story, then, Jesus didn't find his first disciples. They found him. Luke is the only Gospel writer to tell the story behind the stories. He explains why the first disciples followed Jesus. Peter, James, and John became disciples of Jesus because of their miraculous catch of fish (Luke 5:1–11). As a matter of fact, according to Luke, Jesus was by himself for quite some time before he found a single follower. He won over his first disciples with a feat that would snag any fisherman: Jesus caught fish—hundreds of them. There were so many fish, two boats nearly sank. Now that's a fish story few people can top. Peter was so overwhelmed by the irony of having too many fish (can a fisherman ever have too many?), that he left everything to follow Jesus.

That's the way it went according to Luke's Gospel. Time after time, Jesus helped the needy, and they, in turn, became his devoted disciples. The hungry found food, the sinners found forgiveness, the outsiders found acceptance, the sick found healing, the demoniacs found liberation, and the oppressed found hope. Jesus made hundreds of disciples in no time at all. As a matter of fact, at one point (like Peter's net) Jesus had too many disciples, so he pared down the group to twelve (6:12–19). Like a coach choosing his starters, Jesus found twelve "apostles" among the "multitude of His disciples." He had helped so many people his following had become a spectacle. Eventually expanding his effort Jesus chose seventy more disciples, sending out these apostles on a special mission to bring down Satan's reign of terror (10:1–20). Jesus claimed that the success of his kingdom was unstoppable. Satan's demise came just as quickly. Evil was losing its grip. Those who had suffered for so long finally found relief. At one point, an exuberant woman shouted out, "Blessed is the womb that bore You and the breasts at which You nursed" (11:27). Eventually, the crowd of followers became so thick, Luke complains that everyone was "stepping on one another" (12:1). Overwhelmed by the mob, no doubt, the Pharisees tried to shoo Jesus away (13:31). The sinners, on the other hand, flocked to his side (15:1). The reign of God had come, and like sheep breaking through the gate, everyone was "forcing his way into it" (16:16). Isaiah's dream was becoming reality, and everyone wanted in on the action. Momentum was carrying them to Jerusalem, where the Son of Man would be revealed.

"Where the body is, there also the vultures will be gathered" (17:37). In foreboding tones, Jesus tried to warn the crowd that things wouldn't go very well once they reached their goal. He claimed that day would bring great confusion. He knew that his disciples wouldn't be able to see what was going on (vv. 22–23). On that scandalous night, events would

seemingly spin out of control—like lightning flashing or floods rising
(vv. 24–30). Secret arrests in the night, the threat of death hanging over
their heads, Jesus said the vultures in Jerusalem were waiting for them
all (vv. 31–37). Several times he took the twelve aside, trying to prepare
them for that fateful night. But they "understood none of these things"
(18:34). The closer they got to Jerusalem, the more anticipation ran
through the crowd that the "kingdom of God was going to appear immediately" (19:11). And who could blame them? Jesus talked constantly
about the imminence of God's reign. Even though he told them that "the
kingdom of God is not coming with signs to be observed," at times he
made it sound like it could appear at any moment: "Will not God bring
about justice for His elect who cry to Him day and night, and will He
delay long over them? I tell you that He will bring about justice for
them quickly" (18:7–8). Or, even more puzzling, Jesus suggested that
the kingdom of God was already "in [their] midst" (17:21). Blinded by
ambition, caught up in the Passover celebration of Jesus's messianic
entourage, neither the twelve apostles nor the rest of his disciples could
see it coming. The push of humanity made its way like a river through
Jericho, the last stop to Jerusalem. Like blind guides leading the blind,
the Passover pilgrims were lunging toward the kingdom that would appear in David's city, rooting out Roman rule. Ironically, it was there—on
the road through Jericho—where Jesus met three men who couldn't see.
The first man was blinded by wealth. The second man was blinded by
poor eyes. And the third man was blinded by the crowd. Would any of
them see the kingdom of God?

Sight for Sore Eyes

Jesus promised that the blind would see the kingdom of God. He
claimed that Isaiah's vision of the messianic age would not only mean
good news for the poor and release for the captives, but also "recovery
of sight to the blind" (4:18). Of course, when the prophets of old spoke
of blind men receiving sight, they saw the symbolic meaning of their
own words: "On that day the deaf will hear words of a book, And out
of their gloom and darkness the eyes of the blind will see. The afflicted
also will increase their gladness in the LORD, And the needy of man-
kind will rejoice in the Holy One of Israel" (Isa. 29:18–19). A blind man
epitomized Israel's need to see the justice of God. On that day, when
God visited his people, the blind would receive their sight in more ways
than one. Consequently, the reader of Luke's Gospel knows that Jesus
would eventually meet up with a blind man. And it comes as no surprise
when Jesus heals the blind beggar—he promised as much. That's how

the justice of God comes because a blind man sees, making the lasting impression on the one who has eyes to read.

The story of Jesus's encounter with the blind beggar in Luke is sandwiched between two other "blind men" stories that are similar but different (the rich young ruler and Zaccheus). As a matter of fact, Luke strings several episodes together in this series of stories to make the same point over and over again. The literary effect is obvious: for those of us who can't see what he's saying, the same message comes at us again and again. It's Luke's version of "in case you missed it!" First, Jesus tells the parable of the Pharisee and the Publican (18:9–14). Then, the narrator gives a seemingly unconnected account of Jesus blessing the children (vv. 15–17). Next, Jesus meets "a certain ruler" who has kept the commandments all his life (vv. 18–30). Then, Jesus warns the twelve about his version of upcoming events in Jerusalem; but they didn't understand (vv. 31–34). The next story is when Jesus heals the blind beggar (vv. 35–43). Finally, Jesus meets a man by the name of Zaccheus and declares that "salvation has come to this house" (19:1–10). Do you *see* what Jesus was doing? How are these stories connected?

Jesus was being tricky when he told the parable of the Pharisee and Publican. The narrator sets up the story, explaining Jesus's motive: "He also told this parable to some people who trusted in themselves that they were righteous, and viewed others with contempt" (18:9). The parable is about two men who pray in the temple. One, the Pharisee, takes center stage and prays *to himself*: "God, I thank You that I am not like other people: swindlers, unjust, adulterers, or even like this tax collector" (v. 11). The publican hides in the corner, beating his chest, and mutters the prayer, "God, be merciful to me, the sinner!" (v. 13). Speaking of his fictitious characters as if they were real, Jesus said: "I tell you, this man went to his house justified rather than the other; for everyone who exalts himself will be humbled, but he who humbles himself will be exalted" (v. 14). Of course, no one wants to be identified with the self-righteous Pharisee. We would prefer to see our reflection in the face of the tax collector who begs for God's mercy. No one tolerates a judgmental person. So we pray, viewing other self-righteous Christians with contempt, "Lord, I'm glad I'm not like that holier-than-thou Pharisee!" Gotcha! The quest for humility comes at a high price. It is an elusive gift. As soon as we claim it, we lose it. No matter how we do it, those of us who exalt ourselves will be humbled—even by a parable of Jesus meant for the self-righteous.[1] Now comes the "in case you missed it" part of Luke's story.

Immediately, Jesus fleshed out his teaching about humility and exaltation. The disciples tried to prevent Jesus from blessing children. Jesus scolded them for their imperceptiveness and said, "Permit the children to come to Me, and do not hinder them, for the kingdom of God belongs to such as these. *Truly I say to you, whoever does not receive the kingdom of God like a child will not enter it at all"* (vv. 16–17). Remember that. Take a note. Write it down. Whoever humbles himself like a child will see the kingdom of God. Because, as an observant reader, we will meet the man who acted like a child and entered the kingdom. We also get to see the self-righteous Pharisee in living color. Jesus told a parable about two men who went to the temple. Luke shows us who they are.

Meet the Pharisee. He comes to Jesus with confident assertions and inerrant appraisals. "Good Teacher, what shall I do to inherit eternal life?" Even Jesus is taken back by the young man's hubris. "Why do you call me good? No one is good except God alone." That's the way it is with self-righteous people. They're convinced of their perfect vision. They know goodness when they see it. As a matter of fact, the young man claims that he has kept all the commandments *since he was a child* (v. 21). See the irony? Righteous in his own eyes, he's all grown up. Echoes of the Pharisee's prayer can be heard loud and clear. He's a man of impeccable reputation and infallible judgments—he's a "ruler." In every way, he's the opposite of what Jesus required of those who enter the kingdom of God. Remember? Jesus said kingdom people had to become like children. Children have no money. This man is in trouble. "One thing you still lack; sell all that you possess and distribute it to the poor, and you shall have treasure in heaven; and come, follow Me" (v. 22). But the man couldn't do it. He had too much money. Treasure in heaven couldn't compare to treasure on earth. "How hard it is for those who are wealthy to enter the kingdom of God!" Beggars have it easier.

At this point, the disciples remind Jesus that they are as good as beggars. They've left everything to follow him. Mentioning their sacrifice reminded Jesus of his own. After warning his disciples that he would lose everything—even his life—once they came to Jerusalem, the narrator explains how the disciples missed the point. His teaching was hidden from their eyes. They were blind to the fact that he was going to die. Then, as he came into Jericho, Jesus met a blind beggar, literally. Shouting from the margins, the blind man begged for *mercy*. He didn't ask for a miracle; he didn't beg for money. Like the man in the parable, he simply cried out for God's mercy. And, on that day, he found it. Jesus made the blind man see the kingdom of God. "Immediately he regained his sight and began following Him, glorifying God" (v. 43). But that's not all. When God makes blind men see, when his kingdom comes, there will be justice. That's what the prophets had said all along.

The kingdom of God consists of needy people. One cannot beg for what one already has. This is why Jesus was offended by self-sufficient people. They didn't need him. The wealthy didn't beg for money. The rulers didn't ask for power. The healthy didn't need a miracle. The righteous didn't count on the mercy of God. Who needs Jesus? We can get along fine without him. This is why Jesus's response would have been the same even if the rich ruler had approached Jesus like the blind beggar. Can you imagine the scene? A good, wealthy man comes to Jesus and says, "Son of David, have mercy on me." Jesus would have responded in the exact same way: "Sell all you have and give to the poor, then come and follow me." In Luke's Gospel, only the needy find God's mercy. The blind

---

The kingdom of God consists of needy people.

---

beggar is living proof. The ones who humble themselves will be exalted. Being vulnerable, admitting our need doesn't come easy for those of us who have been taught that self-sufficiency is the baseline in fulfilling the American dream. Psychologists say that the hardest part—the first step—in overcoming our problems is admitting that we have a problem. Couples on the verge of divorce don't think they need marital counseling. Addicts dismiss twelve-step programs as a waste of time. Sick people don't want to go to the doctor. To admit our need is to accept our frailty. Broken people have nothing else to do but need God.

Two men in Jesus's parable went to the temple to pray. Besides the self-righteous Pharisee, there was a man who refused to "lift up his eyes to heaven." He beat his chest, praying for God's mercy. He needed it. He was a tax collector. Publicans defined what it meant to be "filthy rich." They were legal thieves. They robbed from the poor and gave to the rich. Excising taxes for the Roman Empire was not only treasonous, it was blasphemous to the Jews. Levying production taxes proved Rome's claim that the "Promised Land" belonged to them. The money was used to pay for the soldiers and procurators, constant reminders of foreign oppression. And, to make matters worse, no one knew how much money was to be made from collecting Roman tribute. There were no official tax tables. Rome had quotas, to be sure. But only the procurators and the publicans knew the amount of monies that needed to be handed over to the emperor. Whatever the publicans collected as their profit margin was their own business. Bilking the public of hard-earned profits was the Roman-backed industry of publicans. No wonder the tax collector in Jesus's parable was punishing himself and begging for God's mercy. By anyone's standards, he was headed straight for hell. Yet, Jesus said that it was this man—the cheat, the scoundrel, the blasphemer—who would go to his house righteous in God's eyes, not the Pharisee who was righteous in his own eyes. How can these things be?

Meet the Publican. He's a short man, unable to see Jesus because of the crowd of citizens watching the parade of pilgrims make their way through Jericho for Passover. Running ahead of the crowd, Zaccheus climbed a tree to get a better view. It must have looked pretty ridiculous—a grown man hanging in a tree. Jesus, no doubt amused by the sight, offered to go home with Zaccheus, honoring the outcast with his presence. *Everyone* complained, "He has gone to be the guest of a man who is a sinner" (19:7). Indeed he had, but that wasn't necessarily the reason why Jesus decided to eat with him. Before he met Zaccheus, Jesus had shared table with *many* sinners—even another publican named Levi, along with all of his money-grubbing friends. This was nothing new, especially to Luke's Gospel. Jesus ate with sinners.

There's another reason why Jesus befriended Zaccheus. Remember what Jesus said after he told the parable of the Pharisee and the Publican? He said, "Whoever does not receive the kingdom of God *like a child* shall not enter it at all." Like a child in a tree, Zaccheus (a man in a child's frame) pictured what Jesus was saying. Now we get to see the eyes of a blind man opened and justice rain down from heaven. "Behold, Lord, half of my possessions I will give to the poor, and if I have defrauded anyone of anything, I will give back four times as much" (v. 8). That pretty much covers all of the bases. The "have-nots" get half; the "haves" get four times back what was stolen from them. That probably didn't leave much for Zaccheus. The rich young man was blinded by his wealth. Zaccheus saw what he needed to do. And, just as Jesus predicted, this man went to his house justified: "Today salvation has come to this house, because he, too, is a son of Abraham" (v. 9). Once a man discovers treasure in heaven, money doesn't mean a thing.

Jesus met three men on his way through Jericho. The first man was blessed by God, wealthy and righteous. The second man was cursed by God, blind and begging. The third man was neither blessed nor cursed by God. He was rich because of his own craftiness, not by God's blessing. He was marginalized as a "sinner" by the town folk of Jericho, not by God's curse. Yet this rich sinner became a poor righteous man because Jesus made the blind see the kingdom of God as a child. His name was Zaccheus, and he was a "wee little man." No wonder children love the story song about Zaccheus. They identify with a little person who wants to see Jesus. This is their story. This is our story. For just like Jesus said, "Whoever does not receive the kingdom of God like a child shall not enter it at all." Money blinds the eyes of a self-righteous man. But here's the good news: Jesus came to make blind men see—rich or poor, cursed or blessed, favored or hated. Zaccheus proves that no one lies beyond the healing touch of God's mercy, because Jesus brings sight for sore eyes.

> Behold, My Servant, whom I uphold:
>   My chosen one in whom My soul delights.
>   I have put My Spirit upon Him;
>   He will bring forth justice to the nations. . . .
> To open blind eyes. . . .

Isaiah 42:1, 7

May his Spirit reign down upon us now.

I am fighting the temptation to sermonize. I have a hundred thoughts running through my head. These stories speak powerfully on so many levels. But I want to stay true to one of the things I think Luke was trying to do. Three parallel worlds are stacked together in this brief episodic narrative: the pious, the poor, and the worldly. As we watched Jesus move effortlessly from one world to the next, I can't help but wonder: How does the American church fare compared to him? Do we relate as easily to the rich, the poor, and the worldly? Or, do we spend most of our efforts proselytizing certain kinds of people? Quite honestly, the rich righteous man would have received much more attention from us than what he got from Jesus. To our way of thinking, he's the perfect candidate for the kingdom of God. He leads a good, clean, moral life. He offers kind, respectful greetings. He's the sort of person most churches are looking for. Perhaps Jesus was too hasty in demanding too much. If this man were to request membership in our church, we would not only receive him with open arms (requiring only 10 percent of his earnings), we would probably make him chairman of finances. Zaccheus, on the other hand, would only get a chuckle out of us as we passed by, dismissing his proclivity for ill-gotten gains as another example of irredeemable humanity (in our part of the country, businessmen who run liquor stores are thought to be beyond hope). And the beggars, I'm not even sure if we hear voices from the margins anymore. The blind beggar reminds me of homeless Americans and the so-called third-world countries that constantly vie for our attention. I get tired of seeing the signs WILL WORK FOR FOOD.

I'm so glad Jesus never ignored pitiful cries for help. I'm grateful that he found a sinner who was looking for a change of heart. I'm even more thankful that he didn't beg a good man to follow him. Because, even though these three men came from three different worlds, they all had the same problem. Jesus could see it when he looked into their eyes. They were blind; all three needed to see God's mercy in their own lives. Two were rich, and one became poor. Two were sinners, and one found righteousness. Two saw the kingdom of God, and one walked away very sad. And what is the difference? Why did a rich publican find the kingdom of God and a wealthy ruler miss it? How did Zaccheus squeeze his way through the eye of a needle? Why did the rich, righteous ruler walk away? How could someone so good be so blind?

Last Sunday morning I was absentmindedly playing with the worship guide before I spoke. I was running the sermon through my head, trying to collect my thoughts, when I noticed a word in the order of service I had partially blocked with my thumb, "offer." Removing my thumb revealed the printed word, "offering." Toggling back and forth, I moved my thumb to cover and uncover the last three letters, "offer . . . offering . . . offer . . . offering." It seems to me that the righteous ruler made an offer; Zaccheus presented an offering. The rich man was an expert in goodness. He knew he was good and he knew Jesus was good. That sounds like good company. So, he made an offer: "What good could a good man do to inherit the good kingdom of God, good teacher?" This man had much to offer. But Jesus wasn't impressed. It's not what a man has to give that matters; it's what he doesn't have that reveals a heavenly treasure. "Truly I say to you, there is no one who has left house or wife or brothers or parents or children, for the sake of the kingdom of God, who will not receive many times as much at this time and in the age to come, eternal life" (Luke 18:29–30). Soon, Jesus would be able to add "money" to that list. Offerings are sacrifices. Indeed, Zaccheus lost it all and found a treasure called the kingdom of God. "For the Son of Man has come to seek and to save *the one who loses*" (19:10, my translation). Blessed is he who has eyes to see.

Imagine the commotion that a minister would cause if the description in the worship guide were changed from "offering" to "offer." Then, the dedicatory prayer would sound something like: "Lord, today we are making you an offer. We are giving our money today hoping that you will take notice of our generosity. Some of us are looking for the promise of your protection. Some here are hoping for job promotions. Many of us are simply praying that you will maintain the status quo—we like what we have, your blessings are evident. Most of us are trying to do what is right. We uphold your standards. We guard your truth. Therefore, we are counting on you to take care of us. We make this offer knowing that you are a God who never forgets. We hope you like what we have given to you this day. For some of us are making significant sacrifices. With these gifts we pledge our allegiance to you. Amen." Who would be so foolish as to offer such a blasphemous prayer? Not many. Yet most of us, at one time or another, have tried to establish such a quid pro quo arrangement with God. We'll do his bidding if he does ours. This is why Jesus told the rich ruler to give everything away. God cannot be bought with our righteousness, our reputations, our promises, or our money. He is no fertility god. He accepts no offers, only sacrifices. This is why it was Zaccheus, not the rich ruler, who went to his house justified. It's not what we have to give that matters, it's what we've given up. For no one can follow Jesus without sacrifice.

> Do not be afraid, little flock, for your Father has chosen gladly to give you the kingdom.
> Sell your possessions and give to charity; make yourselves money belts which do not wear out, an unfailing treasure in heaven, where no thief comes near nor moth destroys. For where your treasure is, there your heart will be also.

Luke 12:32–34

The library of Christian history is filled with stories of believers dedicated to Jesus in selfless sacrifice. Their lives read like Gospel books. Their biographies are narratives of spirituality—witnesses of a life sacrificed to God. "Reasonable service of spiritual worship," Paul would say. Even though they come from different worlds, living at different times, in different places, their lives look the same. There is a familiar, cruciform pattern replicated over and over again in these disciples of Jesus. And, at times, their faith in Jesus seemed to be more of a curse than a blessing. Often, their search for peace of mind tormented their souls. Their bipolar spirituality would throw them into the depths of

---

God cannot be bought with our righteousness,

our reputations, our promises, or our money.

He is no fertility god. He accepts no offers,

only sacrifices.

---

despair and carry them to the heights of rapturous glory. Sometimes, it seems, they were so sure of their sacrifice—a life literally spent for Christ. At other points, nagging doubts of a vain labor would hang over their heads: would they ever find their purpose in the kingdom of God? The tug-of-war between doing the work of God and becoming the work of God forced them to explore the difference between making an offer and becoming an offering. I'm drawn to their stories like a moth to a flame. There is an irresistible quality to their lives that makes me want to learn how to sacrifice. It's almost as if I hear the beckoning call of Jesus in their words, as if I see a portrait of Jesus' sacrifice in their lives. Indeed, they are a sight for sore eyes.

Recently, I've been thinking about two men who picture for many what it means to become an offering to God: Rich Mullins and Henri Nouwen. To some people, I'm sure, these two look more like bookends of the grace of God. Nouwen was a Catholic priest from the Netherlands; Mullins was an evangelical musician who lived in America. Nouwen was an intellectual who lived in Canada. Mullins was a poet. Nouwen was a quiet, unassuming man. Mullins was a megaphone. On the other hand, they lived as if they were paternal twins of God's salvation. Both were celibate. Both were attracted to the monastic life. Both gave up successful careers to live with the underprivileged. Both men died in September. Once prominent, both lived in relative obscurity in their last years on earth. Struggling with their popularity, both men found God's love among simple people—Nouwen was loved by mentally handicapped people, Mullins was adored by Native American children. To the rest of us, their supernatural gifts appeared to be wasted on the "little people." Rich Mullins found his commercial success more of a nuisance than a benefit. He preferred singing his songs for children who danced playfully at his feet. Henri Nouwen left a prestigious faculty position at Yale University to help care for a handicapped boy named Adam. He insisted to the end of his life that he learned more about God's love from his friend Adam than from any book. He was called "Rich," but Mullins gave away most of his money, living below the poverty level. He was a brilliant scholar, but Henri preferred to have his mentally handicapped friends talk during his lectures. Neither man believed that he was making a sacrifice. To Nouwen and Mullins, their friends at L'Arche Daybreak community and on the reservation in New Mexico, respectively, were the benefactors of God's love. It's not what they gave up to live in Toronto or New Mexico that mattered to them. Rich and Henri discovered the abiding joy that comes with becoming an offering to God. Offerings are sacrifices of needy people.

Women's Liberation

Jesus loved women. That's why he helped them. And, consequently, they followed him as devoted disciples. Luke is the only Gospel writer to record the fact that Jesus had women disciples (8:1–3). Indeed, careful students of the Bible have noticed for quite some time that women receive favorable treatment in his Gospel. Only Luke tells the stories about Mary and Elizabeth, Mary and Martha, Anna the prophetess, the widow from Nain, and the hunchback woman. And what do all of these stories have in common? Like all of the people Jesus helped, these women were on the verge or had become marginalized: barren, shamed, widowed, sick, or demonized. As a result, Jesus's effort has been misconstrued as a work to liberate all women as oppressed people. As appealing as that sounds to our ears, that's not what happened in Luke's Gospel. Even though, by our standards, women endured oppressive acts against them simply because they were not men, that's not what Jesus was trying to correct.[2] Jesus was no feminist in the modern sense of the term. If he were, then his response to the woman who exclaimed, "Blessed is the womb that bore You and the breasts at which You nursed" (11:27), would be politically incorrect.[3] He treated women with dignity and respect because he loved them. And they returned his affection with undying loyalty. They followed Jesus to the very end, because, from the very beginning, Jesus was out to "set free those who are oppressed" (4:18).

Jesus tried to explain what he meant that day in Nazareth, but the hometown folk wouldn't hear of it. He knew that his own people wouldn't accept him as the prophet of God who would bring "recovery of sight to the blind, [and] to set free those who are oppressed" (vv. 18, 24). So he used a story from Elijah's ministry to put a sharp tip on his point (1 Kings 17:1–24). It took no time at all for Elijah to earn his reputation as a prophet of God when he kept the clouds from raining for over three years. The resulting famine was God's punishment for the insolence of the king and queen of Israel, the infamous Ahab and his notorious wife, Jezebel. During the blight, Elijah sought refuge in the house of a pagan widow, Zarephath. After she shared her scraps of food with Elijah, God miraculously filled her pots with flour and oil as long as her guest remained. If that were not enough, when her son took ill and died, Elijah prayed that God would revive the widow's *only son*. Elijah's presence would mean God's blessing, even for a Gentile. The boy came back to life, and Elijah's reputation was secure in the mind of the widow: "Now I know that you are a man of God and that the word of the LORD in your mouth is truth" (1 Kings 17:24). In his sermon on the plain, Jesus said: "Blessed are you who hunger now, for you shall be satisfied. Blessed are you who weep now, for you shall laugh" (Luke 6:21). The parallels between Jesus and Elijah are obvious. Both were acclaimed as "prophets" early on because of the miracles they performed. Both were adversaries of the ruling authorities. Both sought refuge outside of Israel. Both found believers among pagans. Both multiplied food miraculously. Both raised a widow's son from the dead.

To the citizens of Nazareth, Jesus was no Elijah. He hadn't performed a single miracle for his own people. To them he was simply "Joseph's son." Jesus anticipated as much: "No prophet is welcome in his home-town" (4:24). To the people of Nain, however, Jesus's ability to replicate the miracle of Elijah made them declare, "A great prophet has arisen among us!" (7:16). Contrast between the two villages couldn't be more dramatic. The difference lies in the beatitude of Jesus: "Blessed are you who weep *now*, for you shall laugh" (6:21). Jesus claimed that as long as he was around, there would be no mourning. He couldn't change the past. Old grievances in Nazareth remained. Jesus could only speak of "today." Therefore, the promise of Isaiah's vision and Elijah's power came to those who were weeping "*now*"! And, in Luke's Gospel, the only people Jesus met who were weeping were women. They were the experts in grief and death. They started the funeral. They prepared the corpse for burial. They led the songs of lamentation. But, in the presence of Jesus, a woman's sorrow wouldn't last long. Her mourning would be turned into laughter because Jesus came to liberate the brokenhearted.

Grief is a dangerous gift. It can help us work through the most difficult times in our lives—like when we bury our own child, or attend to a dying parent, or lose our business to bankruptcy. It can also become a cruel master, enslaving us to bitter feelings over past events that will never change. Grief can be good medicine for the soul. It can also become a filthy habit, polluting our spirits with thoughts of self-destruction. All of us have seen the tragedy of a funeral without burial, where mourners never stop crying over their loss. I know of a pastor whose teenage son died in an automobile accident. His pain is destroying him. He left the ministry, left his wife, and became another man's lover. One year he's preaching sermons against the vices of the world. The next year he's a living example. Therapists talk about stages of grief, or cycles of grief, knowing that grief is the gift that keeps on giving. They also speak of a period of time when grief first comes, when weeping over tragedy is purifying, when bruised souls seek solace. There is a time to mourn. But there also comes a time when grieving souls stop crying. Experts explore how the transition takes place, mapping the terrain of pain and suffering. We never "get over" our loss. No grieving father or mother will ever forget their child. Yet, they learn how to carry on because believers know that God is the one who heals wounded hearts. Death will not spoil life. Loss helps us realize our gain. Despair can evolve into hope. Mourning can turn into laughter. Jesus knew this better than anyone.

Luke records four times when Jesus heard women weeping (7:13, 38; 8:52; 23:27). The first time was when Jesus saw the widow of Nain weeping over her dead son. The second time was when the sinful woman wept at Jesus's feet. The third time he found women crying was when he entered Jairus's house. The last time Jesus heard women crying was when he carried his cross to "The Skull." Death hangs over three of these stories like a vulture. Yet, even in the face of death's pallor, Jesus would have no mourning. Right before her son was buried, the widow heard Jesus say, "Stop weeping." Right after Jairus found out that his daughter was dead, Jesus told the mourners, "Stop weeping." Even as Jesus was about to die, carrying his own cross, he told his faithful disciples, "Stop weeping." For Jesus—the embodiment of Isaiah's promise—there was no reason to cry over death. Laughter would drown out the mourner's sorrow. That happened when the funeral procession burying a widow's son broke out in jubilation: "God has visited His people!" (7:16). What a strange sight, people dressed in grief shouting joyfully, "Glory to God!" One minute they're singing songs of lamentation, the next they are celebrating God's Immanuel with songs of praise. Once again, laughter broke out in the midst of weeping when Jesus silenced the mourners gathered around Jairus's dead daughter. This time, however, their weeping was premature, their laughter insincere (8:52–53). Jesus had questioned their ability to diagnose death, "Stop weeping, for she has not died, but is asleep." Imagine the peculiar sound when laughter meant as scoffing turned into hilarity after the little girl "woke up." Finally, Jesus wouldn't allow the women who followed him to the cross to weep for him. He had already wept for Jerusalem (19:41). Now, it was their turn: "Daughters of Jerusalem, stop weeping for Me, but weep for yourselves and for your children" (23:28). Easter made Jesus's death a cause for celebration, even in Jerusalem (24:52).

These are the pictures of the brokenhearted getting relief, the oppressed finding liberty, the downtrodden recovering hope. It has been said that laughter and mourning come from the same place in our souls. Indeed, hilarity looks much like pure grief: red eyes, flowing tears, wrenched face. Isn't it ironic that our responses to exhilarating news and tragic events are nearly indistinguishable? It doesn't take much, it seems, to go from despair to delight. In the twinkling of an eye sorrow can morph into joy. And, in that very moment, when mourning gives way to laughter, despair dies and hope is reborn. Everyone knows that no one should laugh during a funeral. And yet, how many of us have joined a brokenhearted mother laughing through her tears as friends recounted funny stories about the little girl who died of cancer? Who can laugh at a time like this? Only a woman who knows that she will get her daughter back, someday. This is why Jesus told these women to stop weeping. Isaiah's dream was coming true—for them and for us. "Blessed are you who weep now." If it weren't for the resurrection of Jesus, none of us would stop crying.

I skipped over the story of the sinful woman who wept at Jesus's feet. I want to deal with the significance of that episode in the next chapter of "table stories." There are two other stories in Luke's Gospel, however,

where Jesus's ministry to women illustrates the liberation of the oppressed: when Jesus visited Mary and Martha, and when Jesus healed the
hunchbacked woman (10:38–42; 13:10–17). In both accounts, a woman
has lost her place and guardians of social structures step in to correct
her insolence. In both stories, the women were not trying to act like rebels—bucking social conventions—but innocuously find themselves the
object of scorn simply because they need Jesus. Neither woman speaks;
both only do as Jesus directs—one sits at his feet, the other is touched by
his hands. Yet, in both stories, the lessons learned seem to be more for
the watchdogs of social propriety than the troublemakers who crossed
the line. When Jesus loosed the chains of the down-trodden, the control
freaks got angry. Surprisingly, it wasn't a man who objected to Mary's

*If it weren't for the resurrection of Jesus,
none of us would stop crying.*

behavior, it was her own sister. The twelve disciples didn't seem to mind
Mary's acting like a man. Martha, on the other hand, found her sister's
inactivity intolerable. "Lord, do You not care that my sister has left me
to do all the serving alone? Then tell her to help me" (10:40).

Why did Martha interrupt Jesus's teaching time, appealing to him to
correct Mary? It seems to me that it would have served her purposes
just as well to call *Mary* down for her laziness. As a matter of fact, she
probably could have gotten her sister's attention without raising such
a stink. "Psssst! Mary! Come over here and help me!" But that's not
what she did. Instead, she put the onus on *Jesus*—made it a public
issue. Why? I find at least two reasons. First, I believe Martha was
trying to prove to Jesus that she had been an observant disciple, that
is, not only hearing what he said but doing what he taught. In fact,
prior to her invitation to Jesus to benefit from her hospitality, Jesus
told the parable of the Good Samaritan. I can see Martha, on the heels
of learning a lesson about love in action, intentionally acting out the
part of the hero of Jesus's parable. She will take him home. She will
provide food and drink. She will love her neighbor. Jesus had told the
lawyer for whom the parable was told, "Go and do the same" (v. 37).
Martha heard him well. So, in Martha's mind, who is the better disciple: the one who hears or the one who does? She wanted Jesus to
notice the difference.

The other reason Martha appealed to Jesus comports well with what we know about the roles that men and women played in Jewish society. The home was the woman's domain—her sacred space. As Martha is trying to offer the honorable acts of hospitality, her sister's shameful behavior counteracts her efforts. Normally, under these circumstances, a father, husband, or even a brother would take care of the matter, preserving family honor. In this case, neither Mary nor Martha are married—a questionable status for marriageable women. There were no honorable men in their house. These women seemed to be living by themselves. So, once again in his Gospel, Luke pictures Jesus sharing table with the lowly—this time it's two single women. This explains why Martha appealed to Jesus to correct her shameful sister. According to Jewish Law, only men could handle the Torah. Women were perpetually unclean; they could never be students of the Holy Scriptures. Martha needs a man to take care of the situation. All of this is lost on Mary, who sits at Jesus's feet—a euphemism describing rabbinical students—learning lessons from her rabbi like the rest of the men. Poor girl, she doesn't know any better.

It's a question of who is distracted and who is paying attention. To Martha, Mary is distracted, neither paying attention to what Jesus taught

> *At the feet of Jesus,*
>
> *women find what is necessary.*
>
> *No man, no woman can take that away.*

in the parable of the Good Samaritan, nor to her responsibility as a woman showing honor to a man in her home. To Jesus, Martha is the one who is distracted: "Martha, Martha, you are worried and bothered by so many things." Jesus claimed that what Mary found that day would never be taken away from her. The things that bothered Martha—Mary's impertinence, Jesus's honor, her own responsibilities—weren't worth the effort of removing a girl who lost her place. Indeed, as far as Jesus was concerned, Mary found what was essential: the kingdom of God, where the gospel is preached to the poor, where captives break out of prison, where the blind regain their sight, and *where the downcast find release*. It seems that *Mary* was the girl who understood what Jesus was saying. She saw the line that divides the kingdom of God from the rules of society. She was the disciple that learned the lesson well. At the feet of Jesus, women find what is necessary. No man, no woman can take that away.

Jesus valued people over rules. It's not that he was out to push certain individuals over the edge, to snub social convention, or to threaten the boundaries of conventional wisdom via social anarchy. Jesus was no cynic. Instead, he seemed unrestrained by these unspoken "laws" in his quest for the kingdom of God. It's as if the rules of his society didn't exist when he was about the business of binding up the brokenhearted and liberating the oppressed, giving hope to a wounded world. People mattered that much to him. Of course, to those who liked the rules, who enforced the rules because they benefited from such distinctions of class, sex, race, and wealth, Jesus was a troublemaker. They thought he was after them. Jesus wasn't naïve. He knew that treating all people the same would make waves. But it wasn't about the rule-keepers, or about the rule-breakers. His kingdom was about reclaiming those who needed God regardless of the rules.

She came to the synagogue to worship God. Cursed with a sickness for eighteen years, the hunchback woman was the picture of humility. Bent double, she could never look a person in the eyes. With her face facing the ground, she was *literally* downcast. According to Jesus, she was bound by Satan's shackles (13:16). Indeed, the way she walked probably looked like a prisoner of war, stooped, bound, and led away in chains. She stood at the back of the crowd, minding her own business with the rest of the low-life who always gave way to the honorable members of the synagogue. As a matter of fact, some buildings for certain synagogues were modeled after the temple, where women and children were segregated from the men—on the outside looking in. Whether or not this meeting place divided worshipers like the temple, we know from Luke's account that Jesus had to "call her over" from the margins. First, he pronounced, "Woman, you are freed from your sickness," as if she needed liberation. Then, he laid hands on her, making her stand up straight. Healed from her affliction, she gave glory to God (v. 13; was everyone else silent?). All of this made the head of the synagogue angry. "There are six days in which work should be done; so come during them and get healed, and not on the Sabbath day" (v. 14). Hear the assumption in his words, "so come during them and get healed"? The synagogue ruler acts as if the only reason a hunchbacked woman would come to the synagogue on the Sabbath day would be for healing. His presumption is based on the prejudice that cursed people can't worship God. A woman like this wouldn't be allowed to enter the temple, much less present her offering: "No one who has a defect shall approach: a blind man, or a lame man, or he who has a disfigured face, or any deformed limb, or a man who has a broken foot or broken hand, or a hunchback, . . ." (Lev. 21:18–20). She had no business being there.

To the synagogue ruler's way of thinking, both the hunchbacked woman's presence and Jesus's healing work were contemptuous acts against the holiest day of the week. Sabbath was the day set aside for worship. Her healing and his actions were not acts of worship worthy of the Sabbath. That's what the head of the synagogue told the crowd that day. Jesus couldn't resist playing off the irony of the moment:

> You hypocrites, does not each of you on the Sabbath untie his ox or his donkey from the stall and lead him away to water him? And this woman, a daughter of Abraham as she is, whom Satan has bound for eighteen long years, should she not have been released from this bond on the Sabbath day?
>
> Luke 13:15–16

Fresh on his mind, I can't help but wonder if Jesus had seen that very thing happen as he went to synagogue—a man watering his beast. Then, seeing a woman bent over like an animal, he gets a flash of inspiration. On the Sabbath Jesus will help a woman worship God. What could be wrong with that? Besides, the healing was Jesus's idea, not the woman's. As a matter of fact, there is a very good possibility that the hunchbacked woman came to the synagogue *not to be healed*, but to worship God. She didn't cry out for Jesus's help. She didn't interrupt his teaching during the sacred hour of worship. There was no guarantee that because she showed up that day, Jesus would automatically heal her. Jesus didn't help every sick person he met (see Acts 3:2, which tells of a lame man who was placed outside the temple *every day*—a man Jesus probably passed by several times). The way Luke tells the story, the hunchback wasn't looking for a miracle nor did Jesus plan to heal her that day. He saw her, laid hands on her, and she gave God glory on the Sabbath. Things happen when we worship God. Who knew?

People in control don't like it when things get out of hand. Jesus, on the other hand, relished these moments. After the synagogue broke out in celebration, Jesus compared his kingdom effort to weeds that take over gardens, or yeast that permeates dough (vv. 18–21). That's probably what the head of the synagogue thought: what Jesus did was as threatening as weeds and sinister as yeast. Once it starts, no one can stop it. That's what happens when the downtrodden are released, when the brokenhearted get relief, when the oppressed are liberated, when those who need God's help get it. Jesus left the synagogue in a mess that day. I see the ruler contemplating what this will mean for him as he watches the crowd go wild. From now on, there's no telling who will come to worship. The line that divides the blessed and the cursed is gone. God's mercy rains down on all people: those who think they deserve it and those who know they don't. Who will guard the Sabbath? Who will restore order? Who will make sure that the right people get the right treatment in order to do the right thing? I also imagine Jesus walking away with a grin on his face. He knows what this means. Isaiah was right. God anointed a Galilean prophet with his Spirit to bring good news to the poor, to proclaim release to prisoners, to help the blind see again, and to liberate the oppressed. The year of the Lord's favor had come with a man who believed in the reign of God's kingdom. No evil will stand in his way. No foe will oppose him. Heaven comes to earth. All debts are cancelled. It's time to party!

Sometimes redemption is messy. It scribbles outside the lines of customary pictures of grace. It spills the contents of our souls onto the white sheets that cover the table of forgiveness. The reclamation of wounded people can make a mess of orderly worship. Doesn't it strike anyone odd that we have designated times during church services for God to do his

Sometimes redemption is messy.

work? This is the time for confession. This is how you should praise God in this song. This is the posture you should assume during this hymn. This is the time for all of us to be quiet and listen. This is when you are supposed to respond to God's voice. This is the time to leave. From start to finish, we order the Holy Spirit around as if he were a slave to our schedules. Sometimes I want to fall on my knees and beg God's forgiveness at the *wrong time*. Sometimes I need to scream out in anguish over the suffering of my soul at the *wrong time*. Sometimes I must linger in the presence of God's mercy long after the last "amen." Sometimes it takes an hour to confess my sins. Sometimes it feels like our worship services are designed for those who don't suffer, don't need help, don't need healing, don't need God. Order of worship can sometimes push the needy to the peripheral edge of propriety like a hunchbacked woman. Nevertheless, occasionally, Jesus will call the person doubled over by sin to the front. She comes forward during the time of invitation, falls on her knees and weeps for an uncomfortably long time, then confesses to the congregation, in extremely personal terms, her need of God. A stunned congregation listens in silence, a minister tries to clean up the mess of a life exposed by too much information, and parishioners have something to talk about for the rest of the week. Church is the last place where most of us would want to try and get some help.

When are we going to learn that people are more important than rules, that redemption supercedes propriety, and that healing takes time? Sin can make a mess out of our lives; reclamation of sinners can be messier still. It shouldn't take a bunch of courage to go before a group of Jesus-friendly people and confess our need of God. "It was for freedom that Christ set us free," Paul wrote to Galatian churches imprisoned by rules, regulations, and laws. If Jesus came to announce

> *When are we going to learn that*
>
> *people are more important than rules,*
>
> *that redemption supercedes propriety,*
>
> *and that healing takes time?*

good news to the poor, to liberate prisoners, to bring sight to blind people, and heal the brokenhearted, then it's time for believers to revel in the grace of God without apologies. When we see a hunchback woman find healing, the place should break out in jubilant celebration. When a wounded heart needs consolation, we should take time to minister the oil of healing. When desperate men and women hunger for God's presence, we should stay until we are satisfied. If the truth has set us free, then we are free indeed.

Ironically, the women Jesus liberated followed him to a prison called death. They saw how his body was rushed to burial; they watched Joseph of Arimathea place the corpse in the tomb. They needed to do their work, but had to wait until Sunday morning. It seems that even in his death Jesus threatened the sanctity of the Sabbath. The same women who were exorcized of demons and healed of sickness—Mary Magdalene and Joanna—came to preserve Jesus's body with burial spices. To me it's such a pitiful sight; like sheep without a shepherd they came to the tomb. They had followed him every step of the way, from Galilee to Jerusalem. At this point, they had no one else to follow, no where else to go. Where else could they go? What else were they to do? He was their world. Now he was gone. Echoing in my ears, as I consider these little sheep, are the words of the popular chorus, "And I, I'm desperate for you. And I, I'm lost without you." Brokenhearted, these experts in grief came to do what women did best: deal with death.

"Why do you seek the living One among the dead?" (24:5). Angels announced the good news of Christmas *first* to women. Therefore, it comes as no surprise that women disciples were the first to hear the good news of Easter from angels. And why not? They stayed true to Jesus to the bitter end; they were the disciples who paid attention to what he taught them. Therefore, angels could jog the memory of Jesus's faithful disciples: "'Remember how He spoke to you while He was still in Galilee . . . ?' And they remembered His words" (vv. 6–8). The men, on the other hand, couldn't believe it (v. 11). Isn't it peculiar: those who had the closest association with the horrors of death were the first to believe the impossible, *and* the men who had no stomach for dealing with the unspeakable atrocities of crucifixion refused to believe? All it took for women to believe was an angelic vision and an empty tomb. For the men, it was a different matter altogether. They could stare the resurrected Jesus in the face and still not get it. "O foolish *men* [not women!] and slow of heart to believe in all that the prophets have spoken!" (v. 25).

Before these two men met Jesus on the road to Emmaus, they had heard reports of what the women saw and heard. Yet, "these words appeared to them as nonsense" (v. 11). Hysterics among women were the norm. Now see who are the fools. They walked with him. They talked with him. These men even shared table with Jesus and still didn't recognize him. While the men were trying to figure out what all of this meant, the women were the first to announce the Good News to the poor, to proclaim release of the prisoner, to help blind disciples see again, to bring hope to the brokenhearted. Jesus crushed the shackles of death. No more tears. No more sorrow. No more mourning. No more lamentation. This is why Luke has no stories about women crying at an empty tomb. They knew better.

7

Jubilee!

The confinement of heaven in people's imagination to a *place*
rather than a *time* prevents us from experiencing the depth of
comfort heaven can be to us now.

Marva J. Dawn, *A Royal "Waste" of Time*

What happens when we die? None of us knows for sure. The
holy Scriptures give us only glimpses of the great beyond. Of
course, we know how it ends. The resurrection of Jesus is the goal of
every future. But, in the meantime, we are left to wonder about heaven.
C. S. Lewis dreamed of heaven as ultimate reality, a place where density
defines beauty and evil is so small it can be swallowed by a butterfly.[1]
J. R. R. Tolkien envisioned warm fires, hot drinks, good food, and de-
lightful company as heavenly rest.[2] For Augustine, heaven would be a
lesson taught by Jesus himself.[3] One day, all of us are going to find out
if everything that we've been taught is true. Until then, we search for
clues, inklings of what will be.

John heard a voice from heaven say, "Blessed are the dead who die in the Lord from now on!" (Rev. 14:13). I've heard many stories recalled by grieving families who attended the bedside of believers who died. Sometimes they die quietly. Sometimes they fight death all the way to the other side. But there's one story I shall never forget. Before we buried her husband, the wife of a minister told me what happened when he died. He had suffered for quite a while with a heart problem that eventually landed him in the hospital. His fading in and out of consciousness during the last hours of his life caused the family to cling to his bedside, hoping for any chance of having last words, final good-byes. Suddenly, his eyes shot open, his face brightened, as he began to take in what could not be seen by those around him. "Glory! Glory! Glory! Glory!" His wife called to him from this side of heaven. "Tell us, Wilbur. What do you see? Tell us. What is it? What do you see?" Roused from his vision, the man kept his gaze fixed on the object of his wonderment and replied, "Preach the gospel. Tell them it's worth it. Preach the gospel. Preach the gospel. Glory! Glory!" And then he slipped into a coma and died a few minutes later. Seems that what can be seen when heaven comes to earth cannot be described. Paul heard inexpressible things, too (2 Cor. 12:4). Do these soundings give us a reliable echo of heaven's delight? Perhaps our thorn in the flesh is that we will never know until we cross over ourselves. These celestial beckonings may haunt us more than help us. Unless, that is, someone could show us what heaven is supposed to look like now.

If heaven is heavenly then what must it be? Children playing in grassy, open fields, mountains cradling spring-fed lakes, rivers cascading down hills of tropical flowers, sunsets that never end, friends that never tire, sleep that is always restful, food that is always refreshing. That last image—sitting around a banquet table enjoying good food and drink—was the Jewish ideal of heavenly pleasures. In a world of limited goods, most first-century Mediterraneans rarely went to bed satiated—that full, satisfied feeling most Americans enjoy every evening. As a matter of fact, it was considered wasteful, a sin, to eat more than what was needed to live. Only during festivals did the people have the luxury to eat and drink more than they should. In the Jewish mind, then, heaven should be a place where Israel would celebrate the holy festivals all the time. Of course, to us a buffet is not a heavenly hope but an earthly vice. Nevertheless, the second part of the heavenly banquet scene would have interested us. The Jewish people believed that good conversation around good food would make heaven heavenly. Sharing table with their forefathers, hearing firsthand accounts from Moses about the crossing of the Sea of Reeds, or listening to David tell the story *one more time* about how Goliath fell at the hands of a boy, this would be heaven. Only the most honorable children of Abraham would rub elbows with the great heroes of Israel's faith. The high table hosted by Father Abraham would be reserved for the most honored of them all, the greatest descendants of the patriarch. Heaven would be a never-ending table of food and fellowship for Israel.

Jesus knew what he was doing when he ate with the wrong people. He went about announcing that the kingdom of God had come to earth. And he would attend any party to prove the point. Jesus was celebrating the advent of the heavenly banquet, sharing table with saints, sinners, outcasts, Pharisees, publicans, and prostitutes. Since Isaiah's promise

> *Jesus knew what he was doing when he ate with the wrong people. He went about announcing that the kingdom of God had come to earth. And he would attend any party to prove the point.*

had been fulfilled, Jesus acted as if the favorable year of the Lord had already come. All debts had been canceled. All sins were forgiven. The table of God's mercy was already set. Heaven had come to earth. There was no reason to wait for the great banquet in the great beyond. It was time to party *now*! "Today this Scripture has been fulfilled in your hearing." The righteous, however, didn't care for Jesus's guest list: "This man receives sinners and eats with them" (Luke 15:2). The grace of his open invitation to dine at heaven's table offended scribes and Pharisees. They always stood at a safe distance and scoffed at the spectacle. Now we see why Jesus told the parable of the prodigal son, using a banquet scene to drive home the point:

> Now his older son was in the field, and when he came and approached the house, he heard music and dancing. And he summoned one of the servants and began inquiring what these things could be. And he said to him, "Your brother has come, and your father [Abraham?] has killed the fattened calf because he has received him back safe and sound." *But he became angry and was not willing to go in.*
>
> verses 25–28

It didn't take a genius to figure out whom the elder brother represented in the parable. For Jesus, the banquet table was a living parable of the grace of God's kingdom—a reflection of his reign on earth as it is in heaven. This is why it was time to party. In the words of the father hosting the banquet, "We *had to celebrate and rejoice*, for this brother of yours was dead and has begun to live, and was lost and has been found" (v. 32). The scribes and the Pharisees, on the other hand, found the whole thing distasteful. Bad company ruins good food.

The First Supper

Have you ever noticed what gets Jesus in trouble in Luke's Gospel? Every time Jesus came to the table, controversy followed. The banquet table tended to be a contentious event in Luke's story. The first time it happened was soon after Jesus made a publican one of his disciples. Paying honor for honor, the grateful tax collector threw a party for Jesus (5:29–32). Public banquets signaled to a community the social status of the host. Invitations were sent to persons of equal honor. Persons of high honor would only come to a table worthy of their presence. Guilt by association ruled the honor game. If it was judged that the host's social standing was beneath them, guests wouldn't come. In this case, a man of low status—very little honor—invited his kind to his table. By accepting Levi's invitation, Jesus signaled to all that he belonged there among the "publicans and the sinners," that is, these were his kind of people. So, there he was, drinking and carrying on with the low-life, acting as if he had something to celebrate. This was more than the righteous could take. "And the Pharisees and their scribes began grumbling at His disciples, saying, 'Why do you eat and drink with the tax collectors and sinners?'" (v. 30).

Notice to whom the Pharisees directed their question: they complained to Jesus's *followers*, who were also sharing table with the riffraff. Evidently the Pharisees weren't surprised that Jesus found equal company at Levi's table. Who could forget Jesus's humble beginnings? Besides, he had already made them suspicious when he declared the paralytic's sins forgiven (v. 21). What they couldn't believe was that anyone else would join Jesus in such folly. To share table with the unclean would mean taking in unclean food. Kosher company was as important as kosher food. Before any of his disciples tried to defend themselves, Jesus answered, "It is not those who are well who need a physician, but those who are sick. I have not come to call the righteous but sinners to repentance" (vv. 31–32). In light of what happened before, Jesus's answer must have startled the teachers of the Law. They were expecting him to say something like, "Just as I did for the paralytic, I do for these tax collectors: their sins are forgiven. These people are not sick, they are not unclean, they are no longer sinners. These I declare righteous in God's eyes." Notice, however, that's *not* what he said. Jesus admitted that he was risking defilement: he was eating with sick people, sinful people, people who needed to repent. This he and the Pharisees could agree on. It was the *way* he was calling them to repentance that was the problem.

What is repentance supposed to look like? This was the burning issue that enflamed the holiness police. The Pharisees believed that the more you look like you're grieving over your sins, the better. So, as they fasted and prayed, disheveled hair and loud lamentations accompanied genuine repentance. Sackcloth and ashes had been around for a long time (Job!). Besides, if a man doesn't look like he's broken up over his sin, then maybe he isn't sorry for his transgressions. Several years ago a man bragged to me that he could judge the spiritual condition of any person by the way they prayed to God. He argued that emotional tones and sincere requests revealed true communion with God. A halting voice fumbling for the right words would betray a recalcitrant spirit. This man isn't alone. A famous rabbi believed that if his prayers fell from his lips with ease, then he knew that God would grant his petition. If he had a hard time forming the words, then his prayer would not be heard by God.[4] Evangelists implore listeners to "walk the aisle" and confess their sins. Catholics use a rosary. Pentecostals look for signs of spiritual renewal—tongues, fainting, shaking—to accompany genuine confession. Some think we should weep in remorse of sin. Others require bended knees, or accountability partners, or fasting, or public prayers. In matters of the heart, we all have our preferences as to the proper acts of repentance. "Pray these words," or "kneel down with me," or "do it this way," we say. The arrogance of our spiritual superstitions is seen in the willful compliance of ignorant seekers. We all feel better when everyone repents like they're supposed to.

At this point, the Pharisees took up the issue directly with Jesus: "The disciples of John often fast and offer prayers, the disciples of the Pharisees also do the same, but Yours eat and drink" (v. 33). Why all of this talk about fasting and prayers in the middle of a banquet? Because that's what repentant sinners do: they fast and pray. These are the public acts of repentance, not eating and drinking. The last thing these sick sinners needed to do was celebrate life. They should have acted remorseful, grieved over their sin, mourned their shamefulness. From where the Pharisees were standing (remember this is a *public* banquet), these unrighteous no-accounts were flaunting their sinful ways by acting as if they had *no* reason to fast. Exactly Jesus's point: "You cannot make the attendants of the bridegroom fast while the bridegroom is with them, can you?" (v. 34). As far as Jesus was concerned, this feast resembled a wedding banquet (another occasion when Jews were allowed to eat too much and drink their fill). These are the days when life should be celebrated. When the party's over—when bride and groom start their life together—there will be time for fasting for the friends left behind. But for now, the bridegroom is still single. There's food on the table. Sinners find forgiveness. The sick have their physician. There are no reasons to fast. As far as Jesus was concerned, the party was just getting started.

Jesus assumed that sinners would not grieve over their sin until the bridegroom was taken away. Why? The answer is obvious to those who know the end of the story. His death would eventually make table guests realize their need of repentance. He knew there would come a time when sinners found forgiveness at a table of mercy, where eating and drinking would be acts of repentance, where death and life would mingle together as a somber celebration. In an eerily strange way, the first supper forecast the last—a memorial of his death for our sin. That's why I always wrestle

Need to repent? Join the party.

with conflicted feelings when I break bread and share the cup of Christ with other sinners like me. I don't feel like eating when I think about his death. I don't feel like drinking when I remember my sin. I usually force the little cracker into my mouth, barely washing it down with a gulp of juice. Why would he make us eat and drink at a time like this? Here's why. Eating and drinking keep us alive. Gathered around a table, we take in food and fellowship, celebrating life together. Communion happens in this shared meal of repentance. See? Jesus knew what he was doing. The Pharisees couldn't see how a bunch of sinners could be led to acts of repentance at a banquet table. It must have looked pretty ridiculous to righteous people who believed that prayer and fasting were the only ways we get serious about our sin. Now, two thousand years later, it makes perfect sense. Jesus welcomes sharing table with sinners. They are his kind of people.

Need to repent? Join the party.

Table of Forgiveness

In the second table scene (7:36–50), the situation is completely reversed. This time Jesus was invited to share table with a Pharisee. This time sinners were kept outside looking in. This time a sinner offers the appropriate acts of repentance, weeping and grieving over her sin. This time Jesus comes to a table of judgment not mercy. This time Jesus pronounced the forgiveness of sins. This time Jesus was an unwelcomed guest. Indeed, those who are well don't need a physician. For this table conversation will reveal that Jesus knew what he was talking about when he said that he didn't come to call the righteous to repentance. What's there to forgive?

It seemed that experts devoted to the law of God couldn't be pleased. One prophet of God required the usual acts of repentance; the other took a completely different approach, eating and drinking his way into the kingdom of God. The Pharisees dismissed both of them. Jesus saw through their duplicity: "John the Baptist has come eating no bread and drinking no wine; and you say, 'He has a demon!' The Son of Man has come eating and drinking; and you say, 'Behold, a gluttonous man and a drunkard, a friend of tax collectors and sinners!'" (v. 34). So, regardless of the skepticism of the Pharisees, the question is still begged: which is the better approach? What should repentance look like? Wisdom might dictate that allowing sinners to party their way to heaven would encourage contemptuous behavior. Give sinners too much mercy and they may take advantage of it. Hobnobbing with the heathen may bring a righteous man down (see 1 Cor. 15:33). On the other hand, ascetic practices rarely attract devotees. Sometimes those who take their sin seriously end up taking themselves too seriously. Self-denial can devolve into an egomaniacal art form of self-promotion. The pursuit of holiness often winds up a contest between pious people who feign repentance rather than a quest among sinners who need it. Who's to say which is the wiser approach? Hear Jesus's answer: "Wisdom is vindicated by all her children" (Luke 7:35). Let's meet wisdom's child.

She was a woman whose reputation preceded her, much like Jesus. Even though she was known as the town sinner, we don't know what her sin was. Even though many commentators assume as much, Luke never mentions that she was a whore. All that we know is that her sins "were many," and that the Pharisee was repulsed at the sight of her wiping Jesus's feet with her hair. This is where I am a bit confused. One would think that seeing a sinful woman on her knees, weeping over her sin would be exactly what a Pharisee would want. Perhaps he would have approved if she were weeping at *his feet*. But that's not what happened. Even though she entered Simon the Pharisee's house bearing gifts, she came to see Jesus. At first, she stood behind him as he reclined at table. Then, as her tears fell, washing his feet, she stooped down to wipe them clean. Then, in the ultimate demonstration of self-deprecation, she repeatedly kissed Jesus's feet. To the host, such an erotic act not only

confirmed his opinion of her—"she is a sinner"—it made him realize
what Jesus was not: "If this man were a prophet He would know who
and what sort of person this woman is who is touching Him" (v. 39).
Notice the assumption behind his judgment. If Jesus were a true prophet
of God, he wouldn't let the unclean embrace of a sinner defile him.
Evidently, Jesus was *too imperceptive to know the heart of a sinner.* This
is what Simon thought to himself; this was his judgment in the matter.
No words were exchanged; no dialogue took place. Freeze-frame the
picture for a moment: there was Simon with his thoughts, the woman
with her remorse, and Jesus without comment. Finally, the silence is
broken. Jesus begins to speak. But he doesn't respond to the woman's
overture. Practically ignoring her embarrassing behavior, Jesus struck
up a conversation with *Simon.* While she kissed his feet, weeping over
her sin, Jesus decides—rather callously—to tell the Pharisee a story.
Now that's weird.

It must have appeared for a while that Simon's judgment was true.
Jesus never stopped the woman from kissing his feet. He never even
acknowledged her presence. He displayed no prophetic insight. To the
Pharisee, Jesus must have looked more like a dimwit than an enlightened
teacher. Here comes the parable!

> "Simon, I have something to say to you." And he replied, "Say it, Teacher."
> "A moneylender had two debtors: one owed five hundred denarri, and the
> other fifty. When they were unable to repay, he graciously forgave them
> both. So which of them will love him more?" Simon answered and said,
> "I suppose the one whom he forgave more." And He said to him, "You
> have judged correctly."
>
> verses 40–43

This encounter is dripping with irony. Simon has dismissed Jesus
as a prophet-wanna-be because he is unable to recognize the improper
actions of a sinful woman. This judgment Simon kept to himself. Then
Jesus reveals that he *did know what Simon was thinking* (prophetic powers!) by telling a story about forgiven debts and displays of affection. His
point is driven home when he asks Simon to make a judgment about
two debtors. Notice, Jesus *doesn't* ask the question: "To whom did the
moneylender show more mercy?" In light of Jesus's habit of eating with
sinners, that was the question Simon was probably expecting. Simon's
response would have been, "The one who needed it the most." Pharisees
had no doubts that sinners, like the woman kissing Jesus's feet, were in
greater debt to God than a righteous man. But Jesus turned the parable
the other way when he asked Simon which man would love the credi-
tor more. Hear what Jesus assumes by his question: those who know

they need forgiveness are the ones who truly love God. And, irony upon ironies, Simon *judged the matter correctly* (v. 43). Sure he did.

Is it true that the worst sinners love God more? I always thought that the greatest saints modeled perfect love, that the closer we get to God the less we struggle with sin. But then I read Augustine's *Confessions* or the psalms of David or the biographies of John Wesley and Billy Graham and realize that maybe none of us get to the point where we don't need to fall at Jesus's feet and weep over our sin. It seems that the more of God's mercy we receive the more we need his mercy. God never stops working on us. Purified of one besetting sin, our awareness of five more compels us to draw nearer to God. And the closer I get to God the more I realize how sinful I really am. Is this a good thing? Sometimes I wonder, "Why should I persist in prayer, asking God to draw near to me when his presence brings me such discomfort? Since our God is a consuming fire, who wants to get close enough to get burned?" Only the one who needs to receive forgiveness and to hear the words, "Your faith has saved you; go in peace." This is why we fall at the feet of Jesus. This is why we bring our perfume of confession. We have been forgiven much. He cancels all debts at his banquet table. Even those who have sinned a little need a little forgiveness. Jesus said that God "graciously forgives" *all* of us. But is it enough to drive us to our knees and make us act like a sinful woman? Why should we? Is it really that necessary? Before long many of us could be tempted to think like the Pharisee who sits comfortably at the table of forgiveness. The worst sinners need to do more confessing, that's why they spend so much time on their knees. Then Simon would say, "You have judged correctly." Sure we do.

Simon wasn't as good a judge as he thought he was. Jesus had not been ignoring the sinful woman at all. Actually, he had been talking about her all along. A perceptive man would have caught the implicit references in Jesus's parable. Jesus goaded Simon when he asked, *"Do you see this woman?"* (v. 44). Of course he did. That was the problem. Simon saw too well. He saw who she was. He saw what she did. He even saw what Jesus wasn't. As a matter of fact, Simon had already signaled to all of his table guests that he didn't think Jesus was an honorable guest, much less a prophet. He gave him no respectable greeting. He offered Jesus no acts of hospitality. Simon knew it was a risky thing to have Jesus come to his table. The less contact the better. What Simon lacked, however, the woman more than made up for: she greeted Jesus by kissing his feet, she washed his feet with her tears, she wasted costly perfume by anointing his feet. Why? Because she loved God more. It took a sinner to teach a Pharisee a lesson about repentance and forgiveness. And it all happened at a banquet table. Wisdom is vindicated by her children.

I wonder about her. We never get to hear what she was thinking; she never spoke a word. Everyone else speaks: Jesus, Simon, the other guests. We even get to overhear Simon's thoughts because Jesus *is* a prophet. Although the conversation revolves around her, we never hear from her. All we know is what we see. She pictures repentance at the table of forgiveness. I think it is significant that Luke never tells us what her "many sins" were. We don't even know why she came to see Jesus. Did she see Jesus heal a paralytic and declare that his sins were forgiven? Had she heard what others were saying about Jesus, that he was a friend of sinners? What was she hoping for? Why did she bring the perfume? Why did she kiss his feet? What did she expect? What was she thinking? We don't know. All we know is that she did what every sinner wants to do: fall at Jesus's feet and weep. Weep because sin hurts. Weep because life can be brutal. Weep because loneliness mocks us. Weep because repentance is hard. Weep because evil scares us. Weep because there's nothing left to say. Weep because we all need forgiveness.

Fasting and prayer were protocol for repentance and forgiveness. Yet this sinner didn't refuse food because she was fasting. She simply wasn't invited to the table. She grieved over her sin but never said a word. Her tears were her prayers. Evidently Jesus proved to be more of a prophet than even Simon could have imagined. Jesus saw inside a sinner's heart and pronounced the forgiveness of sins. To Simon and his friends, the whole episode was an odd spectacle. "Who is this man who even forgives sins?" (v. 49). To the woman who loved much, forgiveness meant release. Jesus said, "Your faith has saved you; go in peace" (v. 50). Obviously, when she came to the table she was a troubled woman. Hearing Jesus tell Simon that her sins were forgiven *because she loved much* must have redefined absolution for her (and for us!). Grief over sin without love results in catharsis. Love of Christ compels us to repent of our sins. Repentance without love, repentance that leads to sorrow for sorrow's sake, brings death, to put a turn on a Pauline phrase (2 Cor. 7:10). We need a sorrow for sin that leads to life, a grieving over sin that brings peace. How does that happen? It happens at the banquet table of God's kingdom where all debts are canceled. At the table of Jesus there will be mercy for those who need it the most. And, here's the best part: no reservations are required. Any sinner can come to the table and find forgiveness. You. Me. Anyone. Everyone. "Blessed is everyone who will eat bread in the kingdom of God!" (Luke 14:15). You come to his table brokenhearted over sin. Yet you are blessed because you eat his bread, his body broken for you. He has forgiven you. He knows your heart. Your tears have washed his feet. Let it go. Be at peace. For you know how to weep over your sin like a woman.

Guess Who's Coming to Dinner?

Jesus was invited to the table of a Pharisee two more times. And, as in every table story in Luke's Gospel, there was trouble. In one episode, the controversy revolved around purification rites, that is, making sure table guests were clean (11:37–44). In the other story, the problem was making sure the right kind of guests make it to the table (14:1–24). In both cases, Jesus took exception to table customs that divided people into categories. First, he refused to wash his hands before he ate. Later, he purposefully chose to occupy the last place at the table of honor. His behavior was bombastic. His manners went missing. Jesus would not preserve the customary at the expense of the ordinary. Not every Jew washed his hands before eating. Why did the Pharisees? They believed that they needed to take on the holiness code meant only for Levites as a sign of their extraordinary pursuit of purity. The common people who refused to follow the Pharisaical model were judged to be obstinate. Jesus dismissed the whole idea as manipulative: "Give that which is within as charity, and then all things are clean for you" (11:41). We can't force others to "do the right thing." Instead, we should do the right thing for others. This is holiness. In fact, this is what Jesus was trying to get his table guests to see when he came to the house of a Pharisee for the last time.

At first blush, this story looks like another Sabbath controversy episode. After goading the Pharisees with the question "Is it lawful to heal on the Sabbath?" Jesus in cavalier fashion healed a sick man and "sent him away." But something else is going on here. The fact that the man suffered from dropsy (water-weight gain around ankles, feet, stomach, heart, and neck) *and* that the healing occurred not only on the Sabbath but also in the Pharisee's home, signals to the reader that Jesus was out to teach the Pharisees a lesson that extended beyond what was appropriate labor on the holiest day of the week. Indeed, two questions cry out for answers. First, what was an unclean man doing in the Pharisee's house? Second, since he was healed of dropsy, why didn't the host invite the "clean" man to stay for the meal? Since purity was such an important issue for the Pharisees, the sequence of the story seems backwards. The unclean man defiled the Pharisee's house with his presence—but that didn't stop them from eating. Then, once the man was cleansed *by Jesus*, he was sent away by Jesus. No one caught the inconsistency of the moment. Of course, Jesus couldn't let this slip by unnoticed.

At first, Jesus made fun of the guests tripping over each other trying to get to the honorable places at the table. Luke has already mentioned that this man was a leader among the Pharisees—a person of high social standing. That these dinner guests were invited to eat with the honorable host distinguished them from lowly outsiders. But that wasn't enough. They knew their competition for the best seats at this public banquet signaled social significance to insiders as well as outsiders. Pushing their way to the seats closest to the host made the Pharisee look good. Jesus watched the whole affair from the end of the table—the last place anyone would fight over. He knew where he belonged. "Everyone who exalts himself will be humbled, and he who humbles himself will be exalted" (14:11). Honor does not come through self-promotion but from self-sacrifice. His own death would prove that. Therefore, Jesus believed that the banquet table of God's kingdom would turn the honor game on its head, revealing the ultimate heroes of our faith: a tax collector, a sinful woman, a leper, a man who suffered from dropsy. These are the honorable expressions of the reign of God. These are the kind of people who make it to the table of God's house. These are the persons who should be gathered around the table of a righteous Pharisee.

> When you give a luncheon or a dinner, do not invite your friends or your brothers or your relatives or rich neighbors, otherwise they may also invite you in return and that will be your repayment. But when you give a reception, invite the poor, the crippled, the lame, the blind, and you will be blessed, since they do not have the means to repay you; for you will be repaid at the resurrection of the righteous.
>
> verses 12–14

Why is this so? By now, it's pretty obvious to the reader. Blessed are the poor, the crippled, the lame, and the blind because the reign of God has come through Jesus. And, since he occupied the last place, he shall be given first place. The one who humbled himself will be exalted. Rejects will find their place in the bosom of Abraham. Outsiders will become insiders. The shamed will be honored above all. Heaven's banquet table will tell the story forever.

At this point, the host should have excused himself and run after his most honorable guest, bringing the man healed of dropsy back to his table and telling the person seated to his right, "Give your place to this man" (v. 9). But that didn't happen. Instead, someone at the table exclaimed, "I'm glad *we're* going to be there eating bread when God's kingdom comes!" That's my paraphrase of verse 15. I see him raising his glass and offering something like a "toast" when he said, "Blessed is everyone who shall eat bread in the kingdom of God"—present company included, I'm sure. Jesus, however, had a different guest list in mind. Read the parable he told at this point (vv. 16–24). Here's a story about a man who couldn't get anyone to come to his public banquet (the very opposite of what had occurred prior to the gathering around the

Pharisee's table). Obviously, the guests considered the host their social inferior. Their lame excuses for refusing to come to his demonstration of honor rubbed salt in the social wound. The host was claiming too much by inviting the higher-ups. Making every attempt to preserve the honor of their master, servants took the initiative and brought uninvited low-status citizens, but still there was room at the table (a large table meant a long guest list—this man really thought highly of himself!). In a desperate attempt to save face and food (there were no refrigerators), the host extends his invitation to the country folk outside of town. These are the indigent day laborers and sharecroppers of Galilean life. Now he's reached the bottom of the social barrel. His house will be filled at all costs—even at the risk of ruining his reputation. Now hear Jesus' stinging rebuke, "For I tell you, none of those men who were invited shall taste of *my* dinner" (v. 24). Seems like Jesus was telling more than a story. He was describing *his* ministry, *his* kingdom, *his* banquet table. See who comes when Jesus throws a party?

Who comes to our table? Whom do we invite to eat with us? If we were to throw a party for Jesus, who would make our guest list? We would probably make the same mistake as the Pharisee. We'd bring our friends to our house to celebrate Jesus. I'm not sure I would even think to invite sick people, lost people, sinners—those who need him the most. Confident of my place at heaven's banquet, I would consider a dinner at my house with my friends with my Savior as a sneak preview of life eternal. That's what I want heaven to be: a great reunion where all the persons I expect to be there celebrate for eternity. Earthy fellowship mirrors a heavenly hope. I typically invite my kind of people to my table. Most of us do the same thing. Boy, are we going to be surprised when we finally come to heaven's table. I can see it now. Taking my place—I have no doubts that I will make it—I'm shocked by the guest list. Turning to my right I see a man who struggled with homosexuality his whole life. He's already diving into the food. "What are you doing here?" "Can you believe it?" he exclaims incredulously. "I made it!" Suddenly, I notice the woman sitting across from me. She was the single mom who had five kids by five different men. "What is *she* doing here?" To my left, there's an ex-con. Down my row there are more just like him: liars, adulterers, swindlers, even a murderer. "Wait a minute. I'm at the wrong table. Is this heaven or hell?" "Neither." A voice wakes me from my daydream. "It's the table of our Lord." See who comes when Jesus throws a party.

By eating together Jesus is making us wait on tables together, to confess our sins together, to celebrate life together, to wait for his return together. Where else could one find a more common need—eating and drinking—to unite a more diverse crowd? Some of us are dastardly sinners. Others are admirable saints. Some of us commit the same sin every day. Others justify their sin. Whatever our lot, regardless of the assembly, when disciples of Jesus gather around a table to celebrate redemption, none of us has the right to act like the host and raise the toast. We are all, as C. S. Lewis put it, "jolly beggars" chugging down wine and passing around bread at a table that belongs to no one. All of us bend our elbows to eat; all of us open our mouths to drink. We eat the same food, drink from the same cup. You'll often hear it said that the ground is level at the cross. Indeed it is. We see the evidence of it every time we come to the table of our Lord.

Remembering Jesus

Jesus brokered a kingdom of God for men and women. He claimed that God gave him a kingdom and that he was able to hand over the reign of God to his disciples (22:29–30). The way he did it took everyone by surprise. Jesus would effect the kingdom of God by serving table. Waiting on his disciples, he refused to eat and drink. Instead, he encouraged them to carry on without him, for he had made a vow before they came to celebrate Passover for the last time: "I shall never again eat it until it is fulfilled in the kingdom of God" (v. 16). In fact, Jesus claimed that he had to serve his disciples because he was the bread of suffering they were eating; his blood was in the cup of a new covenant they were drinking. "I will not drink of the fruit of the vine from now on until the kingdom of God comes" (v. 18). Even though he made a vow to quit drinking wine, he encouraged the disciples to keep drinking. Even though he wanted to eat this Passover lamb one last time before he died, he made his disciples eat it, promising that they would never forget him when they broke bread. "This is My body which is given for you; do this in remembrance of Me" (v. 19). He wanted them to keep the party going without him. He wanted the banquet table to be a living memorial to the kingdom of God—a promise that one day the reign of God would come in all its glory. Until then, they would remember his vow. They would remember his sacrifice. They would keep on eating and drinking their way into the kingdom of God without him.

It's a pitiful request. "Don't forget me." How could they forget? He changed everything. Every time they crossed the Galilean sea they would think of him. Every time they saw a farmer sowing seed, they would think of him. Public banquets would never be the same. Seeing people eating and drinking, sharing stories and good food would make them recall good times with Jesus. They would never be able to look at all tax collectors the same way. Indelibly imprinted on their minds, no doubt, was the look of a blind man seeing for the first time, or the sight of a grown man in a tree, or the picture of a woman seated at Jesus's feet. But, there would be one memory they wished they had. It would be the one event that would haunt them the rest of their lives: the crucifixion of Jesus. They wouldn't be there to see him die.

Jesus knew that his disciples would mourn his death, living with the regret of their sin, their cowardice. "Simon, Simon, behold, Satan has demanded to sift all of you like wheat; but I have prayed for you, Simon, that your faith may not fail; and you, after you have returned, would strengthen your brothers" (vv. 31–32, my translation). Jesus prayed the same thing in the Garden. "Pray that you may not enter temptation," he instructed the twelve. Then, praying like he never prayed before— sweating as it were drops of blood—Jesus contended for his friends. He wasn't praying for himself. I believe he was wondering about his disciples—praying that their unfaithfulness would only be a temporary lapse of commitment. That their grief wouldn't get the best of them. That he would see them on the other side. Angels helped him get through the loneliness of that hour while his disciples slept from sorrow (vv. 43–45). Then, everything fell apart so quickly. The powers of darkness invaded (v. 53). His disciples abandoned him. The rulers crucified him. Joseph buried him. There was no funeral, no memorial. Sealed in an unmarked tomb ("where no one had ever lain"), Jesus could have been forgotten. At least, that's what his enemies hoped for. What about his disciples?

The next time they broke bread, would they remember him? The next time they drank wine would they remember him? The next time they celebrated Passover, would they remember him? The next time they saw a man crucified, would they remember him? They next time they grieved over their sin, would they remember him? Luke is the only Gospel writer to record Jesus's request. Of course, to us the whole scenario makes little sense. How could the disciples *not* remember Jesus? We have his words inscribed on our communion tables: "Do this in remembrance of me." Every time we come to his table, we remember him. His body was broken for us. His blood was shed for our sins. At the banquet table of God's kingdom, we celebrate his victory over death. Remembering his last supper, we look forward to the day when Christ drinks the cup of blessing with us. In the meantime, as we confess our sins, as we eat this bread, as we drink from this cup, his presence is undeniable. His memorial speaks louder than words. We live with the regret of our own sins even as we remember his death. How could we forget him? We've been eating *his* last supper for two thousand years.

Paul believed that "as often as you eat this bread and drink the cup, you proclaim the Lord's death until He comes" (1 Cor. 11:26). His memorial is our proclamation. When we remember him at his table, we are announcing his kingdom's reign over death. As we gather around the table of our

Lord, we are proclaiming the year of Jubilee: all debts are canceled. Every time we eat this bread and drink this cup, we keep the party going until he comes. Like the terminally ill who need a transplant, his death means our life. The Great Physician has come to help the sick. Like priests serving the altar of God, his sacrifice is our food. The righteous one has atoned for the sins of the repentant. Every time we eat his last supper we are saying that death didn't win, that our sins are forgiven, that his kingdom comes, that our Lord reigns. This is why his memorial looks more like a celebration than a funeral. This is why eating and drinking are acts of repentance. This is why we believe in a kingdom present but hope for a kingdom come. This is why *every time* we break bread we remember Jesus. We always say grace in his name.

When you think about it, he sure didn't ask for much. Jesus didn't require his disciples to establish an annual memorial or an official

How could we forget him? We've been eating his last supper for two thousand years.

church festival. He didn't anticipate that we would try to celebrate his birthday at Christmas or his resurrection at Easter. He gave no instructions for Christian holidays. Can you imagine? "When you celebrate my birthday, I want you to take an evergreen tree and decorate it with beautiful ornaments and then exchange gifts with family and friends." Or, can you hear Jesus saying, "Now, when it comes time to remember my resurrection, I want you to mark the festivities with a sunrise service and Easter cantatas." He didn't even ask his followers to reinterpret Passover, making it a thoroughly Christian event for all times. No. He simply hoped that we would remember him every time we ate bread and drank wine. Well, I don't drink wine. But I have had my share of bread with many meals. Even though sliced bread isn't something Jesus could count on, I do get the occasional experience of tearing a roll or a bun or a small loaf of French bread. There is an unusual pleasure in ripping a piece of bread in half, a tactile sensation of breaking the outer crust to expose the doughy center. And, sometimes, when I break bread, I think of him. That his body was broken for me, that his life is like bread to me, that he keeps my family alive with hope, that one day I will be with him and he will be with me, forever. When I break bread, sometimes I remember Jesus.

Two men walking on the road to Emmaus thought that the party was over. It wasn't that they had forgotten Jesus. They couldn't see any reason to celebrate. Their downcast gait drew a stranger to their side, accompanying them on their journey. Curious about their forlorn disposition (Passover was festival time!), the stranger asked them, "What are you talking about?" Ironically, they asked, "Are You the only one visiting Jerusalem and unaware of the things which have happened here in these days?" (24:18). Indeed, he was the *only* pilgrim in Jerusalem who knew what had happened. But they didn't know that. The stranger goaded them with what must have seemed like an innocuous question, "What things?" Listen to their tirade. "What things? What things? You've got to be kidding me! The things about Jesus the Nazarene! You *have* heard of him haven't you? Who hasn't? He was a great prophet, worked fantastic miracles, but then Jerusalem got ahold of him and had him killed. They killed all of our dreams along with him. We were hoping that he was the one—you know, the one who would make Israel everything God wanted her to be. But we've lost all hope. The third day is nearly over—a day he promised when we would see his kingdom in all of its glory. Is it over? Really over? Some women are trying to keep hope alive. They say his tomb is empty, that angels appeared to them. But what we want to know is, did they see Jesus? That's all that matters. If he's gone, then all is lost." Then, unbeknownst to them, the resurrected Messiah gave his travel companions a Sunday school lesson that all of us wish someone had written down (v. 27). Yet even a Bible study taught by Christ wasn't enough to convince them of his reign. They wouldn't see the kingdom of God until they broke bread.

Interestingly, Jesus intended to pass by Emmaus, traveling away from Jerusalem (where was he headed?). His companions begged him to stay with them in Emmaus. He complied since the hour was late—the third day was almost over! Then, when they reclined at table, Jesus initiated the meal, which would have been a rather unusual act since he was the guest. Nevertheless, *acting like the host*, he blessed the bread and broke it, distributing the portions. At that very moment, when they broke bread together, they remembered Jesus: "And their eyes were opened and they recognized Him; and He vanished from their sight" (v. 31). Excited by their discovery, the two disciples went straight to Jerusalem to report what they had seen and heard to the apostles: "They began to relate their experiences on the road and how He was recognized by them *in the breaking of the bread*" (v. 35). Indeed, from that time, it became the common practice of early Christians to meet together as often as they could in order to "break bread": "Day by day continuing with one mind in the temple, and breaking bread from house to house, they were taking their meals together with gladness and sincerity of heart" (Acts 2:46).

They never stopped celebrating Jesus's last supper. For every time they gathered around a table, they broke bread and remembered him.

"O, what a foretaste of glory divine." The earliest Christians called them "love feasts." We refer to them as "fellowship suppers." Yet, whatever they are known by, believers have been known to celebrate the kingdom of God with food and drink for a long time. Why? Why is it that believers have the habit of gathering around a table, devouring potluck meals, and call it *koinonia*? It's not that Christians are gluttons. It's not that fellowship meals are social affairs. Instead, there's an intangible reality

We are to keep the party going until Jesus comes back.

of our union, an overwhelming compulsion that beckons us to give our food, eat together, and share our lives at table. Something happens that can't be explained. There's a presence that is greater than the sum of our parts. We enjoy a solidarity that is defined by our common need. All of us are hungry for the mercy of God. We all need Jesus. This is why we keep his last supper. We lift our glasses in his name. We pass around bread in his memory. His vow is our hope. His sacrifice is our reminder. One day he will drink the cup with us. One day his presence will be more than a memorial. One day we will party together, forever. Until then, echoes of heaven will always be heard in good cheer and great joy whenever a table full of grateful hearts gather in his name. We will never forget.

This is what Luke would have us do. We're supposed to keep writing the story of the Acts of the Church, we are to continue celebrating the kingdom of God, we are to live as if Isaiah's dream has become reality. We are to stand before our community—our hometown crowd—and declare good news for poor sinners, liberty for prisoners, sight for blind people, healing for the brokenhearted. We are to announce the favorable year of the Lord. Anointed by his Spirit, we are to tell the whole world, "God forgives you." Jesus believed in the kingdom of God, and so do we. His mission is our calling. His life is our liturgy. His legacy is our destiny. We are to effect the reign of God on earth by his Spirit because Jesus is our salvation. For Luke, this is what it means to follow Jesus. We are to keep the party going until Jesus comes back. His last supper lasts forever.

THE GOSPEL OF JOHN

The Ideal Disciple

8

The Ideal Evangelist

Oh, how clear it is that the smallest crumb of grace in the
service of the Good is infinitely more blessed than to be the
mightiest of all outside that service.

Søren Kierkegaard, *Purity of Heart*

Mirror, mirror on the wall, who's the fairest of them all?" Every
believer who gazes into the looking glass of God's Word cannot help but ask the question: Who was the greatest disciple of Jesus?
Simon Peter? The apostle Paul? John the Beloved? Mary or Martha?
Our response betrays personal preferences. Some disciples strike us
as more appealing than the rest. We like what we see in them—their
courage, their resilience, their loyalty, their boldness inspire us. At the
same time, we also pay particular attention to their shortcomings, their
weaknesses, their failures. Although we may call them, "Saint Matthew"
or "Saint Paul," we find great comfort in knowing that they were human,
too—which is why we ask the mirror, "Who is the fairest of them all?"
Secretly, we wonder if we would have fared any better. What would it

have been like to have actually lived in the days of Jesus? Sometimes I take the quantum leap, transporting myself to New Testament times, and compare myself to the biblical disciples. I wonder, "What kind of a disciple would I be?" So, I dare to ask the question, hoping the mirror responds, "Why, *you* are the fairest of them all!" But, then again, we all know mirrors never lie.

Scripture does something to the reader. We are told that the Word of God is "living and active" (Heb. 4:12). Too often we ask only, "What does the text mean?" when we should be also asking the question, "What does the text *do*?" These are no ordinary stories. God inspired the biblical writers to tell the gospel truth in order to change people (John 20:30–31). For those who have eyes to paint mental pictures and ears to hear narrative sounds, the stories will have their desired effect. We look through the picture window of each Gospel story, transfixed by a world far removed from our own time and space. The Holy Spirit's illuminating light shines on each episode, causing literary characters to come alive right before our eyes. We can see their faces, we can hear their words. The narrator is our guide, taking us along on the journey, following the light of Jesus's path. We delight in the vision. Then suddenly, at the right moment, the spiritual light shifts behind us, and the picture window to the past becomes a mirror. Confused, we try to make out the image—it is no longer a self-righteous Pharisee or a blind beggar that we see. In an instant, the Word of God mirrors our reflection in the faces of Nicodemus or the man born blind. "That's me," we think to ourselves, and the picture is indelibly imprinted in our mind.

This, I believe, is what John was after. His Gospel compels readers to puzzle over their own discipleship as they contemplate the dedication of literary disciples. We meet all kinds of disciples in John's Gospel: secret disciples, disciples who believe because they see the "signs," disciples who believe having never seen "signs," disciples who follow Jesus for a little while, disciples who follow Jesus to the end, disciples who betray him, disciples who would die for him. Some come and go with each episode, others appear as constant companions of Jesus. The reader is left with the impression that Jesus welcomed all kinds of disciples. Due to the great diversity, John's story begs the question: of all the followers of Jesus, which ones would be considered the best examples of genuine discipleship? We read these stories because we want to know how to follow Jesus. What are the ideal qualities of discipleship? Did any disciple of Jesus truly *follow* him? Who was the greatest disciple of Jesus?

Once we've read the entire story of John's Gospel, his answer is not what we expected. It wasn't Peter, or James, or perhaps even John. In fact, none of the twelve qualifies as candidates of ideal discipleship. Despite her ideal messianic profession ("I have believed that You are the Christ, the Son of God," 11:27), Martha does not picture the perfect disciple. Even Mary's insightful act of anointing Jesus for burial *before* the cross does not make her the model of genuine discipleship. Thomas is willing to die with him (11:16), offers the superlative confession of any disciple (20:28), and yet Jesus makes it clear that he is not the favored disciple (20:29). So, who was he (or she)? Who has distinguished himself as the ideal disciple of Jesus? Come forth and identify yourself. What is your name?

According to John, we don't know their names. The ideal disciples of Jesus are anonymous; the narrator never gives their names. A woman from Samaria, a nobleman from Capernaum, a man born blind, the one whom Jesus loved—these are the true models of discipleship; they have the right stuff. They come from every walk of life: male, female, rich, poor, respected, ignored. Yet they all have one thing in common. They do what every disciple wants to do. The Samaritan woman leads her entire city to Christ. The nobleman from Capernaum believes the Word of God when others require a miraculous sign. The man born blind sees things that confound the wise. The beloved one follows Jesus *wherever he goes*. These are the heroes of John's narrative world. Their stories make every reader of John's Gospel wish that they could be just like them. All Christians, whether male or female, rich or poor, respected or ignored, want the same thing. We all want to follow Jesus. These disciples show us how.

The Woman from Samaria

This is a story about the necessities of life: food, water, and love. Food and water are the obvious themes of John 4. Jesus talked with the Samaritan woman about water around a well while the disciples were getting Samaritan food for Jesus. Yet, what hovers over the entire story is the basic human need for love. It's the kind of love that every woman thirsts for, the kind of love that every man hungers for. A love that satisfies our parched soul like a cool drink of water; a love that our bodies crave like a hot meal at noon to get us through a day's labor—this is what we want, this is what we need. Food, water, and love. For all the talk about water and food, this is a story about what we need to live. This is a story about love.

Does this sound familiar? A son of Abraham meets an unmarried woman at a well. He offers her water to drink she could not get on her own. When the woman discovers the special identity of the stranger, she rushes home to tell her people that she has met "the one." As a result of the "chance" encounter, the traveler is welcomed by the family and invited to remain in the foreign village. This is not only a synopsis of Jesus's encounter with the Samaritan woman (John 4:1–42), it is also the story of Jacob and Rachel (Gen. 29:1–20), the beloved romantic tale of "love at first sight."

Jacob met Rachel as he was heading for the north country—he left his home to escape the wrath of his brother, Esau. After a sleepless night, having dreamt of the ladder leading to heaven, Jacob traveled through the heartland of Canaan. He stopped to find refreshment at a popular well where shepherds had gathered their flocks. Impatient and parched, Jacob asked the shepherds to move the stone covering the spring-fed well so that they could water their sheep (obviously, he wanted a drink, too!). They were waiting for a shepherdess, Rachel, who was unable to move the stone on her own since "the stone on the mouth of the well was large" and it took several shepherds to move it (vv. 2–3). When Rachel and her sheep finally caught up with the others, Jacob was so overwhelmed by her beauty that he moved the rock *all by himself*. After this show of masculine bravado, "Jacob kissed Rachel, and lifted his voice and wept" (v. 11). When Jacob revealed his identity to Rachel, the marriageable virgin went straight to her father, Laban, and told him of Jacob's imminent arrival. Laban and his people went out to greet Jacob and invited him to stay. Laban announced, "Surely you are my bone and my flesh" (v. 14). Jacob stayed as a guest of Laban's house for a month.

The obvious parallel between these two stories is no mere coincidence. Like Jacob, Jesus left his "own country" (John 4:44) to travel north to Galilee. He "had to go through Samaria" (the heart of Canaan) as he sought refuge from his enemies. Tired from the journey he stopped *at the same well* and asked for water. In what may have sounded to the woman like the same, typical masculine bravado, Jesus offered her spring water better than Jacob's well. Eventually, Jesus revealed his true identity to the woman. Overwhelmed by her encounter, the woman rushed off to tell her people about the arrival of the one whom they had been "expecting." The people left the village to greet him and invited him to remain with them. They announced, "This One is indeed the Savior of the world" (v. 42). Jesus stayed with them for two days.

Noting the similarities between these two stories enables the reader of John's Gospel to appreciate his literary genius. Although Jesus's encounter with the woman at the well follows the same general story line as Jacob's meeting with Rachel, the ironic twist in the plot takes the reader by surprise, delivering nuances to an old story. Surprise! The single woman Jesus met was no virgin. Surprise! Jesus spoke to the Samaritan woman, who was caustic and practically hostile to his noble intentions. Surprise! Jesus offered water that Jacob could never give. Surprise! Jesus admitted to the woman that he was the Messiah. Surprise! The Samaritans accepted the Jewish Messiah. Surprise! In spite of her station in life, the Samaritan woman behaves more like a follower of Jesus than his own disciples. Surprise! A Samaritan woman is an ideal disciple of Jesus.

Like Jacob, Jesus finds himself at the same well of water, thirsty from his journey as he heads for the north country (vv. 5–6). It was also time for the midday meal. The narrator adds (parenthetically) that the disciples had gone to the city of Sychar to buy food (v. 8). Although this information appears to be rather insignificant to the story, the disciples' whereabouts sets up beautifully the ironic twist at the end. Then, almost on cue, the mysterious woman appears at the well; only this time she is no marriageable virgin from the north. "There came a woman of Samaria to draw water. Jesus said to her, 'Give Me a drink'" (v. 7). There is only one other place in John's Gospel where Jesus asked for a drink. Before Jesus died, he declared, "I am thirsty" (19:28). For John, the timing of Jesus's request is ironic. Throughout his ministry, Jesus claimed to be the source of everlasting water, "Let anyone who is thirsty come to Me, and let the one who believes in Me drink" (7:37c–38a). Now, on the cross, having given his all, the well has run dry. His ultimate sacrifice, surrendering his life, makes the request for water picture perfect. "After this, Jesus, knowing that all things had already been accomplished" (19:28), the well of living water exclaimed: "I am thirsty."[1] The two requests for drink, then, frame the public ministry of Jesus. He is the water of life that winds up thirsty because he has so much to give. A woman drawing water from a well will find out how thirsty he is and how desperate she must be for a drink of his water.

The Cynic

Jesus startled the Samaritan woman. She was puzzled by his request for water since Jews would not share any food or water with the unclean (4:9). For Jesus to drink from the same ladle of water used by this woman would render him unclean. This request is especially shocking since the rabbi who joined the Baptizer in calling the world to ritual purification via water baptism now asks for unclean water.[2] But this woman is about to discover that Jesus does not consider the vessel of service, that is, Samaritan ladle or Samaritan woman, unclean in and of itself—it's what's inside that matters most. Thus Jesus draws her attention away from that which defiles to that which sanctifies, the Spirit of God: "If you knew the gift of God, and who it is who says to you, 'Give

Me a drink,' you would have asked Him, and He would have given you living water" (4:10).

Water in the arid Samaritan mountains was a precious gift of God. Water was always a necessity, never a convenience. The people of Sychar, however, were especially endowed for they inherited a well of water sanctioned by Jacob. Remember, it was Rachel who came to the well, needing someone to move the rock in order to water her flock. This time the woman is able to provide the water and the man needs her help (v. 11). But, in keeping with the story, Jesus claims that he has water she is unable to get on her own. Unlike Rachel, who was overwhelmed by Jacob's show of manliness, the Samaritan woman is not impressed with Jesus's offer. She has probably heard similar boasts from men before. Think about it. What *would* a strange man passing through town want with this woman? Knowing how to take care of "this kind," the woman spares no time in challenging Jesus's manhood. Her response (vv. 11–12) sounds like the typical put-down of any woman who rejects the presumptuous advances of arrogant men. "Who do you think you are? First, you ask *me* for a drink (since I have the bucket) and then offer *me* water (when you have no bucket)." When she asks, "Where then do You get that living water?" (v. 11c), the woman confirms Jesus' suspicions. She doesn't understand. Of course, as it was suggested before, the reader understands. The narrator has already informed the reader that Jesus is the one who "gives the Spirit without measure" (3:34). The woman, trapped in the narrative time of the unfolding story, is not privy to such information. She understands neither that the living water is the Spirit of God nor that Jesus is the source of living water—but she will.

The story operates with the grand assumption that is applicable to all people: thirst. Everyone is thirsty. Of course then, the question is, how will we quench our thirst? We all have needs. We all want more from life than mere survival. God never intended for us to live like animals, barely eking out an existence. Living out animal instincts—thirst, hunger, sexual intercourse—is not what makes us human. We eat; we need more food. We drink; we thirst for more. We copulate; we lust for more. Aren't we built for more than this constant craving? Don't we long for something more than the mundane passing of time, planning for our next meal, our next drink, our next dalliance? Indeed, water from Jacob's well merely delays the inevitable: everyone who drinks will get thirsty again. Quenching implies a temporary fix, a need that persists. Jesus, on the other hand, wants to change the language game. He claimed that he could offer water that makes people never want to drink again—never need to drink again. With such water there is no more "thirst," nor more "quenching"—these are words that cannot be defined anymore. His is the kind of water that turns need into supply, a well into a river, a desert into paradise, a requirement into a reservoir. His claim is his offer. He's talking about a love divine, a spirit everlasting, a life eternal.

> Everyone who drinks of this water will thirst again; but whoever drinks of the water that I will give him shall never thirst; but the water that I will give him will become in him a well of water springing up to eternal life.
>
> John 4:13–14

Now she has heard it all. The Samaritan woman's initial attempt to silence the pretentious stranger had apparently encouraged him to claim more than he ought. Boasting oftentimes leads to more boasting. But she couldn't let this one slip by. Amazingly, many people see the Samaritan woman as a naïve simpleton who innocuously replied, "Sir, give me this water, so I will not be thirsty, nor come all the way here to draw" (v. 15). I hear biting sarcasm in her voice. Consider the source. Here is a weathered woman. She has been used by several men and left for dead, socially. Unlike Rachel, she does not come to the well with a youthful zest for life, wondering whether the mysterious man might

We eat; we need more food. We drink; we thirst for more. We copulate; we lust for more. Aren't we built for more than this constant craving?

fulfill all of her dreams. She is a cynic—a streetwise woman, hardened no doubt by life's disappointments; undesirable, she can only enjoy the company of a man who refuses to honor her in marriage. Who would have her? Without hope she is not living, she is simply surviving. Refusing to become a victim of those who wish to use her for their own advantage, she will be taken in by no one—especially a man. So, when she responded to Jesus's offer, I believe she was mocking him—as if she were saying, rolling her eyes around, "Sure, do me a favor, show me some of this living water so my life won't be so hard, and, by the way, do you have some heavenly manna that you could spare?"

The gospel is too good to be true. I think it's time we give up trying to "sell" it to needy people. When we extol the virtues of our product, unbelievers become even more leery of our pitch. They think we're after something. I don't blame them. Don't we all avoid overbearing salesmen? Aren't we all weary of over-the-top commercials that promise the world but never deliver? By watching television any viewer should think that opening a beer bottle produces an instant party, or that driving a luxury car creates serenity, or that losing weight requires no sacrifices. Everyone wants something from all of us. To withstand the onslaught, we build up our defenses. Americans are developing a fortress mentality. Identity theft, invasion of privacy, investment scams, and child abductions will not allow us to be vulnerable. We can no longer afford the luxury of trusting people. We're forced to be suspicious of everyone. Cynicism has become a way of life for us. In fact it's a matter of survival. Therefore, it shouldn't surprise disciples of Jesus that our genuine concern for the spiritual welfare of our neighbors is met by indifference, suspicion, and sarcasm. To them, our offer is laughable. Eternal life is too good to be true. Only a fool would believe such a story. Drink once and never drink again? Who's going to buy that? The world knows we have nothing to sell.

I think the woman's sarcasm makes more sense of Jesus's response, "Go, call your husband, and come here" (v. 16). He is willing to play along with her in this game of give and take. Here is a woman whose reputation precedes her. Jesus knew of her situation in life, although she callously refuses to admit her own need. He didn't get huffy with her. Rather than respond to sarcasm with sarcasm, Jesus replied tongue in cheek: "Since you so sincerely desire this living water, let's not be selfish—go and get your husband so he can have living water, too." This must have sounded like the typical line used by a man fishing for the marital status of a strange woman. The woman responds, "I have no husband," not knowing that she has fallen into his trap. She is vulnerable; her concealed need is now evident. By her coy response she tells neither the truth nor a lie. She is hiding something. What happened next took the woman by surprise. Rather than carrying the game to the next level, Jesus exclaimed, "You have correctly said, 'I have no husband'" (v. 17c). He admires her ability to reveal yet conceal, for he is the master revealer concealer. "For you have had five husbands, and the one whom you have now is not your husband; this you have said truly." (v. 18). From the woman's perspective, such a revelation would disqualify any interest on Jesus's part. Jewish law allowed a woman to remarry three times. This woman would be off limits to any law-abiding, respectable, Jewish man. Yet, in spite of the fact that Jesus knew the secret of her desperate condition, he still talked to her. He still wanted to share a drink with her. He still cared for her. She probably had never met such a man, one with only noble intentions. This was no ordinary man. "Sir, I perceive that You are a prophet" (v. 19a).

He talked to her. That more than anything bowled her over. At first, their conversation looked more like a sword fight than a dance between lovers. She took a stab at him; he cut her to the quick. Yet, he wouldn't walk away, and she couldn't stop talking. Once he discovered her horrible secret, he stuck around for another repartee. I wonder if she ever had such a meaningful conversation with any man. It must have been refreshing, especially since women never talked theology with men. They never handled the Torah. They never contributed to religious discussions. When it came to spiritual matters, women were seen and not heard. That's why this woman will make the most of it. She's always had her questions, always been told what to believe. Now she will ask this Jewish stranger a thing or two about God, about worship, about Messiah. Her thirst for truth led her to this well. Now she will get her fill. After all, she thinks she's talking to a prophet.

Time for a riddle. Not just any riddle, but a question that puzzled commoners, Jews as well as Samaritans, for centuries. Where is the true temple of God? Jews worshiped Yahweh in Herod's temple in Jerusalem; Samaritans once worshiped God in their own temple. According to Samaritan law, Yahweh gave Moses specific instructions for the ark to remain at Shechem. So, where does God live? On Mount Moriah or Mount Gerizim? The reader already knows the answer to the question. In the first part of his Gospel, John has already established where the true temple of God is found. "The Word became flesh, and dwelt among us, and we saw His glory" (John 1:14). The expression "dwelt among us" is better translated "*tabernacled* among us." Jesus is the tabernacle of God's shekinah glory. Also, when Jesus cleansed the temple, he presented himself as the true temple of God. "Destroy this temple, and in three days I will raise it up" (2:19). The keepers of the temple took his words literally, that is, that Jesus was speaking of the unclean condition of Herod's temple that would result in certain divine retribution (v. 20). But, according to the narrator, "He was speaking of the temple of His body" (v. 21). So we see the irony of the moment: a woman is face-to-face with the true temple of God and asks where it can be found.

"Woman, believe Me, an hour is coming when neither in this mountain nor in Jerusalem will you worship the Father" (4:21). The true temple of God tries to explain to the Samaritan woman that the presence of God can no longer be restricted to one terrestrial location. Before the Word of God pitched his tent among his people, the Jews could claim to have the most significant resident of all; God lived in their "holy" city, Jerusalem. Now, God incarnate is on the move. Meaning is rich here. Jesus established very clearly that the Samaritans worshiped in ignorance what the Jews worshiped in knowledge, "for salvation is from the Jews" (v. 22). The pun cleverly disguises the true identity of Jesus.

His name, *Yeshua*, means "salvation"; indeed, Yeshua comes from the Jews. Looking for their own Savior, the Samaritans were worshiping on the wrong mountain. "But an hour is coming, and *now is*, when the true worshipers will worship the Father in spirit and truth" (v. 23). The temple of God has drawn near to visit the Samaritans on their mountain. The eschatological hour has arrived: old things, past prejudices, historical differences, and ancestral distinctions have passed away; behold, everything is becoming new. "For such people [those who accept the new visitation of God] the Father seeks to be His worshipers. God is spirit, and those who worship Him must worship in spirit and truth" (vv. 23b–24). Those who have eyes to see "his glory" and ears to hear "the Word" recognize the presence of God and become true worshipers of his majesty.

Can you imagine how baffling it was to the woman to hear of worshiping God without a temple? All religions have temples. All gods need a place to live, for devotees to make their offerings. Priests are necessary guardians of the holy. Temples mark out sacred space among the profane. Deities met their followers halfway. They descended from heaven to tabernacle for a while among men, while pilgrims made their way to the temple, ascending the mountain to visit the gods. This time, according to Jesus, God is no longer willing to meet people halfway. This time God comes to us all the way. This time heaven invades all the earth. This time the glory of God's presence will be found on every mountain, every valley. This time truth has a face. The Incarnation changed everything. No more guardians of the holy. No more priests to broker the presence of God. No more sacred shrines. No more turf battles. When the temple of God became a man, every space became sacred, every person became a priest, and every heart could worship God—even an immoral, Samaritan woman. Stone and wood could no longer hold the presence of God. It took flesh and bone to show all of us what is holy. You, brother and sister in Christ, are sacred space.

At this point, Jesus had made two predictions regarding the woman: she would become a well of water though not like Jacob's well, and that she would worship God but not on this mountain. Now the woman will tell what she knows regarding the future: "I know that Messiah is coming. . . . When that One comes, He will declare all things to us" (4:25). Notice how she describes her hero. She doesn't speak of a deliverer, conqueror, or wonder-worker. She doesn't say, "When he comes, he will free us from the Romans," or "When he comes he will perform wonders and signs." Her messiah will be a prophet—one who tells the truth, one who reveals the secrets of the world, one who explains the mystery of God. So Jesus obliges, unveiling the greatest mystery of all time. Who is the Messiah of God? "I *who speak* to you am He" (v. 26).

Jesus's acknowledgment of his messiahship shocks the reader as much as it surprised the woman. Here is the only place in John's Gospel where Jesus admits that he is the Messiah. Throughout the Gospel, Jesus appears reticent to use the popular title when referring to himself. Evidently "messiah" was a dangerous word that provoked a variety of expectations that were alien to Jesus's purposes. He seemed determined to define terms on his terms. After all, how could any old, used, antiquated expression carry the full significance of the new, dynamic, and mysteri-

---

Jesus trusted her with the secret of his soul.

Now that is true love.

---

ous work of God? In light of his reluctance to speak of himself as "the Messiah," Jesus's candid reply to the woman's affirmation shouts for an explanation. Such a rare admission piques the reader's interest. Why, of all people, of all places, of all times, would Jesus tell this woman the secret of his identity? And not just any woman, but a *Samaritan* woman. And not just any Samaritan woman, but an *immoral* Samaritan woman. Jesus trusted *her* with the secret of his soul. Now *that* is true love.

The conversion of a cynic is a wonderful sight to behold. Perhaps because it doesn't happen much anymore. We live in a world of cynics: people who refuse to believe because they can't find anything or anyone believable. Everyone has an angle. No one can be trusted. That is the cruel reality, the plain truth for those who have lost hope. With his diatribe, the cynic mocks humanity's futile attempt to change the world. He delights in reminding us that heroes rarely live up to the expectations of their admirers. Crusaders eventually reveal selfish motives in their campaign for change. Power always corrupts. Notoriety drives discovery. Knowledge breeds arrogance. There is no cure for the common cold much less for what ails the world. Viruses mutate, antibodies become impotent. Death rules over life. There will always be wars and rumors of wars. History rarely teaches us anything. Personal ambition always takes precedence over the greatest good. And, in a world that cannot be saved, faith looks more like hype, and hope is the great pretender. The cynic won't let anyone be fooled by the pretense of those who say they have the answer. No man is sovereign. No woman controls her own destiny. There is no Savior. This may all sound pretty dark, but the cynic claims that he's the only honest man who has the courage to tell the truth, to unmask the hypocrisy of the human heart. It's time to wake up and smell the coffee.

"What's going on here?" Alarming revelations wake us up to the reality that what you see is not necessarily what you get. Most of us move to the steady drum of daily routines, comfortable habits, weekly schedules that lull us to sleep. We carry on without suspicions, mostly taking things as they come. Then something terrible happens. A crime has been committed. A good person has done a bad thing. Embarrassing details reveal the difference between a man and his reputation. Shocked and disappointed, the majority opinion is repeated over and over again, "I never would have suspected him of doing something like that," trying to come to terms with the unacceptable. Conspiracy theorists rush in with their complicated scenarios of sinister forces and the underworld. Alarmists jump to the conclusion of widespread abuse. The intelligentsia debate whither and whence. The naïve refuse to believe that life can really be that bad. The cynics laugh from a distance, chuckling to themselves, "We told you so." To rise above the rest, never taken in by surprise, untouched by tragic twists in the plot of life, never to be fooled by duplicity—to play the cynic—this seems to be the favorite role of most people. And I can see why, since it is easier to be cynical of life in a world filled with surprises. Why get your hopes up?

There's a famous story about Diogenes, the cynic philosopher of the fourth century BC, and his brief encounter with Alexander the Great that sounds more like the modern tale of the new American hero. It is said that Alexander, the most powerful man in the world, once approached Diogenes, who was basking in the rays of the sun. Alexander the Great made an offer, "Ask any favor you wish." Diogenes simply replied, "Get out of my sunlight." For the most part, we act the same way. The people we used to look up to are now only standing in our way. We don't believe anymore in the virtue of public service. Parents don't want their kids to grow up to be president. The church has lost touch with the real world. Preachers are passed off as a bad parody of themselves. Institutions of higher learning have turned into big business, where students are treated like consumers and educators are dismissed as bureaucrats of knowledge. Like Diogenes, we prefer to heckle those who stand over us, those who think they have real answers for real problems. We've been disappointed too many times to be taken in by these professional hucksters. Too many leaders have fallen, too many scandals have rocked our world, too many gullible people have fallen prey to the manipulation of the masses. Cynical of life, it's our job to bring them back to reality, never believe the hype, always look for the loophole, challenge the status quo, never play follow the leader, and above all else, keep our hands clean when things go wrong. Why? So when the world falls apart again, we can say we weren't surprised, we can say we are not to blame, we can shout from a distance the words we long to say, "We told you so."

Distance—that's the problem. It may be safer to live life from a distance, to draw water from a well by yourself, to keep the secrets of your soul vouchsafed in solitary confinement. But where's the joy? Where's the joy in sharing life? Sharing dreams? Sharing time? Sharing a drink

---

It may be safer to live life from a distance,

to draw water from a well by yourself,

to keep the secrets of your soul vouchsafed

in solitary confinement. But where's the joy?

---

of water? Be careful, cynic. A simple request for sharing what you have can make you care when you don't want to. That's what happens when someone invades your privacy, rattles your cage, trusts you with a secret, gets into your heart by taking the terrible risk of being vulnerable. Everyone needs to be needed. That's the lesson a certain woman from Samaria would never forget. Jesus needed her—but not like any other man she had ever known. Jesus trusted her—but not like any other disciple that followed him. He knew what he was doing. Cynics believe again when someone trusts them again.

The Sower

"At this point His disciples came" (4:27). The timing of the return of the disciples from Sychar serves the evangelist well in contrasting the discipleship of the woman and the twelve. The narrator provides a fascinating chain of events juxtaposing the faith of the enlightened woman with the ignorance of the imperceptive disciples, enabling the reader to identify the true disciple of Jesus. First, immediately after Jesus revealed his true identity to the woman, the disciples return to find Jesus talking with the Samaritan. There is a moment of silence, an awkward circumstance where no one said anything. There at Jacob's well stand the slack-jawed disciples, the awestruck woman, and Jesus—staring at each other. Without speaking, the woman leaves the company of men to return to the same city *from which the disciples came.* The narrator simultaneously provides the details of two conversations at two different locations: the report of the woman to the people of Sychar, and the exchange between Jesus and the twelve at the well (vv. 28–37). Then there is a reunion of the woman, the twelve, and Jesus at the well when certain residents of the city follow the woman to meet Jesus. The scene ends when, similar to the Jacob and Rachel story, the traveler is invited to remain in the hometown of the woman. In the end, the reader is left with the inescapable impression that an immoral woman from Samaria proved to be more of a disciple than the twelve men who followed Jesus.

When the disciples found Jesus at the well, "they were amazed that He had been speaking with a woman" (v. 27a). Body language communicated volumes without speaking: "Why do You speak *with her?*" (v. 27c). In their sense of ownership, the disciples were obviously offended by what they saw: Jesus accepting water from a stranger. Possessive of Jesus's affection, the disciples silently took issue with what appeared to be a compromising situation. *They* were the designated caretakers of the master. After all, they had made the trip to Sychar in order to secure provisions for the trip northward. What more could Jesus need? "Yet no one said, 'What do You seek?'" (v. 27b). Eventually, the disciples make an attempt to reclaim their role as the privileged twelve who attend to the needs of Jesus (v. 31). But in their haste to reclaim their "turf" (v. 33), the disciples have missed a golden opportunity to take up the far more noble cause of their calling: to disciple disciples.

Remember what Jesus prophesied regarding the woman? He promised her that if she were to drink of the living water only he could provide, then she would never thirst again, thereby becoming a wellspring of living water herself (vv. 13–14). After drinking the spiritual water that quenches thirst for life, "the woman left her waterpot" (v. 28). Here the narrator knowingly winks at the reader who recognizes the subtlest double entendre of the entire story. A less careful reader would miss the significance of her action, perhaps even attributing her behavior to oversight in haste. Those who have eyes to see and ears to hear understand. She came, a daughter of Samaria, to fetch a jar of water from Jacob's well. She left the well of Jesus a daughter of heaven, without her water pot because those who drink of his living water never thirst again.

The disciples may have dismissed the hasty exit of the woman as evidence of her deference to them since she was out of place in the present company. She left her waterpot, the twelve, and Jesus at the well "and went into the city" (v. 28b). She returned to the city, as any disciple would, to become what Jesus predicted: a wellspring of living water for others to receive eternal life (v. 14). *She* told the people of Sychar, "Come, see a man who told me all the things that I have done; this is not the Christ, is it?" (v. 29). She reported what she witnessed: the stranger was a prophet, for he told the truth. Then she wondered out loud for her Samaritan neighbors, "Could this Jewish man be *our* Messiah?" Because of her faithful testimony—not claiming too much *yet not remaining silent*—the Samaritan people came out to the same well to meet Jesus. We should not be surprised by her actions. Telling other people about Jesus is what disciples do. Her motivation? She was in love. "Come meet the man I've been waiting for my whole life."

I've heard (and even delivered) every sermon imaginable to motivate disciples to share their faith. Sermons that are designed to make listeners feel guilty about the lost spending an eternity in hell; sermons delivered at church growth conferences that employ the modern success ethic—bigger is better; sermons that use the spirit of competition to divide the dedicated from the underachievers; and the worst of them all, sermons delivered by domineering pitchmen intending to drive doubt into the minds of the bashful who never measure up to the model of overbearing salesmen. These sermons work for a while, but they never seemed to stick with me. I kept coming back to the primary motivation that compels us to share our faith and hope: love. We can't help but talk about the people we love.

When I hear a young girl rattle on and on about her soul mate, I listen patiently to her over-the-top accolades about the boy, knowing she's in love. When I hear a little boy brag about his daddy as if he were Superman reincarnated, I smile with admiration and think about the love of my son and daughters. When I'm caught by an irrepressible grandparent with wallet-sized pictures and stories about incidental happenings of toddlers, I settle in for a long conversation, knowing that a grandchild is the finest gift a son or daughter can give his or her parents. This is love. This is why we talk incessantly about our Savior, our best friend, the lover of our souls. We can't help it. We'll talk to anyone who'll listen. Love does that to a person. I've never known anyone who loves me more than Jesus. He came to my well of loneliness. His presence invaded my heart like an arrow. He reminded me of everything I ever did. He trusted me with the secret of his mercy. He loves me every day without fail. I couldn't live without him. Like the rest of us, I need him like bread and water.

"Meanwhile the disciples were urging Him, saying 'Rabbi, eat'" (v. 31). The narrator reveals the ironic timing of these events. "Meanwhile," that is, at the very time the woman was acting like a disciple of Jesus, bringing the citizens of Sychar to him, the twelve were trying to get Jesus to take what *they* had brought from Sychar. To me, the twelve disciples come off looking like the keystone cops. As they rush to take care of the "emergency," the disciples tumble out of the city, bumping into one another as they try to force-feed Jesus. This is where my imagination may take me too far. Reading between the lines, I see the twelve disciples taking upon themselves a distasteful mission: to go to an unclean Samaritan village and buy unclean Samaritan food. This is where my imagination can get the best of me. But I think I can hear one of the Sons of Thunder say, "Okay, gentlemen, this is the plan. Let's go in, find a market, buy food, don't talk, and get out of there as soon as we can. And no matter what, *don't touch anything!*" Can you see their faces as they successfully return to the well with food (albeit Samaritan food), narrowly avoiding defilement, to find Jesus talking with an immoral Samaritan woman? Then, to make matters worse, after all they risked to get the food, Jesus says that he's not hungry. That is what Jesus's response must have sounded like to the twelve (v. 33), but that is not what he said. Jesus, seeing the city of people approaching, led by the woman, said, "I have food to eat that you do not know about" (v. 32). Obviously they were ignorant of such food.

Jesus tried to explain how he found spiritual food offered by a Samaritan woman more desirable than Samaritan victuals offered by the twelve. "My food is to do the will of Him who sent Me and to accomplish His work" (v. 34). Of course, the reader knows what Jesus is talking about. The mission of the Word, outlined in John's prologue, was to enable those who believed in "his name" to become children of God, regardless of race or religion (i.e., "of blood nor of the will of the flesh nor of the will of man"), by the will of God (1:13). And, as disciples of Jesus, they shared in his commission. *They* should have been the ones to announce to the people of Samaria that God's temple had come to their mountain. Instead, they visited Sychar and only brought back food; ideal disciples bring others to Jesus. Ironically, it was the Samaritan woman who used the familiar invitation of Jesus, "Come, and you will see" (1:39; 4:29); it was the Samaritan woman who led the people to Jesus; it was the Samaritan woman who provided true nourishment for Jesus's earthly journey; it was the Samaritan woman who proved to be the ideal disciple of Jesus.

How many disciples, bent on serving Jesus, miss the higher purpose for which they have been called? This picture of the twelve, stumbling over each other as they compete for Jesus's affection, reminds me of American Christianity. Like these twelve disciples, we find ourselves forced to operate a ministry within a world of unclean people. Aliens in a strange land, we work, buy food, live, and raise our families while trying to avoid contact with the ungodly. In our noble service to Jesus, we care for the body of Christ, ensuring that every need is met, while we ignore the ones who need him most. We devote most of our energies to bringing nourishment to the body of Christ—church work—to the exclusion of carrying out the ministry of Jesus among unbelievers—kingdom work. The church was never meant to be an end unto itself. Jesus established the church *to do* the work of the kingdom. Jesus called disciples to make disciples. When all we can think about is avoiding contact with an unclean world, Jesus looks for an ideal disciple who will carry out his mission on earth. We see a moral wasteland; Jesus sees a field ready for harvesting.

The scene of Samaritans ascending the mountain to see him inspired Jesus to teach the disciples a lesson using a "living parable." Apparently, the large number of people flooding the mountainside resembled wheat fields, ripe for harvest, blowing in the wind. Seizing the moment, Jesus shows the twelve in "living color" the divine purpose of his mission. Moving from the metaphor of eating and drinking, Jesus invokes an aphorism of farmers: "Yet four months, and then comes the harvest" (v. 35). Due to the interim, such is the natural order of things: "one sows and another reaps" (v. 37). But God is doing a new thing. In the economy of divine labor, the eschatological hour has brought about the collapse of time. Jesus marvels over the expedience of heavenly farming. Pointing to the fields populated with curious Samaritans, Jesus chides the disciples: "Behold, I say to you, lift up your eyes, and look on the fields, that they are white for harvest" (v. 35). The Sower had just planted the seed of the gospel in the fertile soil of a new disciple, and in no time at all it yields a crop "thirty, sixty, and a hundredfold" (Mark 4:20). Thus sower becomes reaper, "gathering fruit for life eternal" (John 4:36). Consequently, seeing the fruit of his labor, Jesus is able to rejoice in the work of sowing and reaping all at once (v. 36b). While basking in the delight of his profitable exchange with the Samaritan woman, even Jesus was surprised by the immediate, vast yield of his singular effort. It rarely happens that way, even for Jesus. Oftentimes, harvesting the fruit of gospel sowing takes time—days, months, even years. There are times, however, when the eschatological hour enables the sower to reap heavenly harvest.

Jesus, caught up in one of those rare moments of instant spiritual gratification, returns to the reality of his imperceptive disciples whose spiritual development takes time. It must have been quite a scene. There Jesus stands with the twelve looking down on the multitude of Samaritans, led by the woman, scurrying up the mountain. They are coming to see Jesus. These are the same people the disciples visited on their mission. Up to this point, Jesus had spent many days investing in these twelve men, preparing them to carry on with his mission—to see people as he sees them, to understand life as he understands it, to pursue the will of God as he has determined it. In the next few years, the disciples would face many tests, revealing the depth of their commitment to Jesus and his cause. They failed this one miserably. "Look at all these people," Jesus was saying. "They are coming to see me, and it wasn't by your invitation. See who leads them. I have been preparing you to do what she has already perfected. I sent twelve disciples into Sychar on a mission and another fulfills it. Come, let's help her harvest the field of your obligation."

Jesus sent his disciples into Sychar to buy food for which they had not labored. As disciples of Jesus, however, that was not their primary mission. They should always be prepared to reap the harvest of the gospel seed, to work fields they have not sown. As the villagers approach them, Jesus informs the twelve that, in spite of their oversight, they will fall in line and perform their responsibilities as reapers of the Samaritan harvest. "Others have labored and you have entered into their labor" (v. 38b). "For in this case the saying is true, 'One sows and another reaps'" (v. 37); Jesus sows the seed, the woman labors in the field, and the disciples join her in reaping the harvest. All reapers in the gospel field are part of a collaborative effort. We're all in this together. The gospel seed may be planted in a Catholic school, but the harvest may not come until an old-time Pentecostal "camp" meeting. When it comes to farming the gospel, usually one sows and another reaps. Nevertheless, all are disciples of Jesus—everyone joins in the labor. Jews and Samaritans, Presbyterians and Baptists, Catholics and Pentecostals, Asians and Arabs, the unity of our purpose is found in the uniqueness of our labor: we are here to bring all people to Christ, just like a Samaritan woman.

Lest the reader should forget in the midst of the euphoric celebration of the harvest, it all started with her—the immoral, unacceptable, forgettable Samaritan woman. The narrator is quick to remind his readers that "from that city many of the Samaritans believed in Him" because of her (v. 39a). Why did they believe *her* of all people? Because she proved to be the ideal evangelist. She delivered faithfully the word of the Prophet; it was "because of the word of the woman who testified" (v. 39b). What was her testimony? What would convince Samaritans that this Jewish stranger was "the coming one"? That she had witnessed the marvelous "signs" of Jesus's ministry—the salient proof of Jesus's identity according to John? That she had seen him cleanse the Jewish temple, declaring himself the true tabernacle of God? None of these. She simply reported what she knew: he was a prophet who "told me all the things that I have done" (v. 39c). A woman with a checkered past had much to report. Her initial contact with the villagers must have stirred up little interest. After all, how excited could the locals be over a report from this woman about her encounter with a strange man? Yet her testimony must have been plausible enough to convince the people to go out and greet Jesus. Because of *her* word, the Samaritans extended the offer of honorable hospitality to the traveler, and the true temple of God remained on their mountain (v. 40).

Ideally, the true disciple of Jesus not only brings the word to the people but also brings the people to the Word. The narrator emphasizes "many more believed because of *His word*" (v. 41). The testimony of the woman is now eclipsed by the word of the Prophet: "It is no longer because of what you said that we believe, for we have heard for ourselves" (v. 42b). The ultimate revelation of God comes from the logos of God—disciples testify to what they have seen and heard. Her actions replicate those of the exemplary disciple's witness, which has already been established in John's Gospel. The Baptizer, the premier witness, appears at the beginning of the Gospel story as the model of self-deprecation. Servants never surpass their masters. The prologue sounds the early warning, "There came a man sent from God, whose name was John. He came as a witness, to testify about the Light, so that all might believe through him. He was not the Light, but he came to testify about the Light" (1:6–8). In spite of the success of his proclamation, the Baptizer remained true to his purpose. "This is the testimony of John" (1:19): he was (1) a messenger (v. 23), (2) a servant (v. 27), (3) a baptizer (vv. 30–31), and (4) an eyewitness (vv. 32–34). After faithfully proclaiming the word of God, he directed his disciples to listen to the Word of God (vv. 35–39). Even when some followers refused to transfer their allegiances to Jesus, the Baptizer persisted in promoting the superiority of Christ while declaring

> *Ideally, the true disciple of Jesus*
> *not only brings the word to the people*
> *but also brings the people to the Word.*

his own inadequacies (3:27–29). The epitaph to his legacy defines the heart's desire of every disciple: "He must increase, but I must decrease" (3:30). Therefore, as the ideal disciple of Jesus, the Samaritan woman, like the Baptizer, fades from view as new disciples are brought to the feet of Jesus.

The unanimous testimony of the Samaritan people rings true for John's Gospel story. They declared, "We have heard for ourselves and know that this One is indeed the Savior of the world" (4:42c). It is compelling, in light of the episode at Sychar, for Samaritans to declare that Jesus ("savior") is "Yeshua of the world." The world of God's saving activity includes even the outsiders. But, again, this comes as no surprise to the reader. For the prologue had already provided the literary road map for this divine journey. "He came to His own, and those who were His own did not receive Him. But as many as received Him, to them He gave the right to become children of God, even to those who believe in His name" (1:11–12). The Samaritans received the Jewish stranger as the Prophet of God, and they believed in the truth of his name, Jesus. Thus they could declare with confidence the message which has become the banner of all children of God: "We know that this is truly the Savior of the world." Amazingly, it all started with a woman from Samaria, who was looking for water for the day and found water for life. This common woman, who so quickly was thrust into the spotlight of John's narrative world, emerges as the model of true discipleship and then disappears into the crowd of joyful worshipers. Ironically, her legacy proves immortal, yet she remains an anonymous child of God. An ideal disciple of Jesus, and we don't even know her name.

9

The Ideal Believer

Let us then consider it certain and firmly established that the soul can do without anything except the Word of God and that where the Word of God is missing there is no help at all for the soul.

Martin Luther, *The Freedom of a Christian*

Words are powerful things. Authors use them to create literary worlds for their readers. Politicians use them to convince voters of the world they hope to create. God used them to create the world. "In the beginning was the Word, and the Word was with God, and the Word was God. . . . All things came into being through Him" (John 1:1, 3). We should never underestimate the power of the word. Oftentimes, believers come to God looking for "signs and wonders," expecting a supernatural solution to unusual problems. In their distress as they search for hope, answers, and comfort, all they find are words. Yet, somehow, when God speaks, words are enough. His Word heals, assures, and inspires. Believ-

199

ers count on his Word. After all, it is faith that separates a believer from an unbeliever. Taking God at his Word is what sets us apart from the crowd. That's what the nobleman from Capernaum found out.

Jesus left Samaria for Galilee; a nobleman left Capernaum for Cana. Their paths crossed, and the result of their brief encounter provided a lesson of true faith for the church, canonized for the ages. Like the other ideal disciples in John's narrative world, the nobleman from Capernaum appears as a nameless character. We know several things about him, yet he remains an enigma. The narrator gives the reader only enough information to make sense of the story. As informed readers, we can see the clothes he was wearing—the typical dress of royal officials.

> *Those who read the Gospel*
> *do not see "signs and wonders."*
> *Instead, we are left to believe words.*

We recognize the proper speech that marks an educated man of high standing. We empathize with the parent who makes an urgent request on behalf of his son. We see him, but we can't quite make out his face. The anonymity of the solitary figure guarantees the reflective purpose of the mirror image: John wants his readers to see their face on this character. Since all disciples aspire to live as true believers, and this unnamed character from Capernaum exemplifies true faith (he is an ideal disciple), after reading the story of the healing of the nobleman's son, the desired literary effect causes the believer to reply, "That could be me." For the reader knows, like the nobleman, what it means to be among those who "did not see, and yet believed" (John 20:29). Those who read the Gospel do not see "signs and wonders." Instead, we are left to believe words.

"Can anything good come out of Nazareth?"

Although Jesus avoided the title "messiah," he did not hesitate to speak of himself as a "prophet." In fact, Jesus expected honorable treatment as a prophet of God. When the Samaritans provided the honorable acts of hospitality for Jesus, they were merely responding in kind to the honorable presence of their divine guest. In contrast, as the prophet heads for Galilee (John 4:43), Jesus anticipates that he will not receive the same recognition among his own countrymen. "For Jesus Himself testified that a prophet has no honor in his own country" (v. 44). Yet, when Jesus arrived in Galilee, the narrator reports that the villagers welcomed him (v. 45). Was Jesus wrong in his pre-judgment of the Galileans? Not at all. Notice how the narrator characterizes the Galilean reception. They welcomed Jesus not as a prophet but as a wonder-worker, "having seen all the things that He did in Jerusalem at the feast; for they themselves also went to the feast" (v. 45b).

Although John did not record them, Jesus performed many other "signs" in Jerusalem during his Passover visit (2:23). Even though his miracles impressed the Galilean pilgrims in Jerusalem, Jesus was not impressed with their response to his ministry. Evidently, some of the sign-seekers tried to coax Jesus into submitting to mass appeal. "But Jesus, on His part, was not entrusting Himself to them, for He knew all men" (2:24). Later attempts made by miracle-mongers to get Jesus to conform to their own expectations failed as well (6:15, 25–26). The

> *The Galileans were enamored with Jesus the Magician. . . . But according to John's Gospel, miracles were intended to evoke faith not admiration.*

Galileans were enamored with Jesus the Magician. The awesome display of his power created a circus environment where thrill-seekers sought to satisfy their curiosity. But according to John's Gospel, miracles were intended to evoke faith not admiration. For some, the blinding splendor of the miracles of Jesus was evidence of his divine power; for those who had eyes to see, the miracles of Jesus were marvelous "signs" of his divine person. The failure of the Galilean crowd to see the difference between the two explains why they were unable to read the significance of the first "sign" performed in their own backyard.

It is no mere coincidence that the first two "signs" were performed by Jesus in Cana of Galilee. John makes every attempt to show the reader how the first two miracles are correlative. Initially, the narrator is quick to remind the reader that Jesus had returned to Cana, the very place where he changed the water into wine (4:46). Then, as the story unfolds, the reader notices telling similarities between the two signs. For example, both miracles are performed in response to requests Jesus seems to ignore (2:3; 4:47). Like the first sign, the crowd never "sees" the miracle of healing; it is performed for the benefit of those who come to "believe" because they see the "sign" (2:11; 4:53). Finally, both miracles occur due to the spoken word of Jesus. At the end of the story, the narrator includes a reminder that this was the "second sign" Jesus gave to the Galileans (4:54). In all of this, John wants his readers to catch what the Galileans missed. The significance of the first sign explicates the second. Only those who comprehended the meaning of the first sign could understand the significance of the second. So, what is the "*sign*ificance" of the first sign?

When Jesus made the water wine, he was not kowtowing to the demands of his mother, nor was he making some ostentatious display of his mighty power to impress the locals by using extraordinary measures to solve a minor problem. This was no "magic trick." Jesus performed this miracle—the first sign—to initiate his messianic ministry, signaling the arrival of a new order. The water that he used was placed there for ceremonial purification, kept in waterpots outside the house (2:6). Many Jews followed the custom of the Pharisees, who took upon themselves the purity code of the Levites who served Yahweh in the temple. The priests were required by the Torah to wash themselves before they could perform many of their Levitical responsibilities. The Pharisees used the Levitical holiness code as a means of extending the purity of Israel beyond Jerusalem. They engaged in ceremonial washings, and encouraged others to follow their example, in order to maintain the holiness of all of God's people. Therefore, just as the priests were required to wash before eating, so also the Pharisees believed that all Israel should clean their hands, utensils, and uncooked foods before eating (Mark 7:3–4). Throughout the Hebrew Scriptures, especially Leviticus, holiness is defined in terms of washings, cleansings, and purification. Those who came in contact with that which was defined by God's law as "unclean" were required to wash themselves, removing their defiled status. Thus, the Pharisees believed that one could maintain holiness by remaining pure through ceremonial washings. For the most part, these washings were not for hygienic purposes; purification pots contained stale, stagnant, bacteria-infested water. Rather, the ritual washings confirmed the conviction that internal holiness depended upon external purification.

Jesus was out to change all of that. With the advent of his messiahship, Jesus communicated in dramatic form that God was doing a new thing. The old traditions, the expected order, the established ways were about to be eclipsed by a new era. For those who would partake of the gift of God (John 3:10, 14; 7:38), the ineffective purifying quality of the stagnant water would be replaced with that which cleanses from within: wine. Wine was used to purify water as well as combat dysentery. By making the water wine, Jesus signaled the dawn of a new age of divine purification that would produce spiritual holiness. To paraphrase Paul, "What the Pharisees could not do, weak as they were in their attempts to wash away fleshly impurity, God did by sending his Spirit in the likeness of purification, washing away all uncleanness."[1] Only those who had eyes to see the "sign" recognized the true identity of Jesus, the patron of spiritual wine. Pharisees, like Nicodemus, could not make sense of the miracle nor his teaching regarding the Spirit (3:9). From the outset, the religious establishment was challenged by the unfamiliar works and words of Jesus. Jesus was a discomforting presence in the company of those who had grown accustomed to the "usual" ways God works.

Now we are in a better position to make sense of the second sign (4:46–54). By this time, Jesus has a reputation that precedes him. News of his homecoming spread fast, reaching as far as Capernaum. The royal official, having heard of Jesus's return to Galilee, sets off for Cana, which was nearly a day's journey away. Evidently, the nobleman's son was very sick with fever, at the point of death (4:49, 52). The narrator reports that the royal official begged Jesus, asking him "to come down and heal his son" (v. 47). Jesus seems offended by the distressed father's request and counters with the rebuke, "Unless you people see signs and wonders, you simply will not believe" (v. 48). Ignoring the remark, the persistent father is heard pleading with the miracle man: "Sir, come down before my child dies" (v. 49). Why would Jesus respond with such harshness to a situation that would normally evoke compassion? How could one who was known as the friend of the oppressed appear so calloused and cold-hearted? Perhaps the answer to the riddle is found in the way the nobleman made his request. Notice, for instance, the emphasis of the narrator's paraphrase of the first request and the nobleman's words of the second request. Both times Jesus is implored to "come down" to the nobleman's house in Capernaum. Obviously, the royal official wanted Jesus to travel with him back to his home in Capernaum. He expected Jesus to employ the familiar, rabbinical methods of healing. When the nobleman begged Jesus to "come down" to Capernaum, he was simply asking him to do what other rabbis do.

Jesus was not the first rabbi known to have performed acts of healing. The Talmud records the healing activity of other holy men who were members of the rabbinical community. Although their miracles were not as plentiful or dramatic as the works of Jesus, these rabbis employed healing methods that were commonly used by miracle-working sages, for instance, the laying on of hands, washing in certain pools of water, and so on (see Mark 5:23; John 5:2–4). One of the more common methods of healing the blind, for example, was to rub human saliva in the eyes of the blind while offering a prayer to God for the gift of sight. Opening the eyes of the blinded, exorcizing the demon-possessed, and healing the diseased were all part of the religious tradition of the Jewish people (John 9:32; Matt. 12:27; Luke 4:27). Therefore, when the nobleman left Capernaum to fetch the miracle man in Cana, he expected Jesus to "come down" with him to his house and lay hands on his son in order to heal him. That was the intent of his request, which Jesus understood completely.

"Unless you people *see* signs and wonders, you simply will not believe" (John 4:48). There is another reason why Jesus responded to the royal official's request with such a sharp rebuke. Jesus was not merely addressing the nobleman, for the pronoun "you" is in the plural form. A better translation might be, "Unless *you people* see signs and wonders, you simply will not believe."[2] The stinging words of Jesus's rebuke seemed to be directed more against the Galileans than the nobleman. Apparently, Jesus saw the father's request as an accurate characterization of the shallow, imperceptive Galileans. Everyone at Cana understood the implications of the royal official's request. Because of the man's crisis, the crowd would give audience to another miracle. These Galilean sign-seekers, who would hound Jesus's trail for free food and a sideshow (6:24–26), stood ready to go to Capernaum. Much to their chagrin, Jesus did not oblige them. The same Galilean crowd that welcomed Jesus the Miraculous must have been sorely disappointed with Jesus the Prophet. For all that he did, in response to the desperate request of the nobleman, was to speak the words, "Go; your son lives" (4:50). No miracle, no sign, just words. That's what prophets do; they speak the very words of God.

It is no wonder, then, that Jesus knew (as he prophesied) that he would not be honored among the Galileans as a prophet. "Unless *you people see* signs and wonders, you will not believe." The Galileans were looking for Jesus to conform to their expectations. They had witnessed the miracle of the first sign in Cana; they saw him perform miracles when he visited Jerusalem (4:45). Yet they did not have eyes to see the "signs." When Jesus changed the water into wine, God was announcing to the world that old things were passing away and everything was becoming new. The people of Cana of Galilee obviously did not understand the sign. For when they welcomed Jesus back home, they were looking for another obligatory demonstration of the stupendous power of God. Jesus, on the other hand, was out to show them something new—believing is seeing. When it comes to following Jesus, sometimes it takes eyes of faith to see the work of God. For those who demand to see are blind to the suffering of the one who needs the miracle.

We live in a visual world. Magazine ads, billboard signs, television commercials, Internet cookies—images invade our world with promises of what you see is what you want. Music will no longer do, we must have videos to create musicians. Moving pictures take mental images born out of great novels to the masses in order to entertain those who would rather see than imagine. Camcorders chronicle our children's lives for those who live life through the viewfinder—recording for the future but missing the moment. The mystery of the human body is stripped bare as surgeries are performed for cable viewers. Violence entertains, sex sells, and few will admit the contradiction in "Reality TV." Peering and leering we exploit the sanctity of private lives in a world gone public. Misery becomes a spectacle. The innocence of intimacy is lost in the gaze of onlookers who demand to see.

I was lost in the media storm that blew into Jonesboro, Arkansas, during the last week of March 1998. Two boys shot twenty people, killing five persons—four girls and a teacher. Even though I did not know the victims or their families before March 24, their names and faces are etched in my memory. It still hurts to think about the pain they endured before a world trying to make sense of the inexplicable. A little community of fifty thousand residents, Jonesboro was overwhelmed by the hoards of reporters and their entourage who descended upon the scene with their equipment, looking for their own angle to the story that shocked the world. As the senior pastor of a Baptist church with a large membership, I was summoned to the media trucks for interviews. The helicopters flying in additional equipment and personnel made Westside School's parking lot look like a space age RV park—huge cables crisscrossed the pavement, large satellites donned the massive trucks that whined and whirled with strange sounds, strangers took command of their domain, claiming spots for their cameras. While many ministers, counselors, and emergency personnel met with the school's teachers and administrative staff to develop a plan of action to help the students work through the trauma of seeing their classmates and teachers hurt during a "false alarm" safety drill, the media were kept at bay outside. After one of those meetings, one of the news reporters asked me, "What's going on in there?" When I refused to discuss the details, the cameraman blurted out in frustration, "Why won't anyone talk with us? Have they told you not to talk to us?" I recall saying something like, "Look. All we can think about right now is how we can help each other get through this. I'm sorry if it looks like we're ignoring you. This is a very difficult time. Most of us don't feel like talking. We don't know what to say." Then I noticed a look of empathy; the eyes of the reporter told me she understood. She looked like she was hurting, too. She said, "We're sorry," and walked away.

By the end of the week, I had received over 150 requests for interviews. I agreed to six. The telephone at home rang all hours of the night: calls from London, Paris, Hamburg, Sydney, Tokyo. When my wife tried to explain to one reporter from Germany why I refused to talk, he offered his rebuttal: "But the whole world wants to know." At first, the circus environment created by the media was ashamedly exciting. The community was buzzing with nervous energy, watching television reports about themselves. Homefolk became national personalities for a week. Everyone was talking about Jonesboro. The notoriety, however, quickly became a heavy burden. Family members of the victims were thrust into public view trying to cope with private anguish. Jonesboro was labeled by outsiders as a gun-toting, violence-mongering, country town. Cameras seemed to gather like vultures at the wrong places, ogling the wounded at the cemeteries, jails, and hospitals. We couldn't wait until our unwanted guests left town.

I understand that reporters are meeting a need. News makes news because people want to know. What bothers me is not the need to know, but the need to see. Why do we want to see? Why do we crave sensational stories with graphic video? The voyeurism of our culture breeds newscasts that cannot report without sights and sounds. It seems that as long as the public demand to see human suffering, we will wade in a never ending stream of violent images that reduce grief to handy footage for future news stories. Cameras do not have human souls. Their eyes record our pain without emotion. Sadly, humanity's animal instincts drive our desires to watch the misery of others—John called it "the lust of the eyes." We've become cannibals of human despair.

Every time the Jonesboro footage is replayed, they use the same scene: the bloodstained sidewalk where moms and dads lost their little girls and a husband and son lost a wife and mother. It makes me angry every time I see it. I think about the parents who have to endure the indignity of exploitation. What if it were the crime scene of your child's death, played and replayed, over and over again? My parents taught me it was rude to stare at someone else's pain. Shouldn't we collectively turn our heads from the horrible scenes of death and murder we see on television? Remember the next time you casually take in pictures of bloody crime scenes, or even worse, video coverage of corpses strewn out on the pavement like rag dolls thrown down in absentminded ambivalence—a mother still weeps for her baby, a father still cries for his son. Those in the business of gathering news may claim, "Seeing is believing." I can't watch anymore.

Crowds will form around a faith healer. This is inevitable. What seems to have irritated Jesus was the demand to see. Oftentimes, the Gospels record his preference to withdraw from the crowds when ministering to the needy. He never seemed to put on a show for the crowds at the expense of human misery. Even in the more fantastic miracles recorded in John's Gospel, feeding five thousand and raising Lazarus from the dead, Jesus did not play on the crowd's emotion for support of his purposes. Instead, he shied away from the mob's hankering for the sensational. Perhaps what was so repulsive to him has become commonplace today. The exploitation of the desperate makes good tent theater for ministerial showmen who claim to extend the healing hand of Jesus. It's a pitiful sight: common cripples are used as sideshows for faith healers who play to the pleasure of a gawking crowd. Where is the dignity? Where is the mercy? Where is the humility? God heals bodies and broken hearts, no

Heaven will be filled with big surprises—
Jesus warned his listeners about that over
and over again. The biggest of them all will
be finding out how many miracles God never
performed, despite what the crowds may claim.

doubt. I'm convinced that most of the miracles he chooses to perform today cannot be merchandized by the power brokers of faith since they come in the privacy of a moment of desperation known only to those who need him most. Heaven will be filled with big surprises—Jesus warned his listeners about that over and over again. The biggest of them all will be finding out how many miracles God *never* performed, despite what the crowds may claim. Those he performed for an audience of one, on the other hand, will take an eternity to reveal—we'll all have stories to tell, even a nobleman from Capernaum.

A Nobleman from Capernaum

Exhausting every possibility for his son's recovery, the nobleman would be forced to watch his son die. Desperate times call for desperate measures. The father's trip to Cana is reminiscent of the lengths people will go to when their child's welfare is at stake. I'm sure it wasn't a comforting thought for this dignified resident of Capernaum to be forced to rely upon a homeless peasant from Nazareth to save his son from death. Jesus was his last hope. The crushing weight of his own vulnerability, as his son's life hung in the balance, must have made his journey to Cana seem longer than a day. As he approached the little village, a million thoughts probably ran through his mind. "What will I do if he has left Cana? How will I find him? If I do, will I be able to convince him to travel all the way to Capernaum to heal my son? What if he refuses to help me? Should I offer him money for his trouble? What if this doesn't work? Oh God, help me."

When the nobleman found Jesus among the crowd in Cana, he begged the Nazarene to help him. Jesus's reply takes the reader of the story by surprise. Likewise, it must have shocked and stunned those who heard it. His apparent indifference to the plight of the nobleman did not discourage the traveler from insisting, "Sir, come down before my child dies" (4:49). These are the only words spoken by the royal official in the story. Likewise, the only time Jesus addressed the nobleman was with the words, "Go; your son lives" (v. 50). This brief exchange between two strangers not only saved the life of a boy, but also changed the life of a man, forever.

Consider how far the royal official came to get Jesus and bring him back home. His frantic search for the wonder worker brings him to a face-to-face encounter with Jesus that certainly would have left anyone frustrated and confused. Put yourself in his sandals. After traveling nearly a day's journey, you hear Jesus respond to your initial request with some chiding remark about people demanding to see "signs and wonders." Then, as you persist, he turns to you and says, "Go home; everything is all right." That's it? This is all that I get? After coming all this way, he only has time to patronize me with promises? Is traveling to Capernaum too much to ask? Jesus, the mighty miracle worker, merely responds to my crisis, my desperation, my disaster, with words? But that is *not* how the nobleman responded. "The man believed the word that Jesus spoke to him and started off" (v. 50).

No rabbi had ever healed anyone by proxy.[3] How hard was it for the nobleman to turn around and start his trip back home without Jesus? He travels all that way to Cana, hears the word of the prophet, then turns and heads back home, taking nothing with him except what he carries in his heart. This is not what he expected; he did not get what he came for. He came for a miracle; he leaves with a promise. What is he going to say when he gets home? What will his wife say? As the father took to the road, he "believed the word that Jesus spoke to him" (v. 50), trusting in the effectiveness of the prophet's word. While others looked for "signs and wonders," this man was satisfied with the Word of God. This is what distinguished the nobleman as an ideal disciple. He, unlike the Galileans, was willing to take Jesus at his word. He is a true believer who finds faith on the road of life. Simply put, he trusted Jesus. This is what is required of every ideal disciple; it takes ears to hear before eyes can see.

Sometimes we come to God in the midst of our crisis, desperately seeking a sign of God's care for our lives. We come to him with certain expectations, believing that he will answer our request according to our own desires. Carefully crafted prayers are offered to God knowing that he will respond to our need as precisely as we have petitioned him. We've become accustomed to God working in a particular way; we're comfortable with the acceptable arrangement of praying according to our own experience of divine care. We pray, "Please, Lord, let the test be negative," or, "Father, I can't lose this job." Then, when God fails to perform the sign, we question his benevolent care. Our faith falters when we do not see the miracle of God's faithfulness. We beg for a sign, and God speaks the word, "I will never leave you nor forsake you." We cry out for a miracle, and are left with a promise, "I will always be with you, even when your world is falling apart." I see the reflection of my face in the frantic, tired eyes of a father who can do nothing else but beg for the life of his son. My ears have heard those words that cause the heart of a man to fall in his chest, heaving from exhaustion in the panic of a crisis too hard to bear. I have begged God to answer my prayers according to my expectations, only to hear heaven respond with words to be believed: "Everything will be all right." No, Jesus, you must understand. You must *come down* to my house. And the prophet simply says, "Go your way, your son will live."

"The man believed the word that Jesus spoke to him and started off" (v. 50). As the story unfolds, it becomes apparent that the nobleman did not receive word of the welfare of his son until the day after his encounter with Jesus (v. 52). Since Capernaum was more than a half-day's journey, the royal official was forced to spend the night on the road, alone with his thoughts. What a lonely, sleepless night it must have been. How many times did he run the day's events over and over in his mind? Did he really come all that way only to hear Jesus say a few words? Did he feel like a fool? To most people his effort must have looked like a wasted trip. The next day, "as he was going down," that is, moving from the high country of Cana to the lowlands of Galilee, "his slaves met him, saying that his son was living" (v. 51). The nobleman's first inclination was to ask when his son began to recover (v. 52). His question, of course, facilitates the unfolding drama, showing how the "sign" was fulfilled. For when the narrator documents the father's realization that his son began to improve the very hour Jesus spoke the word (v. 53), the reader is enabled to connect word and deed.

On the other hand, perhaps there is more to the father's question than its intended literary purpose. Asking the time of his son's recovery may reveal uncertainty on the father's part as to whether Jesus had anything to do with the good news. After all, Jesus's words "your son will live" could be taken as the carefree blessing of a well-wisher—something like, "Hope everything turns out all right." So much time had expired since he left his son. It was conceivable that the boy began to improve soon after he left for Cana. Maybe the nobleman's question reveals some lingering doubt regarding the efficacy of the prophet's words. But then again, the father's concern to nail down the time of his son's recovery may be the manifestation of a natural curiosity shared by all of us. Mysterious beginnings incite investigation. Besides, the nobleman had already proven that he believed the promise of Jesus. It doesn't necessarily mean that the royal official faltered in his faith when he wanted to know if the prophet's prediction came true. Indeed, he was counting on it.

His faith was poetry in motion. He was a pilgrim looking for hope. His journey brought him to a place where he would kneel at the feet of Jesus and beg for mercy. He wasn't prepared to stand in line. He wasn't going to wait his turn. His emergency was God's opportunity to do what no man could do: heal his son. But coming to Jesus was only half the trip. He had to carry the promise of Christ's word home. It was a faith journey. It took a leap of faith to come to Jesus. It required even more faith to believe without seeing results. This story feels like my story, your story, our story. No wonder we connect the dots of our experience with the nobleman's journey. Like him, we are on a pilgrimage of faith. Like him, we must walk these roads believing that God's word to us will come true once we get home. In the meantime, alone in the middle of the night, waiting by the side of the road of life, we wonder, "Are we fools for believing what no man can see? Is this all we have to go on, words of hope, stories of promise?" Scientists can conduct experiments. Astronomers can see what lies beyond. Believers . . . all we have are words. And, for those of us who sleep peacefully at night, with the stars shining down on six billion people, words are enough. Because, "in the beginning was the Word, and the Word was God." We believe in God because we believe words.

Three times in the story the life of the son is affirmed: (1) when Jesus offers the promise (v. 50), (2) when the servants report to their master (v. 51), and (3) when the father remembers the word of Jesus (v. 53). The emphasis underscores the effectiveness of the prophet's words. Jesus said, "Your son lives," and it was so. For John, this miracle signifies the reality of the church's confession regarding Jesus: he is the Son of God

(20:31). It also confirms what John had claimed from the beginning: Jesus is the Creator of the World. Indeed, the Logos of God broods over this story, bringing significance to the import of the "sign." In the beginning and until the end, God uses words to create life. Jesus is the Word of God who brings life to all who hear the Word. Like God, he speaks and there is life. God's Word is effective; once spoken, the echo of his voice never returns without accomplishing its purpose. See how different we are as creatures of the Word. Remember how ineffective our words can be. As parents, we speak to our children, "Come here!" Nothing happens. Imagine if we were able to speak with divine power, "Come here! . . . and it was so . . . and it was *very* good." But this is what separates

> *Scientists can conduct experiments. Astronomers can see what lies beyond. Believers . . . all we have are words. And, for those of us who sleep peacefully at night, with the stars shining down on six billion people, words are enough.*

creature from Creator; there is a difference between the reliable Word of God and the empty promises of humanity. When Jesus, the spoken Logos of God, speaks, his words bring life and light.

"What has come into being in him was life, and the life was the light of all people" (1:4, my translation). The nobleman from Capernaum did not merely witness a miracle; he saw the sign. The word of Jesus brought life to the nobleman's son and brought light to the nobleman's eyes. "And he himself believed and his whole household" (4:53). Because he had ears to hear, the royal official received eyes to see the true identity of Jesus. In the end, the nobleman was the *only* one who "saw" the sign. The Galileans heard the promise, the nobleman's servants saw his son get better, but it was only the father who witnessed the miraculous. Yet in both respects, in the promise of the Prophet and the report of the servants, the nobleman was left to believe words. Indeed, his faith in the Word made him an ideal believer: He who trusts in his Word believes the Word. For this is the purpose of the signs: that those who see would recognize the glorious presence of the only begotten of God (1:14). And we who are left to read the Word, long to have ears to hear so that we can see God, just like the nobleman from Capernaum.

Great Prophet of God, I want to be a believer. I want to trust the Word when there are no "signs" to see. In the middle of my crisis, in the darkness of my solitary hour, all I need is you. You are my only hope. When I throw myself at the mercy of your feet, even when you refuse to meet my request according to my expectations, help me to trust your words. And, as I head home, remind me that your promise goes with me—even to the end of my world. Amen.

10

The Ideal Teacher

I have come to believe that the chief contribution Christians can make is to keep people from suffering for the wrong reasons.

Philip Yancey, *Where Is God When It Hurts?*

Piety can cause blindness. Many of us who claim perfect spiritual vision are oftentimes blind to our own sin. Pious people rest assured in their infallible judgment of others yet fail to see what has become obvious to everyone else. Calculated displays of self-righteousness, meant to reveal the depth of spiritual maturity, unmask to all the ugly face of pride. We who are the proudest of our relationship with God, out to show the world how dedicated we are to him, end up losing what we never had. Piety, like humility, vanishes with recognition. As soon as we claim it we lose it. Those who say they know God best prove how blind they are, for God reveals himself only to those who admit their blindness. "No one has seen God at any time" (John 1:18); he must *be* seen.

The Pharisees epitomized piety. They were the unquestioned authorities of godliness, able to spot sinfulness without hesitation. Hear the confident assertions of these vigilantes of holiness who claim 20/20 vision when it comes to seeing God: "This man is not from God, . . . We know that this man is a sinner" (John 9:16, 24). A man born blind, the caricature of sinfulness, identified the *same* person as "the man called Jesus," "a prophet," and one who comes "from God" (vv. 15, 17, 33). What is the reader to make of the difference in their judgment of the same person? Only one can be right. In a court of law, credibility often decides the matter when there is such conflicting testimony. The surprising twist in the plot of this story, however, is that those who know God best do not recognize him, and the sinner proves to be the better eyewitness even though he is blind.

John enjoyed contrasting the ideal qualities of discipleship revealed in an unexpected hero of the narrative with a group of characters who function as antitypes. For example, the Samaritan woman proves to be more of a disciple of Jesus when compared to the twelve; the deep faith of the nobleman is contrasted with the shallow, sign-seekers of Galilee. The same technique appears in the story of Jesus's healing of the man born blind (John 9:1–41). The blind man functions as an ideal disciple, able to teach the Pharisees a lesson about the true identity of Jesus. His clear vision is contrasted with the blindness of those who claim "they see." The plot guides the reader as we track the progress of the blind man's vision and the incremental blindness of the sighted. The culmination of the ironical effect occurs when these two trajectories—the progressive perceptiveness of the blind man and the regressive stubbornness of the Pharisees—intersect. At that moment, the sinner teaches the teachers of the law about the work of God (vv. 30–34). The Light of the World illuminated the eyes of one and blinded the eyes of another. Fittingly, Jesus pronounces the moral of the story in the end: "For judgment I came into this world, so that those who do not see may see, and that those who see may become blind" (v. 39).

The Light of the World

Wrestling with the problem of evil and suffering yields few satisfying answers. If God Almighty loves his own, why does he allow them to suffer? Commonly, religious people identify sin as the cause of most human suffering. Sinners bring misery upon themselves when they disobey God. But who sinned to cause a child to be born blind? The disciple's question (v. 2) reveals the prevalent thinking of their day. A few rabbis believed that such birth defects were caused by prenatal sin. They argued that the prenatal struggle of Jacob and Esau indicated sin, which brought the inexplicable judgment of God, "I have loved Jacob; but I have hated Esau" (Mal. 1:2–3). The more common explanation offered by the teachers of the law was that children suffered the effects of their parents' sin (Deut. 5:9). In his answer, Jesus redirected the attention of his rabbinical students from the question of cause to the question of purpose. "It was neither that this man sinned, nor his parents; but it was so that the work of God might be displayed in him" (John 9:3). The pious had too easily dismissed the *why* of his condition in terms of what had been; Jesus chose to think, instead, of *what would be*.

All of us were created for the purpose of revealing the works of God. No group can claim a spiritual monopoly on divine blessings. God's work can be seen in the rich and the poor, the healthy and the diseased, the noble and the dishonorable, the status quo and the disenfranchised. The pious, however, act as if they own the exclusive rights to God. As self-appointed guardians of divinity, these judges determine who evidences the blessings of God and who endures the curses of God. Undesirables often find themselves relegated to a life of begging at the side of the road, discarded by the pious as deserving recipients of the punishment of God. The welfare parent, the AIDS patient, the convict, the migrant

We connect the dots of cause and effect especially when it applies to other people. Yet, while we tend to talk about what has been, God prefers to speak of what shall be.

alien, the indigent high-school dropout are too easily dismissed as sinners who suffer from their own choices. We believe in the power of choice, which makes the blame game easier to play. "They get what they deserve," we say. And, with such confident judgments, we absolve ourselves of all responsibility. Justice must have its desired effect. We connect the dots of cause and effect especially when it applies to other people. Yet, while we tend to talk about what has been, God prefers to speak of what shall be. Jesus came to work the *purposes* of God. He always seemed to have his eyes on the end game. Old things pass away and everything becomes new when God is working redemption.

The symbolism in the words and works of Jesus escaped no one's notice. While Jesus was painting the blind man's eyes with mud, he claimed that he was the source of light. Mud in the eyes of the sighted would naturally bring darkness. But Jesus rubs mud in the eyes of the blind and proclaims, "While I am in the world, I am the Light of the world" (9:5). That image sticks in my mind as I read this story. Certainly, Jesus's action shocked those who saw him rub dirt in the eyes of the blind man. Human saliva was commonly used by certain healers who sought to bring sight to the blind, sound to the deaf, words to the mute (see Mark 7:33). But Jesus mixed dirt and saliva, massaging the paste into the eyes of a man who couldn't tell the difference. The sighted probably winced at the sight. That Jesus smeared mud on the blind man's eyes must have not only repulsed the witnesses of the sign, but also offended the Pharisees. Three times in the narrative the interrogators ask how the blind man was healed (John 9:14, 19, 26), and four times the narrator makes reference to Jesus's unusual method of healing (vv. 6, 11, 14, 15). Why did Jesus use mud to heal the blind man?

The narrator finally informs the reader, shortly before the Pharisees enter the narrative, that Jesus did all of this on the Sabbath day (v. 14). The Synoptic Gospels record that the bone of contention between Jesus and the Pharisees was healing on the Sabbath. John, on the other hand, goes to great lengths to show that there seemed to be more to the issue. For example, it was the fact that Jesus told the lame man to carry his pallet on the Sabbath day that disturbed "the Jews" (5:12), not that he had healed him on the Sabbath. Likewise, when Jesus made mud out of dirt and spittle, he may have broken a commandment that forbade kneading on the Sabbath day. The subject comes up often in the story: "He spat on the ground and made mud. . . . Jesus made mud, spread it on my eyes. . . . it was a Sabbath day when Jesus made mud" (9:6, 11, 14, my translation). Therefore, the Pharisees came to the conclusion, "This man is not from God, because He does not keep the Sabbath" (v. 16). Yet, even though they caught Jesus on a technicality, there seems to be more to the Pharisees' indignation than simply making mud on the Sabbath. Unsatisfied with the blind man's version, they pressed him for more information, repeating the question, "What did He do to you? How did He open your eyes?" (v. 26). Their persistence reveals disbelief: "He put *mud* in your eyes?"

Dirt, the ultimate symbol of uncleanness, was rubbed into the eyes of a "sinner" and it brought light to his dark life. The imagery takes one's breath away. Even the narrator makes much of the irony when the reader is informed that Jesus instructed the blind man to go to the pool of Siloam to wash his eyes. Siloam, "which is translated, Sent" (v. 7), completes the analogy. Jesus had just explained to the disciples that he was *sent* by God to do the works of God "as long as it is day" (v. 4). A blind man with mud in his eyes pictures darkness in almost a cruel fashion. He must go to the pool that was "sent" by God (i.e., Jesus!) in order to find cleansing that brought light to his eyes. "So he went away and washed, and came back seeing" (v. 7). Indeed, as the story goes, the man who was born blind will reveal that he sees the Light of the World, and those who sit in darkness show they still have mud in their eyes. Hence, mud brought sight to the blind and blinded the ones who claimed to see.

We still argue over the work of God. Each Christian group has their own ideas about how God does what he does. How does God reconcile sinners? How can God make a blind man see today? Some say by profession of faith, some say by spiritual baptism, some say by water baptism, some have sacraments, some have ordinances, some have priests, some have elders, some use altars, some have pulpits, some use liturgy, some have Bible studies, some anoint with oil, some use prayer wheels, some see miracles, some hear sermons. Despite the diversity, we all want God's work to conform to our methodology. But why? I believe it's because pious people like ourselves think we control divine labor. We're certain God is honored by our brand of Christianity, but not theirs. We worship God in spirit and in truth, but they don't. Therefore, if anyone wants to see God do his work, you better do it like us and not them. But here's the problem. If God can use mud to make a blind man see, then no method is sacrosanct. When Jesus healed the man born blind, he declared all things clean. To some, new methods look unclean—downright dirty. But to those who watch the eyes of a spiritually blind woman open to the gospel, it's the work of God.

It's called the "emerging church," or the "vintage church," or the "renegade church." But whatever it's called, we're witnessing a revolution in how believers are doing church. These communities of faith are cropping up in the unlikeliest of places, drawing the most bizarre collection of humanity. You'll find them in homes, in warehouses, in strip malls, in old cathedrals, in restaurants, in clubs, in office complexes, in broken theaters. They will be white collar, blue collar, no collar; brown hair, black hair, blue hair, orange hair; kids from nice homes, kids from no homes; dancers, drinkers, smokers; heterosexual and homosexual; pagan and purist; saint and sinner. Their worship services include every genre of music, every medium of communication. They read Augustine and Flannery O'Connor. From coats and ties to piercings and tattoos, all kinds of people are finding Jesus in this postmodern quest of truth. Take the typical Catholic, Episcopalian, Baptist, Vineyard, Pentecostal, Methodist, and Nazarene worship services, mix it all together, and it might resemble their communion with God. They prefer candles and

liturgy, confession and crosses, tears and laughter, hugging and medita-
tion, and, most of all, sacred bonds. They take sin very seriously. Their
vulnerability is intimidating. They want to talk about their weaknesses.
Whatever it takes, they want to see God.

This movement is no paradigm shift. These people are not out to
renovate or innervate our churches. They're speaking a different language. They're walking in forbidden lands. These believers are reaching
people with the Good News of Jesus Christ most of whom would never
go to church. And, quite honestly, the church really doesn't want to have
to deal with this kind of people. These converts are high-maintenance
souls. For a "problem-solving, program-oriented" congregation, it would
be maddening to try to deal with their issues—which is why they don't
come to our churches in the first place. These spiritual vagabonds are
not looking for someone to fix them; they're looking for someone to hold
them. Traditionalists, no doubt, will accuse these renegades of watering
down the gospel, of forsaking our holy calling, of ignoring the essence
of our faith. Others see the work of God in the reclamation of soiled
souls. As long as blind men see, what difference does it make how we
heal these beggars? Here's mud in your eyes.

When the blind man "came back seeing" (v. 7), his neighbors could
barely recognize him. Others refused to believe that he was the same
man who once begged for food (vv. 8–9). Questions regarding the identity
of the blind man persist throughout the story. The Pharisees, in their
cross-examination of the beggar, appear just as incredulous of the blind
man's identity as they are of Jesus's identity. The beggar, throughout the
entire ordeal, only speaks of what he knows. When the neighbors ask,
"Where is he?" he responds, "I do not know" (v. 12). When his exam-
iners ask how he became sighted, the man born blind merely recites
what happened, "He applied clay to my eyes, and I washed, and I see"
(v. 15). (Notice how his story never gets out of hand; now the center of
attention, the beggar never yielded to the temptation to embellish the
story.) Even in the face of the confident judgments of the pious—"We
know that this man [Jesus] is a sinner" (v. 24)—the man speaks only of
what he knows and of what others could never contest, "Whether He is
a sinner, I do not know; *one thing I do know*, that though I was blind,
now I see" (v. 25).

It is compelling to me that the identity of the blind man is as much
of an issue to the Pharisees as the identity of Jesus. They spend as much
time trying to figure out who the beggar is as they do puzzling over Jesus.
They began their two-part investigation, which will lead them to two
"eyewitnesses," with the assumption that the beggar was not the same
man who was born blind (v. 18), and that God did not use Jesus to heal
him (v. 16). The beggar's parents are called upon to establish the fact that

their child was *born* blind. In turn, the man born blind becomes the chief witness in the case concerning Jesus. The Pharisees end up believing the first "eyewitness" and denying the second. They eventually accepted the parents' testimony, acknowledging the fact that the healed man was born blind (v. 18). And yet, the Pharisees rejected the eyewitness testimony of the man for whom the miracle was performed, throwing him out of their "court" (v. 34). As the reader tracks the developments within each "trial," the dual plot becomes more apparent. As the identity of the blind man becomes more clearly established by the council of Pharisees, so does his credibility as a witness concerning the true identity of Jesus. Note the progression of the beggar's opinion regarding Jesus, from ignorance to belief. At first, he doesn't know where Jesus can be found (v. 12). Then, he pronounces with certainty that Jesus is a prophet (v. 17). In the next trial scene, the man born blind claims ignorance as to whether Jesus is "a sinner" (v. 24). Then, he boldly declares that Jesus must be a man of God (vv. 31–33). In the unfolding drama, the beggar proves that he was born blind but now can see, both physically *and* spiritually. "What do you say about Him, since He opened your eyes?" (v. 17). Indeed, he did. One can only see light with open eyes.

Isn't it interesting how skeptics come to disciples of Jesus repeatedly asking the same questions, yet never satisfied with our answers? "So, you believe Jesus is the only way to God?" "Yes; Jesus said, 'No one comes to the Father but by me.'" "You really think that victims should forgive criminals even though they show no remorse for their crimes?" "Yes; Jesus said we're supposed to love our enemies and forgive those who are indebted to us." "Let me get this straight. You used to have it all—fame and fortune—and you're saying that you gave it all up because these things don't matter to you anymore? That your former escapades—wild parties and reckless living—left you unsatisfied? That you've given all of this up for Jesus, and that it's a good thing?" "Yes, yes, and yes." Try explaining your faith once, and they'll ask you again, expecting you to change your answers. Try defending yourself by quoting Jesus and they'll dismiss you as a fanatic. To unbelievers, we look pretty foolish. We're close-minded, stubborn, ignorant, short-sighted fools. They think we've lost our perspective, that we've lost sight of what's reasonable. It's as if our religious zeal has blinded us to reality. No, that's not it at all. The problem is that we were *born* blind, and now we see.

The Man Born Blind

It took the testimony of the parents of a grown man to convince the Pharisees that the beggar was born blind, a fact that only a parent could establish. The parents' role in the Pharisees' investigation is all the more surprising since they were introduced at the beginning of the story as "sinners" who may have caused their son's blindness (v. 2). In the end, the Pharisees were forced to take the word of sinners about the one who does not observe the Sabbath (v. 16)—the parents confirm that their son was born blind, the beggar confirms that Jesus used mud to open his eyes. Their problem was this: "How can a man who is a sinner perform such signs?" (v. 16); in other words, how could a sinner use sinful means to open the eyes of a sinner whom God had cursed with blindness? The Pharisees put their dilemma to the parents of the beggar, "Is this your son, who you say was born blind? Then how does he now see?" (v. 19).

It seems as though the Pharisees were looking for someone to put together for them what was apparently obvious to everyone else. The parents were reluctant to tell the Pharisees what they really thought for fear of being kicked out of the synagogue. "For the Jews had already agreed that if anyone confessed Him to be Christ, he was to be put out of the synagogue. For this reason, his parents said, 'He is of age; ask him'" (v. 22–23). Consequently, the focus of the investigation shifts back to the beggar (vv. 24–34). He's the only one who is giving any answers. He's a blind guide leading the blind. He's the sinner who tries to persuade the pious to believe. He's a man who has never read the Torah (blind men can't read) yet teaches the experts about God.

How we need the experts! We hear from them every Christmas and Easter. Television shows, news magazines, radio interviews—every conceivable medium is bombarded with new, shocking, revealing details about the life of Jesus. Experts are summoned to give their latest theories about the significance of Jesus. Front-page teasers invite inquiring minds to consider sensational stories about Jesus's private life, or the true purpose of his preaching, or why the Gospels are wrong. "Jesus was married, tune in tonight for our exclusive interview," or, "A secret code unlocks the mystery of biblical prophecy," or, "The conspiracy to shut out the fifth gospel: why Matthew, Mark, Luke, and John don't tell the *whole* [said with a sinister tone] story." The more fanciful the story, the more likely it will appear on prime-time network television. After all, who would tune in to hear an investigative news report confirming what we already know? Can't sell commercial time and news ads like that. No, what they prefer to do is line up their "experts" to pass off idiosyncratic views as careful scholarship. I can't take it anymore. There are many qualified biblical scholars who know the meaning of the word "integrity."[1] Their expertise does not yield preposterous ideas because they don't make it up as they go. They read between the lines of the Gospels without ignoring the lines of the gospel. Even though you rarely see them on television, read their work. Listen to their arguments, and you will find out that even scholars know it doesn't take an expert to understand Jesus. Indeed, the simplest of minds can see who he was and figure out what he came to do. Even a man born blind can teach an expert a thing or two.

When the Pharisees exclaimed, "Give glory to God!" (v. 24), they were imploring the beggar to swear an oath and tell the truth (Josh. 7:19). They were convinced that Jesus did not perform the miracle by the power of God. They deduced: anyone who breaks the Sabbath law is a sinner; Jesus made mud on the Sabbath; therefore, "we know that this man is a sinner" (John 9:24). The fact that he performed a miracle was not necessarily a sign of his divine mission. They relied upon a well-established tradition that even false prophets could perform miracles (Deut. 13:1–5). The man who was born blind, on the other hand, speaks of what he knows to be true: "Though I was blind, now I see" (John 9:25). Occasionally, rabbis could heal blinded men; *no one* had ever healed a man *born* blind (v. 32). The Pharisees dismissed the possibility since God made him blind, only God could make him see (v. 33; Ps. 146:8).

> *Even scholars know it doesn't take an expert*
>
> *to understand Jesus.*

(Not even Moses was able to convince God to change the way God made him [Exod. 4:11].) Yet they could not deny that this man, who was born blind, now sees. The Pharisees, looking reality in the face, were left with only one alternative: to question, once again, *how* Jesus healed the man (John 9:26).

The pious Pharisees kept tripping over the sixth "sign" of Jesus's identity. The scandalous manner in which Jesus performed the miracle offended their sensibilities. I can almost hear them say among themselves, "What did he mean by putting mud in the sinner's eyes? What was he trying to prove?" To use dirt to override the just curse of God upon sinners smacks of subterfuge. Yet no one is stronger than God. So they turned to him again, "What did He do to you? How did He open your eyes?" (v. 26). And it is at this point where the man born blind begins to see the blindness of the Pharisees. They keep asking him the same questions; they cannot see what he is saying. It is as if they had mud in *their* eyes. "Why do you want to hear it again? You do not also want to become His disciples too, do you?" (v. 27). Looking into their blinded eyes, the beggar invites the Pharisees to go to the pool Sent by God in order to wash the mud out of *their* eyes—to which the Pharisees appropriately replied, "You are His disciple, but we are the disciples of Moses" (v. 28). Thus, according to John, the blind man sees the sign and the Pharisees cannot see past the Law.

How shocking it must have been for the beggar when he realized that the religious experts could not recognize the work of God. Here he is, a blind beggar who had never worshiped God in the temple, never participated in a synagogue service, never handled the Torah with his own hands, and yet he can see the handiwork of God. And then there are the Pharisees, teachers of the law of God, leaders of the synagogue, constables of holiness, who can only speak of what God has done (v. 29). They know that God spoke to Moses; but Jesus, "we do not know where He is from" (v. 29). "Here is an amazing thing" (v. 30). The beggar says what the reader is thinking. How could these who hear the voice of God in Moses *not* see the work of God in Jesus? After all, one of the common, expected signs of the presence of God's coming kingdom on earth, predicted by the prophets, was the restoration of sight to the blind (see Isa. 29:18; 42:7, 16; Jer. 31:8; Luke 4:18). The beggar, therefore, persists in taking the implication of his (in)sight to its logical conclusion: Jesus performs the kingdom work of God on earth. "The Law was given through Moses; grace and truth were realized through Jesus Christ" (John 1:17).

"We know that God does not hear sinners" (9:31). I hear pathos in the beggar's voice. No one knew the truth of that theologically correct statement more than the man who was born blind. How many times did he ask God to heal him, and how many times did he despair realizing that God would never answer his prayers? He was born a sinner! Resigned to a life of begging, having shamed his parents to the point that they were unwilling to care for him, the blind man's daily darkness was the constant reminder that he would never see the blessing of God. Convinced by the pious that God never hears the prayers of a man born in sin, the blind man had given up any hope of seeing. God only listens to anyone who "is God-fearing and does His will" (v. 31). He heard that his whole life. Then, on a day like any other day, "the man called Jesus" opened his eyes. There was no prayer; the blind man made no request. Jesus simply said something about "work[ing] the works of Him who sent Me" (v. 4), and then sent him to the pool to wash his dirty eyes. "Since the beginning of time it has never been heard that anyone opened the eyes of a person *born* blind" (v. 32). Things like this don't happen. The beggar brings the point home: Since Jesus heals the blind, and God only hears the prayers of one who does his will, then God's will is accomplished through Jesus. "If this man were not from God, He could do nothing" (v. 33).

To do the work of God, we must become the work of God. It's amazing how many of us have forgotten that simple reality of grace. It is evident in the way we look to our own heroes—champions for the kingdom—to get the job done. Those who have the most to give are hand chosen to deliver the Christian message to the masses. Christian celebrities are made by entrepreneurs of the church, trying to market faith to outsiders. Only the brightest stars share the stage with well-known evangelists, like trophies on the mantle of God's greatest accomplishments. We *assume* that outstanding musicians are outstanding disciples. Movie stars shine the light of salvation the brightest. Sports idols give God high profile.

Here's the boring truth:
God doesn't need a public relations department;
weak people are God's best work;
and the world will never understand grace.

We are led to believe that God saves the best in order to save the rest. Then, when our heroes fall, everyone becomes disillusioned. Everyday Christians feel betrayed, disgraced celebrities are discarded like trash, and the world laughs once again at our delusions of grandeur. Here's the boring truth: God doesn't need a public relations department; weak people are God's best work; and the world will never understand grace. This is why we never tire of singing the song for the ages: "Grace has brought me safe thus far, and grace will lead me home." We all tell the same story: once I was blind, but now I see.

The irony of the situation finally hit the Pharisees. A blind man, born in sin, tries to dispel the ignorance of the learned, enlightening the eyes of the pious about God. They took offense: "You were born entirely in sins, and are you teaching us?" (v. 34). Notice, however, they offered no counterargument, no persuasive rebuttal. All they could do to the one who had seen the Light (v. 5) was to throw him out (v. 34). But this action does not take the reader by surprise, for the narrator had warned us in the prologue that, "The light shines in the darkness, and the darkness did not comprehend it" (1:5). Darkness cannot tolerate light. Yet everyone knows it takes light to see. The man with enlightened eyes shines in the face of those who dwell in darkness, unable to see because their eyes had become accustomed to the night. Then the light of the blind man's confession blinded the Pharisees. I can hear someone with dilated eyes cry out, "Somebody turn that light off!" So they drove him out, dousing the light.

The beggar probably showed no remorse when he was removed from the presence of the religious elite. Unlike his parents, the man born blind did not fear the repercussions of his confession of Jesus as one who comes from God. As a reject of society, the beggar had never experienced recognition. He was accustomed to severe treatment by the insiders. He was never welcome in the synagogue, so getting kicked out of the community was no loss. He was indifferent to their approval, numb to the sting of rejection. He was back where he started—a social pariah who was still a sinner in the eyes of the pious. Yet, despite their attempts to put him in his place, there was one significant, life-changing difference—he could see. He could see! And no one could take that away.

At this point, Jesus reenters the narrative. Since he was the subject of debate throughout the story, his absence was barely noticeable. He appears, like bookends to the story, at the beginning and the end. Rather innocuously, Jesus started the entire controversy by doing a good work. Jesus did not force the issue. Notice that he did not send the healed man to the Pharisees; he did not orchestrate the validating of the miracle by bringing the beggar's parents to offer testimony on his behalf; he did not encourage the beggar to confront the religious leaders with the significance of the "sign." Jesus preferred to let the sign speak for itself. He simply stood back and watched the whole episode play out before him. Then, when he heard that the beggar was rejected by the Pharisees, Jesus found him (9:35). The before-and-after scene of Jesus with the beggar completes the story. The last time Jesus saw the blind man, he was headed for the pool with mud in his eyes. Now the Light of the World looks into eyes brightened by light and asks, "Do you believe in the Son of Man?" (v. 35).

"You are His disciple" (v. 28). The Pharisees' derogatory remark was the highest tribute anyone had ever paid the beggar. What the Pharisees saw as the ultimate insult, the narrator reveals as the ultimate point of the story. Jesus found an ideal disciple in a blind beggar, whose simple teaching confounded the wise. In their second face-to-face encounter, the beggar laid eyes on Jesus for the *first* time. "Do you believe in the Son of Man?" (v. 35). The beggar responds, "'Who is He, Lord, that I may believe in him?' Jesus said to him, 'You have . . . seen him'" (vv. 36–37). Although the beggar sees him for the first time, Jesus implies that the blind man has seen him before. The blind man had already revealed that he could see the Son of Man when he professed that Jesus was a prophet come from God (vv. 17, 33). When Jesus brought light to his eyes, the beggar showed everyone that he could see physically and spiritually. Because of his perceptiveness, Jesus tells the man who

> *It is no wonder that readers of John's Gospel identify with the blind man. He captured for all time the universal testimony of every Christian: "Once I was blind, but now I see."*

meets him for the first time with seeing eyes, "We've already met." It is no wonder that readers of John's Gospel identify with the blind man. He captured for all time the universal testimony of every Christian: "Once I was blind, but now I see." His journey epitomizes the pilgrimage of every seeker. For we all find ourselves believing in the man we have never seen. And one day, as we profess our faith in the presence of doubters and naysayers, Jesus will come and find us. In the meantime, it is a beggar who inspires us to have eyes of faith to see him until we meet him face-to-face.

That's the hardest part about being a Christian: waiting. We walk by faith that is sight until we see him in whom we have believed. We wait for God's work to become complete in us. We wait for heaven. We wait for his coming. We wait for the last day. We wait until sin has power over us no more. That will be the day—when we no longer have to fight to win. In the meantime, the skeptics will persist in their disbelief, the pious will judge the unfit, the crowds will marvel over a changed life, and blind men and women will continue to claim that Jesus touched their eyes. Now they see clearly for the first time in their lives. The Light of the World overpowers the darkness of any soul. This is why we wait in the shadows. This is why we search the evening sky for signs and wonders. We wait for a man who will ask us on the last day, "Do you believe in the Son of Man?" Then we will say, "Yes, Lord. We have seen you, and we are beholding you now and forevermore."

When faith becomes sight there is worship. Here the beggar reveals what the reader has known all along: the blind man sees and believes.

After the revelation of Jesus's identity, the beggar confesses, "Lord, I believe," and worships Jesus (v. 38). The blind man sees the Light of the World, beholding the shekinah glory of God, and falls prostrate in his presence. His example is in stark contrast to the teachers of the law. This scene, with the beggar kneeling before Jesus like a prodigal son and the pious scoffing at a distance, illustrates the point of the story: "For judgment I came into this world, so that those who do not see may see, and that those who see may become blind" (9:39). The final frame captures the culmination of the plot of this story: the Light of the world enlightened the eyes of the blind and blinded the eyes of the sighted. "This is the judgment," the narrator had warned the reader, "that the Light has come into the world, and men loved the darkness rather than the Light, for their deeds were evil" (3:19).

The Pharisees, strangely enough, "saw" what Jesus was saying and were offended, "We are not blind too, are we?" (9:40). Jesus's response brings the story full circle: "If you were blind, you would have no sin; but since you say, 'We see,' your sin remains" (v. 41). See now who is the blind sinner. As the Light of the World, Jesus performed signs to show the works of God, revealing his true identity. Those who had eyes to see and ears to hear recognize him. The Pharisees, on the other hand, remain in darkness, blinded by their sin. Unable to see the signs, they prove that they are as blind as a beggar on the side of the road (Isa. 42:18–20). And there they shall remain, for only *Jesus* can heal the blind and forgive sinners. At this point, the reader is brought to the beginning of the story, only the roles are reversed. This time, the pious are left by the side of the road, blind to their sin. And the reader, following the Light as he leaves this place, looks at the pitiful sight and asks, "Jesus, who are blind, these men or their parents?" I imagine Jesus would reply, "Neither, they think that they see."

> For a little while longer the Light is among you. Walk while you have the Light, so that darkness will not overtake you; he who walks in the darkness does not know where he goes. While you have the Light, believe in the Light, so that you may become sons of Light.
>
> John 12:35–36

11

The Beloved Disciple

To endure the cross is not a tragedy; it is the suffering which
is the fruit of an exclusive allegiance to Jesus Christ. When it
comes, it is not an accident, but a necessity.

Dietrich Bonhoeffer, *The Cost of Discipleship*

A ll of us, at one time or another, think we are God's favorite. This
abiding conviction is evident when we compare ourselves to
those who are less fortunate. We say, "There, but by the grace of God,
go I"; but what we really mean is, "God would never let something like
that happen to me, I hope." We reveal our true feelings when something
worse befalls us, and our impulse is to question the benevolent care of
God. "Why did you let this happen to me? What have I done to deserve
this? I thought you loved me more than this." Every believer would like
to think he is the ultimate, ideal disciple: the one whom Jesus loves
the most. It's a natural conviction. Even the twelve debated the issue
on more than one occasion (Mark 9:34; 10:35–44). But would any of
us qualify as the ideal disciple of Jesus? What would it take to be the

greatest disciple of Jesus? Certainly one of the twelve would make the top ten, but which disciple did Jesus appreciate the most? Who would qualify for the distinct honor of being called "the one whom Jesus loved"?

John answered the question. In his Gospel the beloved disciple appears as the quintessential follower of Jesus. He first appears at the Lord's table, in the seat of honor, sharing intimate fellowship with Jesus (John 13:23). Then he appears as the faithful follower of Jesus, the *only* disciple who followed Jesus to the cross (19:26). The beloved disciple was the first to believe that the empty tomb was evidence of Christ's resurrection (20:8). His superior insight enables him to recognize Jesus, the resurrected Messiah, before the others (21:7). He seemed to possess every quality of true discipleship. His faithfulness even inspired Jesus to entertain the idea of allowing this loyal disciple to remain on earth, to continue the work until he returned (21:22). Who was this mysterious disciple? He doesn't say much in John's Gospel; the narrator records only two expressions as coming from the beloved one: "Lord, who is it?" and "It is the Lord" (13:25; 21:7)—symmetrical statements that seem to incite more curiosity than provide information. His anonymity teases the reader, inviting us to puzzle over his identity. We don't know his name; yet his reputation in the early church became so widespread that everyone knew him by the moniker any Christian would cherish: "the beloved disciple." Who was he?

Traditionally, the author of the Gospel has been identified as the beloved disciple. John is the only disciple of the twelve never mentioned in the narrative. Furthermore, the postscript to John's Gospel appears to attribute the authorship of the Gospel to the beloved one (21:24). John's close association with Jesus, the outstanding characteristic of the beloved disciple, is also corroborated by the Synoptic Gospels (cf. Matt. 17:1; Mark 14:33). There are some objections, however, to this association. For example, would John distinguish himself from the other disciples in such pretentious terms? It is hard to imagine John referring to himself as "the one whom Jesus loved" when Jesus discouraged such competitive claims among his disciples (Matt. 18:1–4; Mark 10:35–45). More than likely, John used a recording secretary (like Paul, cf. Rom. 16:22); hence, one can certainly see how the transcriber would refer to the apostle as "the beloved one" when he wrote down the stories of John. Another problem is that the beloved disciple appears for the first time in the narrative at the end of Jesus's ministry. If the beloved disciple was John, why would there be no mention of him before chapter 13? Some have linked the beloved disciple with other anonymous disciples who appear throughout the narrative: Andrew's associate (John 1:35), Peter's friend, (18:15), and the disciple witness

(19:35). But this association is assumed more than proven. It could just as easily be assumed that Andrew's associate and Peter's friend *are* anonymous references to John, but that "the one whom Jesus loved" is someone else. But who?

One suggestion is especially compelling to me. The conspicuous appearance of the beloved disciple at the Lord's table in John 13:23 may not take some observant readers by surprise. One who has followed carefully the narrator's depiction of certain characters in the episodes prior to the final scenes of the story has already been informed as to the identity of this one who enjoys unique status. The beloved disciple may have been Lazarus.

Three times in the story of the seventh sign, Lazarus is described as one whom Jesus loved (11:3, 5, 36). Then, after the miraculous raising of Lazarus from the dead, Jesus and his disciples visit Bethany, Lazarus' home. The narrator specifically indicates that, along with the disciples, "Lazarus was one of those reclining at the table" with Jesus (12:2). From that point on, Lazarus and Jesus are as inseparable as Jesus

The beloved disciple may have been Lazarus.

and the beloved disciple. The crowds flock to see Jesus *and* Lazarus (12:9); the chief priests planned to put Lazarus to death along with Jesus (12:10); then, the crowd who witnessed the raising of Lazarus orchestrated Jerusalem's reception of Jesus as the "King of Israel" (12:12–18). Lazarus becomes the focal point of Jesus's ministry since he embodied the ultimate demonstration of Jesus's messiahship. The miracles were signs, according to John, that Jesus was the Messiah, the Son of God (20:31). As the seventh sign, the raising of Lazarus was the decisive revelation of the work of God in the public ministry of Jesus. Indeed, Lazarus *was* the seventh sign—the sign to end all signs, the perfect sign of Jesus's identity. No other miracle could reveal more clearly the deity of Christ, for only God has power over death. As a result, no one could contest the significance of Jesus with Lazarus around:

> It was also because they heard that He had performed *this* sign that the crowd went to meet Him. The Pharisees then said to one another, "You see, you can do nothing. Look, the world has gone after Him!"
>
> John 12:18–19, my translation

Consequently, for John, this ended the public "signs" of Jesus's ministry. After the raising of Lazarus, Jesus "departed and hid from them" since there was nothing more he could do to convince the Jews of his true identity (12:38–40).

Seeing Lazarus as the beloved disciple seems to resolve certain ambiguities in the text. For example, the evidence that he is the "one whom Jesus loved" is clearly seen in Jesus's anguish over the loss of Lazarus, expressed in graphic terms, "He was deeply moved in spirit and was troubled . . . Jesus wept. So the Jews said, 'See how He loved him!'" (11:33–35 my translation). It explains why Lazarus becomes the target of the enemies of Jesus, "because on account of him [Lazarus] many of the Jews were going away and were believing in Jesus" (12:11). Lazarus is to die with Jesus, but neither man is afraid of the death threats of the chief priests—Lazarus, because he has already died; Jesus, because he is supposed to die. Therefore, no longer fearing death, Lazarus is the only disciple of Jesus (in addition to the women) willing to follow Jesus to the cross (19:26). It is fitting, then, that he is the first to believe that the empty tomb could mean that Jesus came back to life, for he himself once walked out of a tomb, leaving his grave clothes behind (11:44; 20:5–8). Finally, if Lazarus were the beloved disciple it would explain how the legend of the immortality of the beloved one could become such a popular rumor spread throughout the Christian community (21:23). Since Lazarus died once, many Christians believed that Jesus's prediction regarding the beloved one meant that he would not die again (vv. 22–23).

But, then again, John may have intended for the beloved disciple to remain an anonymous figure to the reader of his Gospel. After all, despite various attempts to unmask the beloved disciple, no single person qualifies as an unquestionable candidate for the title "the one whom Jesus loved." The fact that his identity remains a mystery may reveal the narrator's purpose. Like the other disciples, the beloved one appears as the nameless benchmark of genuine discipleship. The literary effect of his anonymity is to get the reader to toy with the idea that he or she *could* be the beloved disciple. Christians who visualize the story of Jesus sometimes imagine what kind of disciples they would have been in the narrative world of John's Gospel. Would you be the faithful disciple who shares intimate table fellowship with Jesus, in whom Jesus confides his deepest, darkest secret? When the rest of the twelve abandoned him, would you courageously follow him to the cross and carry out his dying wish to take care of his mother? Could you, after discovering the empty tomb, believe the impossible, seeing with eyes of faith that Jesus was alive? Perhaps any one of us *could* have been the beloved disciple—which is why none of us will ever really know who it is.

The Honorable Guest at the Table

In every scene with the beloved disciple, the narrator uses Peter as
the photographic "negative" to bring into sharp focus the difference
between ideal and common discipleship. In the first episode, Peter finds
himself at the end of the table while the beloved disciple, reclining next
to Jesus, is privy to inside information regarding the traitor. Then, the
familiar story of Peter's denial is contrasted with the loyal friendship
of the beloved one who stays with Jesus until the bitter end. In the next
scene, the beloved disciple gets to the empty tomb first (he knows the
way) and is the first to believe that Jesus had been raised from the dead.
In the final episode, the resurrected Jesus first questions the commitment of Peter and then commends the beloved disciple as one who could
remain until the return of Christ. Together, these individual episodes tell
the whole story. Peter and the beloved disciple characterize two kinds
of disciples: those who want to follow Jesus (13:36–38) and those who
do (12:26). They appear as bookends which frame the wide range of discipleship found in the library of Christianity. Indeed, most readers would
find more affinity with Peter than with the ideal disciple. Nevertheless,
the narrator puts forward the ultimate, ideal disciple as the character
"whom Jesus loved" in order to encourage would-be followers of Jesus
to become carbon-copy witnesses with impeccable integrity—the kind
of witness whose legacy would inspire an entire community of faith to
testify, "We know that his testimony is true" (21:24 my translation).

It is no wonder, then, that the beloved disciple appears for the first
time at the Lord's table, next to Jesus (13:21–30). The narrator introduces
the familiar scene by picturing Jesus as one who "became troubled in
spirit" (v. 21). Jesus was "troubled" two times before this story: at the
death of Lazarus (11:33) and at the arrival of the eschatological hour
(12:27). His reaction to the disturbing news of Lazarus' death was to
bring him back to life. The seventh sign revealed his glory. Later, while
contemplating the hour of his glorification (his own death and resurrection), Jesus speaks of wheat falling to the ground, dying, then yielding more wheat. This will not only be required of Jesus but of any who
would follow him: "If anyone serves Me, he must follow Me; and *where
I am, there My servant will be also*; if anyone serves Me, *the Father will
honor him*" (12:26 my translation).

Jesus, refusing to shy away from his destiny, will show the way for all
who would follow him (v. 27). Messianic suffering precedes messianic
glory. The heavenly voice confirms "the way." "I have both glorified it
[the seventh sign], and will glorify it again [the resurrection of Jesus]"
(v. 28). The people do not understand, so Jesus explains to the crowd
what must come: "And I, if I be lifted up from the earth, will draw all

men to Myself" (v. 32)—to which the narrator adds what has become obvious to the reader (v. 33). Just as God was glorified through the ultimate sign of Jesus by raising Lazarus from the dead, "the resurrection and the life" (11:25) will glorify the Father through the ultimate sign of God's glory: the death and resurrection of his Son. Jesus approached both "signs" with a troubled spirit (11:33; 12:27). Yet he will not face the trouble alone. Linked by a common destiny, the beloved disciple will serve him by following him. So that, wherever Jesus is, there will be the beloved one also. And, whoever serves Jesus, the Father will honor (12:26). Consequently, when Jesus comes to the table "troubled," the beloved disciple is right there with him (13:21–23).

Most scholars believe that the seventh sign is paradigmatic for the glorification of Jesus. And, if Lazarus is intended to be read as the beloved disciple, the association between the story of the raising of Lazarus and the passion story becomes even more intriguing. Betrayal, for example, sets up both stories. When Jesus receives the report of Lazarus' condition he prophesies, "This sickness is not to end in death, but for the glory of God, so that the Son of God may be glorified by it" (11:4). But Jesus seemingly "betrays" Lazarus when he delays his trip to Bethany (vv. 5–6). Indeed, Lazarus dies before Jesus arrives, which leads Martha and Mary to question Jesus's devotion (vv. 21, 32). Later, there is an eerie similarity in the circumstances leading to the death of Lazarus and Jesus. Like Lazarus, a friend will "betray" Jesus. This "betrayal" will set into motion the sequence of events that will lead to a tomb. And, like the seventh sign, it will not end in death, "rather it is for God's glory, so that the Son of God may be glorified through it."

"Truly, truly, I say to you, that one of you will betray Me" (13:21). The disciples are concerned that they could be the one. When would it happen? How would it happen? Who could it be? No one was willing to ask Jesus to identify the traitor except the only one who knew it couldn't be him, the beloved disciple. Even Peter is afraid to ask, fearing it could be him. And, much to Peter's chagrin, shortly after the exit of Judas, Jesus's prediction regarding Peter's denial (v. 38) must have sounded to the rest of the disciples like the unmasking of the traitor! Peter, therefore, motions from the end of the table—the least honorable seat—to get the beloved one to ask Jesus of whom he was speaking (John 13:24). Notice, Jesus tells the secret only to the beloved one—not even Peter is aware of the identity of the betrayer (v. 28). And yet, the manner in which Jesus reveals the traitor is in word *and* deed, for all to see: "This is the one for whom I shall dip the morsel" (v. 26). Jesus could have just as easily told the beloved one, "It is Judas." Instead, he reveals the significance of his actions (giving the bread to Judas), which was seen by all, only to the beloved one. Why all the public drama in the midst of private revelation? The reader knows.

Every public act of Jesus reveals the significance of his mission to those who have ears to hear his word. The disciples didn't understand what Jesus meant when he told Judas, "'What you do, do quickly.' Now no one of those reclining at the table knew for what purpose He had said this to him" (vv. 27–28)—not even Peter. Evidently the disciples did not correlate Jesus's prediction of the betrayer with his symbolic gesture of handing a piece of unleavened bread, dipped in bitter herbs, to Judas. In this case, only two people at the table knew what Jesus was doing: the beloved one and Judas. We as readers, on the other hand, have been clued in by the narrator regarding the significance of the moment. Eavesdropping on the conversation between the beloved one and Jesus, we share the vantage point of the beloved disciple, enabling us to make sense of the word and deed of Jesus. The symbolism is overwhelming.

When Jesus handed the morsel to Judas, he signaled to the traitor the significance of his betrayal. Unleavened bread pictured for Israel Yahweh's desire to deliver a pure people from Egyptian slavery. They were to dip the bread baked without yeast in bitter herbs as they left Egypt by stealth, to remind them of the bitter experience of slavery. Jesus, the "bread of life" (6:35), offered himself as the unleavened bread to be

> *Judas did purchase what was necessary*
> *for Passover; with his betrayal*
> *Judas secured a paschal lamb for the poor.*

dipped in the bitter herbs of his passion. The betrayer, who now holds Jesus's life in his own hands, becomes Satan incarnate, but still yields to the command of the Master, "What you do, do quickly" (13:27). The disciples don't realize what is happening. They tried to interpret Jesus's command in the context of their Passover experience. They thought that Jesus was giving orders to the treasurer to buy what was necessary "for the feast," or to make the obligatory offering for the poor during Passover. Yet, even though the twelve did not understand the significance of Jesus's word and deed, their innocuous guesswork proved to be prophetic. Judas *did* purchase what was necessary for Passover; with his betrayal Judas secured a paschal lamb for the poor.[1]

The Faithful Friend at the Cross

The second appearance of the beloved disciple occurs at the crucifixion of Jesus. There is no mention of what he does prior to the famous scene at the cross (19:26–27). Peter, on the other hand, appears as one of the three characters—Jesus, Peter, Pilate—which dominate the story leading up to Jesus's death (18:1–19:22). In the first section (18:1–27), Peter and Jesus are the main characters of the story; then, in the second section (18:28–19:22), the story centers around Pilate and Jesus. Notice how the narrator juxtaposes the trial of Jesus and the interrogation of Peter. As the investigation focuses initially on his disciples (18:19), Jesus affirms that his private testimony can be confirmed by *"those* who have heard what I spoke to them" in public (v. 21), including the disciples. Just as Jesus was encouraging the Sanhedrin to question the disciples, Peter was denying that he even knew Jesus. The irony, of course, is that Peter, "the rock," had recently promised to die for Jesus—a promise even Jesus knew Peter couldn't keep (13:36–38). But he tried.

When Jesus was arrested, Peter was prepared to fight to the death to protect his friend. How serious was he in his attempt to fight for the life of Jesus? He tried to kill the servant of the high priest . . . *the high priest!* He was the most powerful ruler in Jerusalem, besides Pilate. The assassination of the high priest's servant would be interpreted as a major act of insurrection, resulting in the immediate execution of the criminal. A man's slave was supposed to be treated as if he were the master himself (Matt. 21:34–36; 22:3–7). For all practical purposes, it was as if Peter were trying to kill the high priest. But such an act of heroism was not what Jesus wanted. His utmost concern was for the welfare of his disciples (John 18:8–9). Peter's reckless behavior reveals, once again, that he misunderstood the purpose of God: Jesus was supposed to die (v. 11). And regardless of what the "rock" tried to do, Jesus's word would come true: Jesus would die, and Peter would deny him three times (13:33–38).

Jesus warned the disciples that where he was going they could not follow (13:36). But Peter tried. Peter followed Jesus as far as *the high priest's court* (18:15–18, 25–27). He tried to remain inconspicuous, lurking in the darkness outside the doorway to the high priest's chamber. But then a friend insisted that he come inside (v. 16). His safety in peril, Peter sheepishly entered the court of the same man whose servant he tried to kill. Would anyone recognize him? Immediately he is found out. As he enters the court, the doorkeeper (another high priest slave) identifies the stranger (v. 17). Peter decides to return outside. Every impulse must have directed him to flight. Instead, so as not to confirm the girl's suspicions, he joins more slaves of the high priest at the fire just outside the door. They recognized him (v. 25); the glow of the fire, no doubt, cast light on Peter's face in a familiar way—not too different from the garden scene when the soldiers were carrying lanterns and torches (v. 3). Then one of the slaves, a *relative* of the servant whom Peter tried to kill, fingered the disciple as "the one" who was in the garden (v. 26). Three times Peter denied that he was the disciple of Jesus, while his master was interrogated by the high priest. Just when Jesus was speaking "rightly" in the well-lit court of the high priest, giving testimony to what he had done publicly (vv. 20–23), Peter was trying to hide in the darkness of his denial. Finally, after the third lie, Peter escaped with his life. The dark night was over; morning had broken; the cock crowed; and Peter was gone with the darkness (v. 27).

The disciple whom Jesus loved, on the other hand, followed Jesus to the cross. Although Jesus anticipated that all of his disciples would abandon him (16:32), the beloved one stayed with him to the end. As men were scavenging like dogs through Jesus's only possessions (19:23–25), the beloved disciple stood in the company of faithful women ready to fulfill Jesus's dying wish. Seeing the loyal company standing at the cross, Jesus entrusted to his friend the care of his mother (vv. 26–27). The novelty of Jesus's directive, "Woman, here is your son," not only brings into sharp focus the pain of Mary's sacrifice (she is losing her boy), but it also put the beloved disciple in a new category of relationship. Jesus was treating his friend as if he were his brother, for the care of a mother fell to the eldest son's brother. The friend, who was closer than a brother, was honored by Jesus's request, and "from that hour the disciple took her into his own household" (v. 27).

"Were you there when they crucified my Lord?" Just thinking about being there would make anyone tremble. The disciples abandoned him, Peter denied him, Judas betrayed him, but the beloved disciple watched him die. Most believers can identify with most of the characters of the story. We see ourselves often in the faces of the faithless disciples—cowardice makes traitors of us all. Many times we can identify with the thief on the cross—we should have died for our crimes, not Jesus. Sometimes we see unbelievers act cold and hardened at the sight of the cross as if they were the soldier who stabbed the corpse of Jesus. In our life story, it always seems that women who love Jesus are more faithful than men in their devotion to him. Few of us, on the other hand, can say that we would have been there for him in his darkest hour. To watch him die is a sight too horrible to imagine. To hear him cry out, "It is finished," would sound more like the final epitaph of a life snuffed out too soon than any triumphant declaration. Would we have eyes to see and ears to hear and understand the meaning of this splendid tragedy? Would our eyewitness testimony inspire an entire community of faith to believe (v. 35)? Would we risk our lives *before* Easter, following him to the bitter end as a faithful friend? He did. He was the one whom Jesus loved. He was there when they crucified our Lord.

The First Believer at the Tomb

Peter and the beloved disciple were running to the tomb. It was the first day of a new week, before sunrise, when Mary Magdalene discovered the empty tomb and reported her concerns to the two disciples (20:1–2). Mary thought that the makeshift arrangements for the interment of Jesus's body in another man's tomb caused the owner enough grief to have the corpse removed (v. 2). Alarmed by the report, the two ran to the tomb. The beloved disciple arrived first since he knew the way (v. 4); Peter would not have known where they buried Jesus, he wasn't there—the three Marys, the two secret disciples (Joseph and Nicodemus), and the one whom Jesus loved were the ones who made sure that Jesus received a proper burial (19:38–42; see also Luke 23:50–56).

When the beloved one arrived at the tomb, he stopped short of going inside the burial chamber in order to avoid defilement (Num. 19:11–16). Evidently, there was enough light from the dawn to see into the tomb. There the beloved disciple first noticed the burial wrappings that once clothed the corpse. This must have been a peculiar scene, for if the body had been moved, no Jew would have unwrapped the corpse before carrying it to another location. The sight hardly confirmed the disciple's expectations. Despite the curious circumstances, however, the beloved disciple remained outside the tomb (John 20:5). Peter was not so careful. As soon as he arrived, he impetuously stumbled into the tomb before noticing the grave clothes (v. 6). Once inside, Peter saw something that caused even the beloved one to lose every inhibition. He found "the cloth that had been on Jesus's head, not lying with the linen wrappings but rolled up in a place by itself" (v. 7). When the disciple whom Jesus loved saw *this*, he joined Peter in the tomb. According to the narrator, there was something about the head wrapping that not only caused the beloved disciple to defile himself but also "to see and believe" (v. 8)—the code word for interpreting signs (6:30; 7:31; 12:37). What was the significance of the head wrapping? Why would *this* sign inspire the beloved one to believe *before* he saw the resurrected Messiah? How could a head wrapping give evidence to the beloved disciple that Jesus was alive?

Notice how the narrator suggestively recorded that the cloth that once covered Jesus's head was "rolled up in a place by itself" (20:7). Burial practices varied among the Jews, especially when it came to preparing the corpse. Customarily, a sheet would cover the entire body (Mark 15:46), then strips of cloth would be used to bind the corpse (John 19:40). A separate cloth would be used to cover the head (11:44). The tomb scene as described by the narrator gives the reader the impression that there was nothing conspicuous about the arrangement of the linen wrappings that once covered the body of Jesus. They were simply "lying there" in the tomb (20:5). The head cloth, on the other hand, was not found in the pile of wrappings. It was deliberately *placed* by someone in a different location. Remember, the beloved one came to the tomb expecting to find evidence that someone had moved the body of Jesus. Finding the head wrap "rolled up in a place by itself" would not be any more of an unusual sight than finding the rest of the grave clothes of Jesus. There must have been something unique about the *way* the head cloth was "rolled up" that caused the beloved one to "see and believe."

According to the Mishnah, the second-century collection of rabbinical teachings, two teachers had a difference of opinion regarding the placement of the napkin used prior to table fellowship. Shammai and Hillel, the two leading rabbis of Jesus's day, taught that a man should use a napkin to dry his hands after the required rite of water purification before mealtime. Shammai believed that it was permissible for the napkin to be placed on the table; Hillel taught that the cloth should be placed on the cushion upon which the rabbi would recline during the meal.[2] Could this custom provide some explanation as to why the beloved disciple came to believe that Jesus was alive when he saw the napkin "rolled up in a place by itself"? He "sat" next to Jesus during the "last supper." He would have noticed how Jesus rolled up the cloth before the meal. Such minor idiosyncrasies are insignificant habits in the daily affairs of life. But imagine how powerful the scene would be if the beloved disciple were to find in the tomb a head cloth rolled up in the same way that Jesus used to fold up his napkin at the table.

The beloved one first came to the tomb expecting to find nothing in it. When he arrived at the scene, he found that Jesus was gone—just as Mary said—but grave clothes were left behind. While the beloved disciple stood outside the tomb, puzzling over the site, Peter rummaged around inside the tomb and found the head cloth. I see a look of anguish on the face of the one whom Jesus loved, disturbed by the prospect of someone having first stripped the body of Jesus before moving him from the borrowed tomb. Who would do such a thing? Perhaps an enemy, wishing to add indignity to Jesus's humiliating death, was trying to deny him an honorable burial. But then, the beloved one noticed something peculiar. The head wrap was folded up in a familiar way. His mind races back to the times of table fellowship with Jesus. In a sudden shock of discovery he *sees*. "Wait a minute. That's the way Jesus used to . . . He's alive!" Only one disciple would have eyes to see "the sign"; he's the one who used to sit next to Jesus.

This is my conjecture. Indeed, it is speculative. There is no specific literary evidence that the head cloth was rolled up by Jesus in the same way he may have folded a napkin during table fellowship. We are told that Jesus sometimes kept the custom of washing his hands before meals, even though he allowed some of his disciples to eat with "common hands," that is, unwashed hands (see Mark 7:1–8). We are not told, however, what he did with the napkin. These ambiguities notwithstanding, the narrator's inviting details regarding the sequence of the discovery of the head cloth and the resulting behavior of the beloved one still raise the eyebrows of any curious reader. What was so intriguing about the head cloth that it would cause the beloved one to ignore purity codes, enter the tomb, see and believe? Only the beloved one knows for certain. But whatever the implication, it was not *the* sign of Easter, "for as yet they did not understand the Scripture, that He must rise again from the dead" (John 20:9). The ultimate proof of Easter was not an empty tomb nor a pile of grave clothes, but a resurrected Messiah!

"I have seen the Lord" (v. 18). Mary's claim became the disciples' reality, "We have seen the Lord" (v. 25), which led to Thomas's request. He did not ask to see the empty tomb; he did not ask to hear the testimony of the beloved one. Thomas wanted to see the resurrected Jesus (v. 25). Although he offered the most profound profession of messianic faith, "My Lord and my God!" (v. 28), Thomas did not rate as the ideal disciple. "Because you have seen Me, have you believed? Blessed are they who did *not* see and yet believed" (v. 29). Once again, the beloved one is approved by Jesus as the model disciple. He is blessed because he believes before faith becomes sight. Even though the appearance of a resurrected Messiah was the ultimate vindication of Easter faith,

> *The ultimate proof of Easter was not an empty tomb nor a pile of grave clothes, but a resurrected Messiah!*

the beatitude of Jesus affirms any who would walk by faith and not by sight—the lot of every reader. To be like Thomas, to see and feel, might be held up as the ideal experience of any believer. But make no mistake;

although Thomas sees and believes, he was the last of the disciples to believe. The one whom Jesus loved was the first.

The Beloved Disciple by the Sea

The last chapter of John's Gospel functions as an epilogue to the entire story of seeing and believing. Once again, Peter and the beloved disciple appear in the episode as fraternal twins of discipleship—although they belong together, they don't look anything alike. Peter is impetuous, the beloved one is perceptive. Peter is unpredictable, the beloved one is reliable. Peter is asking questions, the beloved one knows the answer. Like the first episode at the Lord's table, the three men are brought together again. The scenery is different but the actors seem to be reading from a familiar script. They break bread. The question of betrayal hovers over the conversation. The disciples speculate over the identity of one of the guests. Jesus predicts the fate of one of his disciples and speaks of his departure. The similarities between the two episodes, nevertheless, give way to the differences. This time the meal includes bread and fish. This time Jesus questions the devotion of Peter three times rather than predicts his triple denial. This time the disciples question the identity of Jesus. This time Jesus anticipates the faithfulness of the beloved one rather than the disloyalty of the traitor. This time Jesus talks about coming back. After the resurrection of Jesus, life *seemed* to be the same—but then again, everything seemed to change.

Peter's fishing trip and the miraculous catch of fish take the reader by surprise. The narrator tells the story as if the disciple's vocation and the previous episode of the miraculous catch were well known to his community. But this information is not found in John's account. The familiar story of Jesus calling fishermen to "fish" for men is never mentioned in the Gospel of John. And, Luke was the only Gospel writer to record the story of the miraculous catch. Therefore, for the reader of John's Gospel, Peter's desire to fish does not necessarily reflect the actions of an inadequate disciple who "reverts" to his previous lifestyle as if nothing had happened. This is the first time we are told that Peter was a fisherman. Furthermore, in John's narrative world, this is the first time Jesus performed such a miracle—the miraculous catch of fish is not one of the seven "signs." Therefore, the reader is led to the conclusion that the beloved disciple was the first to recognize the resurrected Messiah (John 21:7) because of his perceptive abilities rather than his collective memory, *and* that Peter's fishing trip simply provides the unusual circumstances under which Jesus "manifested Himself" (v. 1).

It was dark and the disciples "caught nothing" (v. 3). Jesus arrives with the dawn's light and confirms their unproductive effort with a goading question, "Children, you do not have any fish, do you?" (v. 5). He stands on the seashore some distance from the boat, "about one hundred yards away" (v. 8). At that distance, even a familiar face would be difficult to identify, so the narrator states, "The disciples did not know that it was Jesus" (v. 4). But as soon as the disciples followed the advice of the stranger on the seashore, filling their nets with an abundance of fish (v. 6), the beloved one declares, "It is the Lord"! Without hesitation, Peter jumps into the water and swims to the shore (v. 7), leaving the other disciples to drag the net full of fish to the bank (v. 8). Once again, the sequence of events provides a telling contrast of two kinds of disciples. The disciple whom Jesus loved sees a "sign" and recognizes Jesus; Peter cannot "see" for himself. Instead, he relied upon the witness of a faithful disciple—he went to Jesus when he "*heard* that it was the Lord" (v. 7). As a matter of fact, the disciple's witness was unquestionable in the minds of the others. Even when the disciples saw Jesus face-to-face and failed to recognize him, they did not ask, "'Who are You?' Knowing that it was the Lord" (v. 12). The beloved one could "see" Jesus a hundred yards away, yet the other disciples were unable to recognize him even though they were standing next to him. They couldn't believe their eyes, but they could trust what they heard from the one who had eyes to see.

Peter found himself, once again, uncomfortable with the discussion that developed around a warm fire. The last time he was the subject of conversation, the intense heat of the interrogation of that dark night resulted in his triple denial. Now, in the light of day, around a fire that cooked his breakfast, Jesus is asking questions of Peter that will purify the heart of the one who claimed that he would die for the Lord (13:37). "Simon, son of John, do you love Me more than these?" (v. 15a). Peter's response reveals the humility that often follows the failure of youthful hubris. "Yes, Lord; You know that I love You" (v. 15b). Before, Peter claimed that he loved the Lord more than the other disciples; he promised to follow Jesus to the end. "I will lay down my life for You" (13:37). Peter's boast, in fact, put him in a category of obedience equal to the Son of God. Jesus marveled over Peter's pretentious pledge, "Will *you* lay down your life for *Me*?" (v. 38). Of course, the opposite came true; Jesus was the one who laid down his life for his friends—even Peter, the one who denied him. Now Peter must face the lessons that are learned by those who claim too much.

In John's Gospel, the resurrected Messiah questioned the devotion of Peter with good reason. Unlike the synoptic accounts, Peter showed no remorse over his denial in John's account. After he denied Jesus the third time, Peter simply disappears from the narrative. The narrator does not record how Peter responded to the call of the rooster. There is no scene in John's Gospel of Peter weeping bitterly over the realization that Jesus's prediction has come true. Peter fades from view, with no mention of his exit, and reappears in the narrative at the discovery of the empty tomb. Therefore, in John's Gospel, there is unfinished business between Jesus and Peter. The "absence" of Peter's contrition makes his actions before his face-to-face encounter with Jesus even more compelling. Even after his own failure to live up to his lofty claims, Peter is seen *still* trying to outdo the other disciples and go beyond the expectations of Jesus. For example, after the disciples had rowed the boat ashore with the net full of fish (21:8), Jesus instructed the disciples, "Bring *some* of the fish which you have now caught" (v. 10). Jumping at the chance, Peter returns to the boat and drags the entire net full of fish to the fire—153 large fish, more than enough for breakfast, lunch, and dinner! I see Jesus smiling to himself, perhaps even thinking, "Oh Peter, when will you ever learn?" So he asked him three times, "Simon son of John, do you love me?"

Rather than make the same mistake as before, this time Peter will make no claims for himself, deferring to the judgment of Jesus, "Lord, You know all things" (v. 17). Indeed he does. He knew that Peter would not follow him to the cross. He knew that Peter would not die for Jesus. He knew that Peter would deny him three times before the dawn. He knew that Peter was not the beloved one. He knew that Peter needed to be taught what it meant to be an ideal disciple. "Peter do you love me? Then obey me." That, in essence, is the mark of genuine discipleship. "Feed my lambs; tend my sheep; feed my sheep." For every denial there

> *True discipleship is not found in the claims of those who follow him. True disciples obey him.*

was a call to obedience. True discipleship is not found in the *claims* of those who follow him. True disciples obey him. Those who follow him, those who obey him, find a cross at the end of their journey.

Here stands the resurrected Messiah. The glory of his power comes *after* the humiliation of his suffering. Now he has shown Peter, in living color, what it takes to obey, and challenges him to follow the same path. "When you were younger, you used to gird yourself and walk wherever you wished; but when you grow old, you will stretch out your hands and someone else will gird you, and bring you where you do not wish to go" (v. 18). If Peter obeys, he will follow in Jesus's footsteps; he will die on a cross (v. 19a). Knowing this, having predicted the way Peter would die as an obedient disciple, Jesus turns to the one who makes promises and commands, "Follow Me" (v. 19b).

Christ's prediction may have sounded to Peter more like a form of punishment than a call to discipleship. He wanted to know if all disciples would get the same treatment. "Lord, and what about this man?" (v. 21). Peter was referring to the beloved one, who was *already* following Jesus (v. 20). Before, Peter thought too highly of himself, compared to the other disciples. Now, Peter wonders if he is being singled out for remedial work. Jesus's response probably confirmed Peter's suspicions. "If I want him to remain until I come . . ." (v. 22). Jesus toys with the idea of keeping the faithful disciple in the service of the church until the end. To Peter and the rest of the church (did Peter spread the rumor?), Jesus's "wishful thinking" was to be taken as a prediction of the beloved disciple's escape from death (v. 23). But, according to the narrator, such an interpretation missed the point. "Jesus did not say to him that he would not die" (v. 23). Instead, Jesus was trying to get Peter to see that he was not the beloved disciple, in word, in deed, in destiny. What Jesus desired for the beloved one was none of Peter's business. What the Lord wanted Peter to do was to follow *him*, in word, in deed, in destiny (v. 22). The beloved one had already followed Jesus to the cross; now it was Peter's turn.

"What if I want him to remain until I come?" Ideally, faithful disciples stay true to the end. This is *the* model of discipleship—there can be no other. To be Jesus's closest friend, to obey his commands, to follow him to Golgotha, to see with eyes of faith, to believe when others doubt, to serve him until he comes back, this is the disciple whom Jesus loves. Most of us, however, look more like Peter than the ideal disciple. We find ourselves at his table, yet we are not close enough to him to know what troubles his heart. We boast, in the company of other Christians, of our devotion to him. Then we deny him, in the company of unbelievers, trying to escape the shame of his cross. Too often we can't make sense of what we see, blind to the signs of God's resurrection power. Then, when we gather with other disciples around the fire of his glorious company, we compete for his favor, wondering if he notices that we love him more "than these." Finally, when others seem to enjoy a more favorable journey, we question the justice of God. And so Jesus turns to us, just as he did to Peter, and commands, "Follow me. Follow me to the celebration of my death. Follow me to the cross of my humiliation. Follow me to the empty grave of faith. Follow me until I come again. Follow me." This is the path taken by the ideal disciple. This is the destiny of every true believer. This is the one whom Jesus loves.

Via Sanctus

Heroes are too easily admired from a distance. Sometimes we idolize human icons not so much for the purpose of imitating their laudatory achievements but to beg off our responsibilities. Magnifying the successes of those who rise above the rest reinforces our own convictions that some people are destined for greatness. We say, "he's gifted," or "she's fortunate," attributing the accomplishments of others to superhuman abilities or perfect timing. By putting heroes on a pedestal, we not only enshrine their greatness but also put their achievements at a safe distance, making ourselves more comfortable with mediocrity. *We* make idols. And these superheroes are meant to do what the rest of us cannot do. To cheer them on is the obligation of our veneration.

John did not spotlight four ideal disciples for our admiration. The commonness of their circumstances helps the reader to see that Jesus found ideal disciples in ordinary people. *Any one of us* could be the Sower who plants the gospel seed into the hearts of all people, perhaps even bringing to harvest the entire city of our residence. If a Samaritan woman can become an ideal disciple of Jesus, surpassing the dedication of twelve men, then so can I. *All of us* have faced life-or-death situations, agonizing over choices that must be made, then coming to a place where we realize that there is nothing we can do to change things. When I am

> *To share in the fellowship of his sufferings, to follow him to Golgotha, to believe that he is alive when the world questions the meaning of an empty tomb, to remain faithful until he comes again—this is the one whom Jesus loves.*

alone in the despair of my crisis, I want to be the Believer who trusts the Word of God, just like the nobleman from Capernaum. *Every believer* can identify with the testimony of the man born blind: "Once I was blind, but now I see." But will we boldly speak of what we see, risking exclusion and isolation? The Teacher tells the truth regardless of the consequences. *Every disciple wants* to follow Jesus. Ideal disciples *actually* follow Jesus.

To share in the fellowship of his sufferings, to follow him to Golgotha, to believe that he is alive when the world questions the meaning of an empty tomb, to remain faithful until he comes again—this is the one whom Jesus loves.

"For if anyone is a hearer of the word and not a doer, he is like a man who looks at his natural face in a mirror; for once he has looked at himself and gone away, he has immediately forgotten what kind of person he was" (James 1:23–24). As the Word of God, John's stories of ideal discipleship work like a mirror. Every flaw and distinctive feature of our own reflection can be seen in the mirror image of genuine discipleship. Vanity would compel us to look away, without taking in the true-to-life critique of our commitment to Jesus. When compared to these super-models of discipleship, the lines on our face become more pronounced, the image too hard to bear. But we keep looking; something draws us back. The before-and-after pictures of each disciple remind us that the Samaritan woman did not start out as an ideal disciple, the nobleman *became* a believer, the teacher of the Pharisees was once blind, and the one whom Jesus loved was just a man. We witnessed the transformation; we saw with our own eyes what God can do.

If seeing is believing, then John has fulfilled his purpose in telling the story. Jesus did so many things, there was so much to report. Yet the evangelist's choice of these particular stories reveals his specific intention. He wanted his Gospel to change people (John 20:30–31). These stories were preserved not only for what they say about Jesus, but also because of what they do to the reader. Just as Jesus changed his life, John knew that our encounter with the Living Word would change our lives. We call it "conversion." Primarily used by the church to describe the experience of a new "convert," believers soon realize that God's Word never stops converting our lives from what was to what shall be. That's why we are continually drawn back to the Mirror. Every time we return we notice a slight change in our appearance. We don't look the same. The more we read, the more we see, the more we follow him, the more we recognize that God's creative work is producing *in us* a transformation of heart and mind, soul and strength, desire and resolution.

Celebrating the regenerative experience of following Jesus, we notice others heading down the same path. Confident that a Samaritan woman, a nobleman from Capernaum, a man born blind, and the one whom Jesus loved have taken the same road, pilgrims find joy in the journey knowing that God will finish the work. Taking in the sight, believers begin to recognize familiar faces. "Look there! Doesn't she *look like* the Sower? And over there, isn't that the Believer?" Then another traveler approaches us and says, "I know you! Aren't you the one who was born blind? Jesus touched your eyes and now you can see!" Taken back by the comparison, we take in the sight of a road filled with so many pilgrims. Different faces, names, colors, dress, ages—yet, the farther down the path we go the more we look alike. Whispers circulate through the crowd that the footprints of the beloved disciple can be seen straight ahead. Then we realize that we're all headed for the same destination. Golgotha waits for every cross-bearing disciple of Jesus. This is our story. We will share in his suffering, we will die in Christ, and we will partake of the glory of his resurrection—the day we all become ideal disciples. For we are the ones whom Jesus loves. This is the Via Sanctus.

Conclusion

Being Good News

It is certain, my Lord, that in these days withdrawal from the
world means no sacrifice at all.

Teresa of Avila, *The Way of Perfection*

Disciples of Jesus live holy lives because we follow a holy man.
As far as we're concerned, no one else measures up to him. He
defines what it means to be human and divine. What sets us apart from
unbelievers, therefore, is this: we all have one dream, one goal, one
purpose, one faith—his life. He incarnated truth. He revealed the glory
of God. He showed the most excellent way. This is what makes us different from devotees of all other religions. We want to live the life of Jesus
Christ. We want to be good news for all people. This is why we study the
Gospels. This is why we memorize his life. This is why we meditate on
his words. To us, Jesus is more than a theological idea—he is a necessary
sacrifice for our sins. We thank God not only for his perfect death that
atones for our sin, but also for his beautiful life that inspires perfection.
His grace makes us want to live for him and no one else. We want to live
holy lives. We follow Jesus.

He had the same effect on Matthew, Mark, Luke, and John. And,
ironically, he has the same effect on us because of Matthew, Mark, Luke,
and John. Think about it, if all we had were the letters of Paul, what

would Christianity look like? We would know what to believe, but we wouldn't know how to live. Indeed, the only reason we can make sense of what Paul, Peter, or John were trying to say is because we have literary Gospels. We can see the Gospel as well as hear the Gospel because Matthew, Mark, Luke, and John have shown us how to live the gospel. For example, Jesus makes disciples of anyone who has eyes to see or ears to hear the Gospel according to Matthew. But that's not all. Matthew has carefully shown *how* Jesus made disciples in his absence—turning them into believers—so that they would never doubt his presence when *they made* disciples. Fulfilling the great commission reveals the presence of Christ. When disciples make disciples, then the student has become the teacher and the believer can say with every confidence: "Jesus is with us always, even to the end of the world." Still, some might say, "Lord, when did we see you?" And what is Jesus's reply? "When you've seen the least of these you've seen me." Perhaps this is one reason why Paul insisted on claiming, "I am the least of the apostles." Littleness defines greatness in the kingdom of Christ according to the Gospel of Matthew.

Mark tells the story of a man who risked everything for God. He never hedged his bets, or developed contingency plans, or diversified his investments, or kept his options open. He kept to one plan. He had one mission. He pursued one dream. Jesus believed in the reign of God. He knew the odds were stacked against him. Roman Empire, evil powers, selfish people, hard times—these are the forces that would bring down any dreamer, making him give in to these cruel realities. Not Jesus. He pushed back the darkness. He overcame the powers. He found fertile soil for his gospel seed in selfless hearts discarded by life. He mocked weeds with mustard seed faith. He ploughed deep fields of faith among shallow disciples. He counted on children to model enduring faith. And he never got to hear the most profound profession of faith, "Surely, this man was a son of God." Jesus was God's farmer who planted a generous crop of gospel seed and yielded a miraculous harvest. We are evidence of his faith in God's kingdom. His gospel seed has been planted in our hearts, and we have Mark to thank. For we have ears to hear the Good News and we have seed to sow for the kingdom because this Gospel writer has shown us how to farm the gospel of Jesus Christ, the Son of God. Every heart can be fertile soil. We prove that we are seed-bearing disciples because we've read the Gospel according to Mark. Sow the seed!

For Luke, the question isn't "when?" it's "why not?" It's time to party! Heaven has come to earth because Jesus is good news for poor people. Because God's Spirit has been poured out on Jesus, then the end of the world has come. Isaiah dreamed about it. Jesus lived it. So what happens when heaven's blessing becomes earth's reality? The poor are favored, the captives find liberty, the blind see the kingdom of God, and the downcast finally get some relief. All debts are cancelled! Jesus threw a party announcing the year of Jubilee and invited everyone to his table. Party poopers dismissed the whole ordeal as presumptuous. Party crashers reveled in a banquet of forgiveness. According to Luke, Jesus taught us how to celebrate the reign of God by eating broken bread and drinking a cup of sacrifice. We keep the party going when we remember him at table. Eating and drinking our way to the kingdom of God's reign, we lift our glasses knowing that, one day, he will eat his last supper with us, forever. In the meantime, we have a bold confession to make, a preposterous claim to stake. Isaiah's dream has already been fulfilled in our hearing, too. For Jesus *still* brings good news to the poor, release to captives, recovery of sight to the blind, and hope to the downtrodden. God forgives all debtors. Hallelujah! Hallelujah! Hallelujah! Jesus, we remember you; how could we forget? Remember us when you come into your kingdom.

Love, faith, humility, and faithfulness—these are virtues of an ideal disciple. It's one thing to hear about such admirable qualities, it's something else to see them. John tells the story of incarnation. In the beginning and to the end, Jesus revealed God's Word in human flesh. Throughout the narrative, John also fleshed out four ideal disciples for readers to see: a Samaritan woman, a Capernaum nobleman, a man born blind, and a beloved disciple. These nameless, faceless characters inspire us to be like them. Because we love Jesus, we want to be the one to lead our whole community to find living water. Because we believe in the power of God's Word, we want to lock the promises of Christ in our hearts and carry them until we all come home. Because we know what it means to be blinded by sin, we want to give personal testimony to what Christ

We are the narrative of God's grace

because he is our story.

has done for us: "Once I was blind, now I see." And, because we want to be faithful followers of Jesus, we will carry his cross until he comes again. Who are these ideal disciples of Jesus? They are the ones whom Jesus loves. People like you; people like me. Male and female, rich and poor, blind and sighted ("It is the Lord!"), ideal disciples follow Jesus to the end.

We will never give up. We will never stop loving him. We will never forget him. We are disciples of Jesus—nothing more, nothing less. We are good news for all people because he is our life. We are the hope of the world in Christ Jesus because he is our future. We are the narrative of God's grace because he is our story. In a world filled with messiahs, we need only one Savior. Matthew, Mark, Luke, and John have made sure of that. Indeed, Jesus makes for a good study. So the Gospels show us how to be his students. "Let the reader understand," Mark liked to write because literary Gospels make disciples out of anyone who has eyes to read. The Scriptures work. We are living proof for we are the Master's apprentices. Live and learn.

Notes

Introduction: Strapping on Sandals

1. Several years *after* entering the monastery, Thomas Merton wrote, "I have a terrific undefined longing to give everything to God and a constant feeling that I am not doing so here—or not now." *The Intimate Merton: His Life from His Journals*, ed. Patrick Hart and Jonathan Montaldo (New York: Harper-Collins, 1999), 59.

2. As indicated on the copyright page, unless otherwise indicated all Scripture quotations are taken from the *New American Standard Bible*.

Chapter 1 Fit for Faith

1. See Paul S. Minear, *The Good News According to Matthew: A Training Manual for Prophets* (St. Louis: Chalice, 2000).

2. The expression, "learn from Me," is the verb form of the noun, "disciple."

Chapter 2 Fitted for a Crown

1. Interestingly enough, it was a minister to children, Daron Evans, in a church in southwest Missouri that helped me see the obvious. Certain children need special attention because they don't understand. That fits Peter, James, and John—the only disciples Jesus gave nicknames.

2. Perhaps Jesus kept the three close at hand for their own safety. Remember, it was Peter (according to John's Gospel) who brandished the sword and foolishly tried to protect Jesus from his captors. If Peter were part of the company guarding the outer perimeter, his impetuous behavior might have led to disastrous results before Jesus's arrest.

3. I owe this insight to Ken Gire, *Windows of the Soul: Experiencing God in New Ways* (Grand Rapids: Zondervan, 1996), 167–68.

Chapter 3 Sowing the Seed

1. The word "messiah" is a synonym for the Greek word "Christ." Both terms mean "the anointed one."

2. Philip Yancey, *The Jesus I Never Knew* (Grand Rapids: Zondervan, 1995), 23.

3. See Mary Ann Tolbert, *Sowing the Gospel: Mark's World in Literary-Historical Perspective* (Minneapolis: Fortress Press, 1989), 148–75.

4. Pliny, *Natural History* (Cambridge: Harvard University Press, 1967), 18.21.94–95.

5. The original ending of Mark's Gospel is 16:8; the last twelve verses were added by scribes disturbed, no doubt, by what Mark leaves out of his last chapter: a resurrection appearance of Jesus, a gathering of rehabilitated disciples, a great commission, and the ascension of Christ.

6. Of course, Jesus originally spoke in his native tongue, Aramaic, the language the Jews learned in exile during the Babylonian captivity.

7. Tolbert notes that when Jesus came into his glory, that is, was crucified for the sins of the world, there were two men, "one on his right and one on his left," who followed him to a cross—and they weren't James and John! (15:27). *Sowing the Gospel*, 154–55.

Chapter 4 Finding Good Soil

1. Chapter divisions were added by scribes several centuries after the Gospels were written and copied.

2. See Richard A. Horsely, *Hearing the Whole Story: The Politics of Plot in Mark's Gospel* (Louisville: Westminster John Knox, 2001), 141.

3. After a boy's bar mitzvah, he was considered to be a man. Yet there was the acknowledgment that a "young man" retained childish immaturity (1 Cor. 13:11). Philo quoted Hippocrates for the distinction between a boy and a young man: when he begins to grow a beard he is no longer a "child." Philo, *On Creation* (Peabody, MA: Hendrickson, 1993), 105. Indeed, a "young man" could very well be, according to our terminology, a teenager.

4. A correlation I hadn't made until a friend of mine, David Capes, suggested it with the question: "Do you think Mark intended for his readers to see the young man at the end of the story as the same person as the streaking disciple?"

5. Notice that Mark does not describe the boy as an angel; that is the assumption of those who import Matthew's version.

6. Richard B. Hays, *A Moral Vision of the New Testament: A Contemporary Introduction to New Testament Ethics* (New York: HarperCollins, 1996), 338–39.

Chapter 5 The Reverse of the Curse

1. My translation/paraphrase of Isaiah 61:1–2 as it appears in Luke 4.

2. A saying, by the way, that does *not* appear in Luke's Gospel.

Chapter 6 Blessed Are the Cursed

1. I owe this insight to Brad H. Young, *Jesus the Jewish Theologian* (Peabody, MA: Hendrickson, 1995), 181–93.

2. If that were the case, then his comment regarding his own mother would make little sense (Luke 8:19–21).

3. What he *should* have said, according to our way of thinking, was, "Yes, mothers are the power brokers of God's sustaining love," or some other proverb that would empower the disenfranchised, such as "The hand that rocks the cradle is the hand that rules the world" (from a poem attributed to William Rose Wallace, http://www.theotherpages.org/poems/wallace1.html).

Chapter 7 Jubilee!

1. C. S. Lewis, *The Great Divorce* (New York: Macmillan, 1946), 122.

2. J. R. R. Tolkien, *The Lord of the Rings* (New York: Houghton Mifflin, 1954, 1965, 1966).

3. Augustine, *Confessions*, trans. R. S. Pine-Coffin (Baltimore: Penguin Books, 1961), 9.10.

4. Haninah ben Dosa said, "If my prayer is fluent, then I know that it is accepted [and the person will live]. But if not, I know that it is rejected [and the person will die];" *The Mishnah*, trans. Jacob Neusner (New Haven: Yale University Press, 1988), *Berakhot* 5.5.

Chapter 8 The Ideal Evangelist

1. See R. Alan Culpepper, *Anatomy of the Fourth Gospel: A Study in Literary Design* (Philadelphia: Fortress Press, 1983), 195.

2. The Pharisees believed that unclean vessels contained unclean water; see Luke 11:39.

Chapter 9 The Ideal Believer

1. Taking liberties with Paul's words in Romans 8:3.

2. According to the *New American Standard Bible*.

3. Except, of course, for the times when rabbis were called upon to pray for the sick. The difference between these stories in the Mishnah and the healing ministry of Jesus is apparent: Jesus never prayed to God to heal the sick—he simply pronounced them cured of the affliction.

Chapter 10 The Ideal Teacher

1. Here are a few of my favorite New Testament scholars: Richard Hays, Ben Witherington, Charles Talbert, N. T. Wright, E. P. Sanders, G. B. Caird, James D. G. Dunn, Gordon Fee, Douglas Moo, Adela Yarbro Collins, Robert Jewett, Craig Evans, and Leander Keck.

Chapter 11 The Beloved Disciple

1. According to John's Gospel, the "Lord's Supper" did not include the paschal lamb (18:28).

2. *Mishnah, Berakhot* 8.3, 8–9.

Rodney Reeves (Ph.D., Southwestern Baptist Theological Seminary) is currently dean and professor of biblical studies at the Courts Redford College of Theology and Church Vocations, Southwest Baptist University in Bolivar, Missouri. An ordained pastor in the Southern Baptist Convention, he has served churches in Arkansas, Texas, and Missouri.